Starting an Online Business For Dummies®

Cheat Sheet

Contact Information to Keep Close at Hand

Nobody runs a business alone. You need to know where to go for help if problems arise. Take a moment to jot down the following names and phone numbers/e-mail addresses so you have them when you need them:

Your Internet Service Provider's access number (the number you usually dial to connect to the Internet):

_____

An alternate ISP access number (if the first number is busy, call this one):

W9-CCB-276

_____

Your ISP's technical support number (where to call if you can't connect or access your e-mail):

_____

Your Web hosting service (the company who posts your Web site on its server) — this may be the same as your ISP:

_____

Your Web site designer (if you hire a friend or a firm to help you build your Web site):

_____

Your technical support contact (be it a neighbor, a toll-free computer support company, or a paid service):

_____

Your employees or business partners:

_____

_____

_____

Your credit card network (where to call when you want to process a credit card order):

_____

Your accountant:

_____

Other contacts:

_____

_____

_____

...For Dummies: Bestselling Book Series for Beginners

Starting an Online Business For Dummies®

Cheat Sheet

Legal Requirements

- **Decide what type of business you're going to be:** Are you going to be a sole proprietorship, a partnership, or a corporation?

- **Collect sales tax:** Be sure to charge the sales tax rate applicable in the state in which the purchase is made — that is, the state where your customer lives, not where you live.

- **Choose an accounting method:** You can either do cash-basis or accrual-basis accounting.

- **Choose an accounting period:** Calendar year is simple, but you can also choose fiscal year.

- **Record your revenue:** Write down the amount you receive, the form of payment, the date, the name of the client, and the goods or services you provide in exchange.

- **Keep track of expenses:** Write down the date the expense occurs, the name of the person or company that receives payment, and the type of expense.

- **Avoid copyright and trademark infringement:** Conduct a thorough trademark search before deciding on and posting a trade name.

- **Be aware of local restrictions:** Some cities, towns, or counties have zoning restrictions preventing businesses from operating from home, or requiring home-based businesses to pay licensing fees.

Web Site Checklist

You can put almost anything you want on your Web site, but here are some essentials:

- ___ Your contact information
- ___ Your company name and logo
- ___ Your business mission statement
- ___ Titles that match each Web page's contents.
- ___ META tags that help search services index your site
- ___ Copyright notice
- ___ Links to main areas of your Web site
- ___ Feedback form or guestbook
- ___ Endorsements from satisfied customers/clients
- ___ Photos of your merchandise for sale
- ___ Online order form
- ___ Frequently Asked Questions
- ___ Customer service information
- ___ Payment options (credit card, check, escrow account)
- ___ Shipping options (overnight, two-day, ground)

Referral List

Smart businesspeople build goodwill and develop loyalty by referring customers to other sources when they can't provide the services needed. Write down the names, e-mail addresses, Web site URLs, or phone numbers of companies or individuals you can personally recommend:

Name: _____ Contact Info.: _____

Name: _____ Contact Info.: _____

Name: _____ Contact Info.: _____

Name: _____ Contact Info.: _____

Name: _____ Contact Info.: _____

...For Dummies: Bestselling Book Series for Beginners

™

References for the Rest of Us!®

BESTSELLING BOOK SERIES FROM IDG

Are you intimidated and confused by computers? Do you find that traditional manuals are overloaded with technical details you'll never use? Do your friends and family always call you to fix simple problems on their PCs? Then the *...For Dummies*® computer book series from IDG Books Worldwide is for you.

...For Dummies books are written for those frustrated computer users who know they aren't really dumb but find that PC hardware, software, and indeed the unique vocabulary of computing make them feel helpless. *...For Dummies* books use a lighthearted approach, a down-to-earth style, and even cartoons and humorous icons to diffuse computer novices' fears and build their confidence. Lighthearted but not lightweight, these books are a perfect survival guide for anyone forced to use a computer.

> *"I like my copy so much I told friends; now they bought copies."*
>
> — **Irene C., Orwell, Ohio**

> *"Quick, concise, nontechnical, and humorous."*
>
> — **Jay A., Elburn, Illinois**

> *"Thanks, I needed this book. Now I can sleep at night."*
>
> — **Robin F., British Columbia, Canada**

Already, millions of satisfied readers agree. They have made *...For Dummies* books the #1 introductory level computer book series and have written asking for more. So, if you're looking for the most fun and easy way to learn about computers, look to *...For Dummies* books to give you a helping hand.

STARTING AN ONLINE BUSINESS FOR DUMMIES®

by Greg Holden

IDG BOOKS
WORLDWIDE

IDG Books Worldwide, Inc.
An International Data Group Company

Foster City, CA ♦ Chicago, IL ♦ Indianapolis, IN ♦ New York, NY

Starting an Online Business For Dummies®

Published by
IDG Books Worldwide, Inc.
An International Data Group Company
919 E. Hillsdale Blvd.
Suite 400
Foster City, CA 94404
www.idgbooks.com (IDG Books Worldwide Web site)
www.dummies.com (Dummies Press Web site)

Library of Congress Catalog Card No.: 98-89940

ISBN: 0-7645-0464-9

Printed in the United States of America

10 9 8 7 6 5 4 3 2 1

1B/SR/QR/ZZ/IN

Distributed in the United States by IDG Books Worldwide, Inc.

Distributed by Macmillan Canada for Canada; by Transworld Publishers Limited in the United Kingdom; by IDG Norge Books for Norway; by IDG Sweden Books for Sweden; by Woodslane Pty. Ltd. for Australia; by Woodslane (NZ) Ltd. for New Zealand; by Addison Wesley Longman Singapore Pte Ltd. for Singapore, Malaysia, Thailand, and Indonesia; by Norma Comunicaciones S.A. for Colombia; by Intersoft for South Africa; by International Thomson Publishing for Germany, Austria and Switzerland; by Distribuidora Cuspide for Argentina; by Livraria Cultura for Brazil; by Ediciencia S.A. for Ecuador; by Ediciones ZETA S.C.R. Ltda. for Peru; by WS Computer Publishing Corporation, Inc., for the Philippines; by Contemporanea de Ediciones for Venezuela; by Express Computer Distributors for the Caribbean and West Indies; by Micronesia Media Distributor, Inc. for Micronesia; by Grupo Editorial Norma S.A. for Guatemala; by Chips Computadoras S.A. de C.V. for Mexico; by Editorial Norma de Panama S.A. for Panama; by Wouters Import for Belgium; by American Bookshops for Finland. Authorized Sales Agent: Anthony Rudkin Associates for the Middle East and North Africa.

For general information on IDG Books Worldwide's books in the U.S., please call our Consumer Customer Service department at 800-762-2974. For reseller information, including discounts and premium sales, please call our Reseller Customer Service department at 800-434-3422.

For information on where to purchase IDG Books Worldwide's books outside the U.S., please contact our International Sales department at 317-596-5530 or fax 317-596-5692.

For information on foreign language translations, please contact our Foreign & Subsidiary Rights department at 650-655-3021 or fax 650-655-3281.

For sales inquiries and special prices for bulk quantities, please contact our Sales department at 650-655-3200 or write to the address above.

For information on using IDG Books Worldwide's books in the classroom or for ordering examination copies, please contact our Educational Sales department at 800-434-2086 or fax 317-596-5499.

For press review copies, author interviews, or other publicity information, please contact our Public Relations department at 650-655-3000 or fax 650-655-3299.

For authorization to photocopy items for corporate, personal, or educational use, please contact Copyright Clearance Center, 222 Rosewood Drive, Danvers, MA 01923, or fax 978-750-4470.

is a trademark under exclusive license to IDG Books Worldwide, Inc., from International Data Group, Inc.

About the Author

Greg Holden is founder and president of a small business called Stylus Media, which is a group of editorial, design, and computer professionals who produce both print and electronic publications. The company gets its name from a recording stylus, that reads the traces left on a disk by voices or instruments and translates those signals into electronic data that can be amplified and enjoyed by many.

One of the ways Greg enjoys communicating is through explaining technical subjects in nontechnical language by writing computer books, which help other people use the Web to share their own personal and professional interests. *Starting an Online Business For Dummies* is his ninth book. Recently, Greg also coordinated a chat event on the Internet, prepared content for a CD-ROM tutorial that shows small business owners how to create their own Web sites, and helped produce technical manuals on Java and Lotus Notes.

Greg balances his technical expertise and his entrepreneurial experience with his love of literature. He received a M.A. in English from the University of Illinois at Chicago, but that only gave him an official credential for what he had been doing since he was a tiny tot. As a preschooler, barely big enough to hold the book, he was displayed by his proud but rather puzzled parents as the kid who read from the encyclopedia to impress his relatives at family gatherings. You can read about some of his past and present triumphs and traumas in the poetry and short stories that he scribbles down at odd moments.

After graduating from college, Greg became a reporter for his hometown newspaper, first covering sewers and school boards and then working his way up to having his own column (called "So It Goes"), in which he voiced his perspective on the world. Working at the publications office at the University of Chicago was his next job, and it was there that he started to use computers. He discovered, as the technology became available, that he loved desktop publishing (with the Macintosh and LaserWriter and, later on, the World Wide Web).

Greg loves to travel, but since his two daughters were born, he hasn't been able to get around much. However, through the Web, he enjoys traveling vicariously and meeting people online. He lives with his family in an old house in Chicago that he has been rehabbing for — well, for many years now. He is a collector of objects such as pens, cameras, radios, and hats. He is always looking for things to take apart so that he can see how they work and fix them up. Many of the same skills prove useful in creating and maintaining Web pages. Greg is an active member of Jewel Heart, a Tibetan Buddhist meditation and study group based in Ann Arbor, Michigan.

ABOUT IDG BOOKS WORLDWIDE

Welcome to the world of IDG Books Worldwide.

IDG Books Worldwide, Inc., is a subsidiary of International Data Group, the world's largest publisher of computer-related information and the leading global provider of information services on information technology. IDG was founded more than 30 years ago by Patrick J. McGovern and now employs more than 9,000 people worldwide. IDG publishes more than 290 computer publications in over 75 countries. More than 90 million people read one or more IDG publications each month.

Launched in 1990, IDG Books Worldwide is today the #1 publisher of best-selling computer books in the United States. We are proud to have received eight awards from the Computer Press Association in recognition of editorial excellence and three from Computer Currents' First Annual Readers' Choice Awards. Our best-selling ...*For Dummies*® series has more than 50 million copies in print with translations in 31 languages. IDG Books Worldwide, through a joint venture with IDG's Hi-Tech Beijing, became the first U.S. publisher to publish a computer book in the People's Republic of China. In record time, IDG Books Worldwide has become the first choice for millions of readers around the world who want to learn how to better manage their businesses.

Our mission is simple: Every one of our books is designed to bring extra value and skill-building instructions to the reader. Our books are written by experts who understand and care about our readers. The knowledge base of our editorial staff comes from years of experience in publishing, education, and journalism — experience we use to produce books to carry us into the new millennium. In short, we care about books, so we attract the best people. We devote special attention to details such as audience, interior design, use of icons, and illustrations. And because we use an efficient process of authoring, editing, and desktop publishing our books electronically, we can spend more time ensuring superior content and less time on the technicalities of making books.

You can count on our commitment to deliver high-quality books at competitive prices on topics you want to read about. At IDG Books Worldwide, we continue in the IDG tradition of delivering quality for more than 30 years. You'll find no better book on a subject than one from IDG Books Worldwide.

John Kilcullen
Chairman and CEO
IDG Books Worldwide, Inc.

Steven Berkowitz
President and Publisher
IDG Books Worldwide, Inc.

*Eighth Annual
Computer Press
Awards ≥1992*

*Ninth Annual
Computer Press
Awards ≥1993*

*Tenth Annual
Computer Press
Awards ≥1994*

*Eleventh Annual
Computer Press
Awards ≥1995*

IDG is the world's leading IT media, research and exposition company. Founded, in 1964, IDG had 1997 revenues of $2.05 billion and has more than 9,000 employees worldwide. IDG offers the widest range of media options that reach IT buyers in 75 countries representing 95% of worldwide IT spending. IDG's diverse product and services portfolio spans six key areas including print publishing, online publishing, expositions and conferences, market research, education and training, and global marketing services. More than 90 million people read one or more of IDG's 290 magazines and newspapers, including IDG's leading global brands — Computerworld, PC World, Network World, Macworld and the Channel World family of publications. IDG Books Worldwide is one of the fastest-growing computer book publishers in the world, with more than 700 titles in 36 languages. The "...For Dummies®" series alone has more than 50 million copies in print. IDG offers online users the largest network of technology-specific Web sites around the world through IDG.net (http://www.idg.net), which comprises more than 225 targeted Web sites in 55 countries worldwide. International Data Corporation (IDC) is the world's largest provider of information technology data, analysis and consulting, with research centers in over 41 countries and more than 400 research analysts worldwide. IDG World Expo is a leading producer of more than 168 globally branded conferences and expositions in 35 countries including E3 (Electronic Entertainment Expo), Macworld Expo, ComNet, Windows World Expo, ICE (Internet Commerce Expo), Agenda, DEMO, and Spotlight. IDG's training subsidiary, ExecuTrain, is the world's largest computer training company, with more than 230 locations worldwide and 785 training courses. IDG Marketing Services helps industry-leading IT companies build international brand recognition by developing global integrated marketing programs via IDG's print, online and exposition products worldwide. Further information about the company can be found at www.idg.com.   10/8/98

Dedication

To my best friend Ann Lindner, who makes everything possible.

Author's Acknowledgments

As any businessperson knows, most large-scale projects are a team effort. In the course of writing this book, I met a lot of businesspeople. I was struck by the fact that the most successful entrepreneurs also tended to be the ones who were the most generous with their time and experience. They taught me that the more helpful you are, the more successful you'll be in return.

I want to thank all those who are profiled as case studies in this book, particularly Caroline Dauteuille, Dave Hagan Jr. of General Tool and Repair, Dan Podraza of the Collectible Exchange, John Moen of Graphic Maps, John Raddatz of SoftBear Shareware, Nancy Roebke of Profnet, Inc., Dr. Werner Steurenberg of Art Quarter, Kathie Turner of Health Care Provider Services, Judy Vorfeld of Office Support Services, and Joseph Wu of Joseph Wu's Origami Page.

Madonna Gauding (madonna@interaccess.com) gave me a refresher course on how valuable it is to have a right-hand person who cheerfully and competently responds to many requests. She worked extensively on Chapter 10 and the Internet Directory.

I would also like to acknowledge some of my own colleagues who helped prepare and review the text and graphics of this book, and who have supported and encouraged me in other lessons of life. Thanks to my friend and Stylus Media partner John Casler (jcasler@paranet.com), who taught me multitasking, and Ann Lindner, whose teaching experience proved valuable in suggesting ways to make the text more clear.

For editing and technical assignments, I was lucky to be in the capable hands of the folks at IDG Books Worldwide: my project editor, Shannon Ross; technical editor, Allen Wyatt; and Carmen Krikorian, Heather Heath Dismore, Joell Smith, and the rest of the Media Development staff.

Thanks also to David Rogelberg of Studio B, and to Joyce Pepple of IDG Books for helping me to add this book to the list of those I've authored and, in the process, broadening my expertise as a writer.

Last but certainly not least, the future is in the hands of the generation of my two daughters, Zosia and Lucy, who allow me to learn from the curiosity and joy with which they approach life.

Publisher's Acknowledgments

We're proud of this book; please register your comments through our IDG Books Worldwide Online Registration Form located at http://my2cents.dummies.com.

Some of the people who helped bring this book to market include the following:

Acquisitions, Editorial, and Media Development

Project Editor: Shannon Ross

Acquisitions Editor: Joyce Pepple

Copy Editor: Shannon Ross

Technical Editor: Allen Wyatt, Discovery Computing, Inc.

Media Development Editor: Joell Smith

Associate Permissions Editor: Carmen Krikorian

Editorial Manager: Mary C. Corder

Media Development Manager: Heather Heath Dismore

Editorial Assistant: Paul Kuzmic

Production

Project Coordinator: Karen York

Layout and Graphics: Lou Boudreau, Angela F. Hunckler, Jane E. Martin, Brent Savage, Jacque Schneider, Brian Torwelle

Proofreaders: Christine Berman, Kelli Botta, Laura Bowman, Vickie Broyles, Rebecca Senninger, Ethel M. Winslow

Indexer: Tech Indexing

Special Help: Suzanne Thomas; Publication Services, Inc.

General and Administrative

IDG Books Worldwide, Inc.: John Kilcullen, CEO; Steven Berkowitz, President and Publisher

IDG Books Technology Publishing: Brenda McLaughlin, Senior Vice President and Group Publisher

Dummies Technology Press and Dummies Editorial: Diane Graves Steele, Vice President and Associate Publisher; Mary Bednarek, Director of Acquisitions and Product Development; Kristin A. Cocks, Editorial Director

Dummies Trade Press: Kathleen A. Welton, Vice President and Publisher; Kevin Thornton, Acquisitions Manager

IDG Books Production for Dummies Press: Michael R. Britton, Vice President of Production and Creative Services; Cindy L. Phipps, Manager of Project Coordination, Production Proofreading, and Indexing; Kathie S. Schutte, Supervisor of Page Layout; Shelley Lea, Supervisor of Graphics and Design; Debbie J. Gates, Production Systems Specialist; Robert Springer, Supervisor of Proofreading; Debbie Stailey, Special Projects Coordinator; Tony Augsburger, Supervisor of Reprints and Bluelines

Dummies Packaging and Book Design: Patty Page, Manager, Promotions Marketing

♦

The publisher would like to give special thanks to Patrick J. McGovern, without whom this book would not have been possible.

♦

Contents at a Glance

Cartoons at a Glance

By Rich Tennant

"I've been in hardware all of my life, and all of a sudden it's software that'll make me rich."

page 9

"Come on Walt—time to freshen the company Web page."

page 281

"Games are an important part of my Web site. They cause eye strain."

page 81

"So far our Web presence has been pretty good. We've gotten some orders, a few inquiries, and nine guys who want to date our logo."

page 175

"Just how accurately should my Web site reflect my place of business?"

page D-1

"Face it Vinnie— you're gonna have a hard time getting people to subscribe online with a credit card to a newsletter called 'Felons Interactive!'"

page 229

Fax: 978-546-7747 • E-mail: the5wave@tiac.net

Table of Contents

Introduction

• •

*Y*ou've been thinking about starting your own business, but until now, it's been just a dream. After all, you're a busy person. You have a full-time job, whether it's running your home or working outside your home. Or perhaps you've been through some life-changing event and are ready to take off in a new direction.

Well, I have news for you: *Now* is the perfect time to turn your dream into reality by starting your own online business. Many people just like you are making money and enriching their lives by operating businesses online. The clock and your location are no longer limiting factors. Small business owners can now work any time of the night or day in their spare bedroom, local library, or neighborhood coffee shop.

If you like the idea of being in business for yourself, but you don't have a particular product or service in mind at the moment, relax and keep yourself open for inspiration. Many different kinds of commercial enterprises can hit it big on the Internet. Among the entrepreneurs I interviewed for this book are a man who sells artwork created through origami (the art of paper folding), a mapmaker, a woman who provides office services for the medical community, a hardware salesman, a dealer in fine art, and several folks who create Web pages for other businesses. With the help of this book, you can start a new endeavor and be in charge of your own cyberbusiness, too.

You Can Do It!

What's that? You say you wouldn't know a merchant account, profit-and-loss statement, or clickthrough advertising rate if it came up to you on the street and introduced itself? Don't worry: The Internet (and this book) level the playing field, so a novice has just as good a chance to succeed as those M.B.A.s who love to throw around business terms at cocktail parties.

The Internet is the new frontier for business. Whether you've been in business for 20 years or 20 minutes, the keys to success are the same:

✔ **Having a good idea:** If you have something to sell that people have an appetite for, and if your competition is slim, your chances of success are hefty.

> ✔ **Working hard:** When you are your own boss, you make yourself work harder that any of your former bosses ever could. But if you put in the effort and persist through the inevitable ups and downs, you will be a winner.
>
> ✔ **Preparing for success:** One of the most surprising and useful things I learned from the online businesspeople I interviewed was that if you believe that you will succeed, you probably will. Believe in yourself and proceed as though you're going to be successful. Together with your good ideas and hard work, your confidence will pay off.

If you're the cautious type who wants to test the waters before you launch your new business on the Internet, let this book lead you gently up the learning curve. After you're online, you can master techniques to improve your presence. This book includes helpful hints for doing market research and reworking your Web site until you get the success you want. Even if you aren't among the lucky small business owners who make a fortune by connecting to the Net, the odds are very good that you will make new friends, build your confidence, and have fun, too.

Where This Book Is Coming From

Online business is not just for large corporations, or even just for small businesses that already have a storefront in the "real" world and simply want to supplement their marketability with a Web site.

The Internet is a perfect place for individuals who want to start their own business, who like using computers, and who believe that cyberspace is the place to do it. You don't need much money to get started, after all. If you already have a computer and an Internet connection and can create your own Web pages (as this book describes), making the move to your own business Web site may cost only $100 or less. After you're online, the overhead is pretty reasonable, too: You may only pay $50 to $100 per month to a Web hosting service to keep your site online.

With each month that goes by, the number of Internet users increases exponentially. Whether you believe the surveys that count 40 million users or the ones that provide a more conservative estimate of 20 million users, you have to admit that a whole lot of people are out there in cyberspace. We are now beginning to reach that critical mass where *most* people are using the Internet regularly for everyday shopping and other financial activities. Very soon, the Internet will be a powerhouse for small businesses.

So why wait to fall behind your competition? The goal of this book is to help you open your fledgling business on the Internet now, while the Net is still new and cutting-edge. Let this book guide you through the following steps:

- ✔ Preparing a business plan, defining your target market, and setting goals
- ✔ Purchasing the hardware and software you need to run your business
- ✔ Making your Web pages content-rich and interactive
- ✔ Marketing to customers around the world
- ✔ Creating a secure environment for shopping and receiving payments online
- ✔ Keeping your business records and observing legal requirements

How to Use This Book

Want to get an overview of the whole process of going online and be inspired by one family's online business success story? Zip ahead to Chapter 1. Want to find out how to accept credit card payments? Flip ahead to Chapter 8. Feel free to skip back and forth to chapters that interest you. I've made this book into an easy-to-use reference tool that you will be comfortable with, no matter what your level of experience with computers and networking. You don't have to scour each chapter methodically from beginning to end to find what you want. The Net doesn't work that way, and neither does this book!

If you're just starting out and need to do some essential business planning, see Chapter 2. If you want to prepare a shopping list of business equipment, see Chapter 3. Chapters 4 through 9 are all about the essential aspects of creating and operating a successful online business, from organizing your Web site to providing effective online customer service. Later chapters get into security, legal issues, and accounting. The fun thing about being online is that it's easy to keep revising. So start where it suits you and come back later for more.

What This Book Assumes

This book assumes that you have never been in business before but that you're interested in setting up your own commercial site on the Internet or America Online or CompuServe. I also assume that you're familiar with the Internet, have been surfing for a while, and may even have put out some information of your own in the form of a home page.

It also assumes that you have or are ready to get the following:

- **A computer and a modem:** Don't worry, Chapter 3 explains exactly what hardware and software you need.

- **Instructions on how to think like a businessperson:** I spend a good amount of time in this book encouraging you to set goals, devise strategies to meet those goals, and do the sort of planning that successful businesspeople need to do.

- **Just enough technical know-how:** You don't have to do it all yourself. Plenty of entrepreneurs decide to partner with someone or hire an expert to perform design and technical work. This book can help you understand your options and give you a basic vocabulary so you can work productively with the consultants you hire.

What's Where in This Book

This book is divided into five parts, and each part contains chapters that discuss a stage in the process of starting an online business. In addition to the parts, this book also includes an Internet Directory and an appendix.

Part I: Starting Your Own Online Business

Part I describes what you need to do and how you need to *think* in order to start your new online business. The first chapter follows the story about how a business started by an 11-year-old boy and his family has grown into an Internet success story. Subsequent chapters also present case studies profiling other entrepreneurs and describing how they started their online businesses. This part describes the software you need to create Web pages and perform essential business tasks, and any computer upgrades that will help your business run more smoothly.

Part II: Putting Your Web Site to Work

Even if you use an online service that isn't technically part of the Web, such as America Online, you need to create a Web site — a series of interconnected Web pages that everyone in cyberspace can view with a Web browser. The Web is where it's at as far as online business is concerned. This part explains how to create a compelling and irresistible Web site, one that attracts paying customers around the world and keeps them coming back to make more purchases. This part also includes options for accepting electronic cash or credit card payments from your customers.

Part III: Promoting Your Online Business

Your work doesn't end after you put your Web site online or start to make a few sales. In fact, what you do after you open your cyberdoors for business can make the difference between a site that says "Wow!" and one that says "Ho-hum." This part describes cost-effective marketing and advertising techniques that you can do yourself to increase visibility and improve customer satisfaction.

Part IV: Law, Security, and Accounting

This part delves into some less-than-sexy but essential activities for any online business. Find out about general security methods designed to make commerce more secure on the Internet. I also discuss copyright, trade-marking, and other legal concerns for anyone wanting to start a company in the increasingly competitive atmosphere of the Internet. Finally, you get an overview of basic accounting practices for online businesses and suggestions of accounting tools you can use to keep track of your e-commerce activities.

The Starting an Online Business For Dummies Internet Directory

If you're running your online business in your off-hours or between other activities, you don't have time to scour the Web for help. Not to fear: You can find everything you need in this directory. It's a collection of Web sites and other Internet resources of special interest to individuals starting an online business — especially if you're working alone or at home and need to find people to help you. (You can also find a set of links to all the sites listed in this directory on the CD-ROM that accompanies this book.)

Part V: The Part of Tens

Filled with tips, cautions, suggestions, and examples, the Part of Tens presents many tidbits of information that you can use to plan and create your own business presence on the Internet.

Appendix

The appendix at the back of this book provides detailed explanations of the business, Web page, graphics, and other cool software programs included on the CD-ROM. It tells what you need in order to use the programs, how to install them, and where to go for more information.

Conventions Used in This Book

In this book, I format important bits of information in special ways to make sure that you notice them right away:

- ✔ **In This Chapter lists:** Starting at the very beginning, every chapter begins with a list of the topics covered in that chapter. This list represents a kind of table of contents in miniature.

- ✔ **Numbered lists:** When you see a numbered list, follow the steps in a specific order to accomplish a given task.

- ✔ **Bulleted lists:** Bulleted lists (like this one) indicate things that you can do in any order or list related bits of information.

- ✔ **Web addresses:** When I describe activities or sites of interest on the World Wide Web, I include the address, or Uniform Resource Locator (URL), in a special typeface like this: `http://www.idgbooks.com/`. Because the newer versions of popular Web browsers, such as Netscape Navigator and Microsoft Internet Explorer, don't require you to enter the entire URL, this book uses the shortened addresses. For example, if you want to connect to the IDG Books Worldwide site mentioned previously, you can get there by simply entering the following in your browser's Go To box: `www.idgbooks.com`.

  Don't be surprised if your browser can't find an Internet address you type or if a Web page that's depicted in this book no longer looks the same. Although the sites were current when the book was written, Web addresses (and sites themselves) can be pretty fickle. Try looking for a missing site by using an Internet search engine. Or try shortening the address by deleting everything after the `.com` (or `.org` or `.edu`).

Icons Used in This Book

Starting an Online Business For Dummies also uses special graphical elements called *icons* to get your attention. Here's what they look like and what they mean:

This icon points out some technical details that may be of interest to you. A thorough understanding, however, is not a prerequisite to grasping the underlying concept. Non-techies are welcome to skip items marked by this icon altogether.

This icon calls your attention to interviews I conducted with online entrepreneurs who provided tips and instructions for running an online business.

This icon flags practical advice about particular software programs or about issues of importance to businesses. Look to these tips for help with finding resources quickly, making sales, or improving the quality of your online business site.

This icon points out potential pitfalls that can develop into more major problems if you're not careful.

This icon alerts you to facts and figures that are important to keep in mind as you run your online business.

This icon alerts you to software programs and other resources that I consider to be especially good, especially for the novice user.

This icon marks software programs and other goodies that are included on this book's CD-ROM.

We're in It Together

Improving communication is the whole point of this book. My goal is to help you express yourself in the exciting new medium of the Internet and to remind you that you're not alone. I'm a businessperson myself, after all. So I hope that you'll let me know what you think about this book by contacting me online or by regular (snail) mail. Check out the IDG Books Worldwide Book Registration page at the back of this book for information about registering this book and sending your feedback. And remember to check out the ...*For Dummies* Web site at www.dummies.com.

You're also welcome to contact me directly if you have questions or comments. Send e-mail to Greg Holden at gholden@interaccess.com.

Part I
Starting Your Own Online Business

The 5th Wave   By Rich Tennant

"I've been in hardware all of my life, and all of a sudden it's software that'll make me rich."

In this part . . .

*W*hat all does starting an online business involve? This part answers that question with a brief overview of the whole process. The following chapters help you set your online business goals and draw up a blueprint for meeting those goals.

And just as dentists prepare their drills and carpenters assemble their tools, you need to gather the necessary hardware and software to keep your online business running smoothly. This part discusses the business equipment that the online store owner needs, and suggests ways that you can meet those needs even on a limited budget.

Let the step-by-step instructions and real-life case studies in this part guide you through the process of starting a successful business online.

Chapter 1

Opening Your Own Online Business in Ten Easy Steps

These days, virtually every existing company seems to be adding a Web site with an address like www.company.com to its arsenal of business tools. But the steps required to conduct commerce online are well within the reach of individuals like you and me, who have no prior business experience. Companies are continually releasing new programs that make creating Web pages and transacting online business easier than ever. All you need is a good idea, a bit of start-up money, some computer equipment, and a little help from your friends.

One of my goals in this book is to be one of the friends who provides you with the right advice and support to get your business online and make it a success. This chapter gives you a step-by-step overview of the entire process of starting an online business.

Step 1: Identify a Need

Statistically, the Internet is a hotbed of commerce — and it just keeps getting hotter. Listen to what the experts are saying:

✔ eMarketer (www.emarketer.com) estimates that anywhere from 25 to 40 million individuals use the Internet worldwide, and that this number will balloon to 142 million users by 2002.

✔ The director general of a Canadian electronic commerce task force recently estimated that electronic commerce conducted in that country will to grow from $1 billion in 1998 to $13 billion by 2002. Worldwide, revenues from e-commerce are expected to grow from $20 billion to $300 billion over the same period.

Check out the Starting an Online Business For Dummies Internet Directory, later in this book and on the accompanying CD-ROM, for more sites where you can gather "fast facts" and background information on doing business online.

But all this online buying and selling doesn't mean that starting an online business is a sure thing. After all, you can't expect Web surfers to patronize your online business unless you identify services or items that they really need. Your first job is to get in touch with your market and determine how you can best meet its needs.

Seeing what's out there

Many people decide to start an online business with little more than a casual knowledge of the Internet as a worldwide, interconnected network of computers to which people can connect either from work or home, and through which people can communicate via e-mail, receive information from the Web, and buy and sell items using credit cards or other means.

But when you decide to get serious about going online with a commercial endeavor, it pays to get to know the environment in which you plan to be working. The more information you have about the following aspects of the online world, the more likely you are to succeed in doing business there:

✔ Other online businesses that already do what you want to do

✔ The kinds of customers who shop online and who might visit your site

✔ The special language and style of online communication — in other words, the culture of the Internet

One of your first steps should be to find out what it means to do business online and to determine the best ways for you to fit into the exploding field of electronic commerce. For example, you need to realize that the Internet is a personal place; that customers are active, not passive, in the way they absorb information; and that the Net was established on a culture of people sharing information freely and helping one another.

Some of the best places to learn about the culture of the Internet are the newsgroups, chat rooms, and bulletin boards where individuals gather and exchange messages online. Visiting discussion forums devoted to topics that interest you personally can be especially helpful, and you're likely to end up participating yourself. Also visit commerce Web sites, such as online shopping malls, making note of ideas and approaches that you may want to use yourself.

As you take a look around the Internet, notice the kinds of goods and services that tend to sell in the increasingly crowded, occasionally disorganized, and sometimes complex online world. The things that sell best in cyberspace are

- Items sold at a discount
- Hard-to-find or unique items
- Items that are easier to buy online than at a "real" store, such as a rare book that you can order in minutes from Amazon.com (`www.amazon.com`), or an electronic greeting card that you can send online in seconds (`www.greeting-cards.com`)
- Publications available by subscription, such as newspapers and magazines, or electronic publications *(e-zines)* that only exist online

Figuring out what's missing

After you take a look at what's already out there, the next step is to find ways to make your business stand out from the crowd. Direct your energies toward making your site unique in some way and providing things that others don't offer. The things that set your online business apart from the rest can be as tangible as half-price sales, contests, seasonal sales, or freebies. They can also involve making your business site higher in quality than the others.

What if you can't find other online businesses doing what you want to do? Lucky you! In electronic commerce, being first often means getting a head start and being more successful than latecomers, even if they have more resources than you do. (Just ask the owners of the online bookstore Amazon.com.) The whole field of online business is still in its pioneering days, so don't be afraid to try something new and outlandish. It just might work!

CASE STUDY

The Podraza family finds its online niche

When 11-year-old Michael Podraza received his first two Beanie Babies as gifts in the fall of 1996, he decided to become an avid collector. In case you don't know, Beanie Babies are little plush animals produced by Ty Inc. (www.ty.com). Since they first appeared in 1996, Beanies have become hot items, especially those that have been strategically "retired" by Ty. Although the critters retail for about $5, some scarce varieties can sell for $300 or more. One particularly rare model (the royal blue elephant) recently sold for $5,000.

Michael's father, Dan Podraza, drove him to flea markets and swap meets, where they looked long and hard for particular Beanies. Sometimes, they didn't find what they were looking for at all. After many hours of driving, Dan started to think that there must be a better way to locate these little treasures — and that there must also be lots of collectors like Michael who were eager to buy and sell them.

One day, Michael heard two women in a store discussing how difficult it was to find certain varieties of Beanie Babies, and how much they might pay for the Beanies if they could find them. Michael had two of the plush animals the women were discussing. He ended up selling the toys, which had originally cost $5, to the women for $25 and $30.

It was Dan Podraza's 15-year-old son, Christopher, who introduced him to the Web. The Podrazas didn't know much about the Internet or online commerce at the time they jumped on the cybercommerce bandwagon.

"I've been a high-school math teacher for 28 years," Dan explains. "I've never sold anything before." He sensed that there was a business need, and he was simply looking for an easy way to fulfill that need.

Although Beanie Baby publications, businesses, and Web sites are plentiful these days, in mid-1997, no Web sites at all were set up to exchange Beanie Babies. "We visited other Beanie Baby Web sites, but none of them sold Beanies," says Dan Podraza. "We knew that lots of people were interested, though. We often saw messages that people left on electronic bulletin boards, asking where they could go to find these things."

The family decided to start the Collectible Exchange, Ltd., a Web site that brought buyers and sellers together to make transactions. They had no idea how well it would do, but they had determined two essential things: There was a market for this product, and there was a need for a service that did not yet exist online.

The Collectible Exchange now employs six full-time and three part-time workers (all family members and neighbors), and its Web site (www.beaniex.com) receives 50,000 visits *each day*. But not so long ago, the Podrazas, like you, were just starting out, and they, too, had only a dream and the courage to explore something new. I hope that their story will inspire you to turn your own online business into a reality, as well.

Step 2: Determine What You Have to Offer

Determining what you have to sell, another early step in the process of putting together a new business, often occurs before or at the same time as the previous step — identifying your likely customers. That's what business is all about, either online or off: identifying customers' needs and figuring out exactly what goods or services you're going to provide to meet those needs.

Make a list of all the items you have to put up for sale, or all the services you plan to provide to your customers. Next, you need to decide not only what goods or services you can provide online, but also where you're going to obtain them. Are you going to create sale items yourself? Are you going to purchase them from another supplier? Jot down your ideas on paper and keep them close at hand as you continue developing your business plan.

The Internet is a personal, highly interactive medium. Be as specific as possible with what you plan to do online. The medium favors businesses that specialize. After all, the more specific your business, the more intimate you can be with your customers.

Step 3: Set Your Cyberbusiness Goals

The process of setting goals and objectives and then designing strategies for attaining them is essential when starting a new business. What you end up with is called a *business plan*. A good business plan applies not only to the start-up phase but also to a business's day-to-day operation. It can also be instrumental in helping a small business obtain a bank loan.

Creating a business plan

To set specific goals for your new business, ask yourself these questions: Why do you want to start a business? Why do you want to start it online? What would *you* want to buy online? What would make you buy it?

Sure, I can give you plenty of reasons for setting up virtual shop on the Internet. But only *you* can answer these questions for yourself. Make sure that you have a clear idea of where you're going so you can commit to making your venture successful over the long haul. (See Chapter 2 for more on coming up with goals and envisioning your business.)

To carry your plan into your daily operations, observe these suggestions:

✔ Write a brief description of your company and what you hope to accomplish with it.

✔ Draw up a marketing strategy (see Chapters 7 and 11 for tips).

✔ Keep track of your finances (see Chapter 14 for specifics).

Consider using specialized software to help you prepare your business plan. Programs such as Business Plan Pro by Palo Alto Software (www.palo-alto.com) lead you through the process by asking you a series of questions as a way of identifying what you want to do. The program retails for $89.95; however, you can find a version of this highly regarded software right on this book's CD-ROM.

Working without a storefront

Although doing business online means that you don't have to rent space in a mall or open a real, physical store, you *do* have to set up a virtual space for your online business. You do so by creating a Web site and finding a host for your site. (A *host* is a company that, for a fee, makes your site available 24 hours a day by maintaining it on a special computer called a *Web server.*)

Chapter 2 describes two methods for selling your wares online that don't require a Web site — online classifieds and auctions. But most online businesses find having a Web site indispensable for generating and conducting sales.

In addition to your virtual storefront, you also have to find a real place to do your business. You don't necessarily have to rent a large space with both men's and women's bathrooms, as the Podrazas did. Many online entrepreneurs use a home office or perhaps a corner in a room where computers, books, and other related equipment reside.

If you set aside part of your home for business purposes, you are eligible for tax deductions. Exactly how much you can deduct depends on how much space you use. (For example, I have a nine-room house, and one room serves as my office, so I am able to deduct one-ninth of my utility and other housing costs.) You can depreciate your computers and other business equipment, too. On the other hand, your municipality may require you to obtain a license if you operate a business in a residential area; check with your local authorities to make sure that you're on the up-and-up. You can find out more about tax and legal issues, including local licensing requirements, in Chapters 13 and 14 of this book.

Step 4: Assemble Your Equipment

Not all businesses cost thousands of dollars to start up. As many of the entrepreneurs profiled in the case studies throughout this book report, you can start an online business with an investment of only a few hundred dollars, or perhaps even less.

Finding a Web host

Any business needs a place to call home. In the offline world, stores rent space in malls or other buildings. In cyberspace, your landlord is called a Web hosting service. Your Web host is a company that makes your online store accessible to shoppers who connect to you by using Web browsers or other software.

A Web host can be as large and well-known as America Online, which gives all of its customers a place to create and publish their own Web pages. Some Web sites, like GeoCities (www.geocities.com) or Tripod (www.tripod.com), act as hosting services and provide easy-to-use Web site creation tools, as well. In addition, the company that gives you access to the Internet — your Internet Service Provider — may also publish your Web pages.

Make sure that your host has a fast connection to the Internet and can handle the large numbers of simultaneous visits, or *hits,* that your Web site is sure to one day get. You can find a detailed description of Web hosting options in Chapter 4.

Getting the hardware you need

For doing business online, your most important piece of equipment is your computer. Other hardware, such as scanners, modems, and monitors, are essential, too. You need to make sure that your computer equipment is up to snuff, because you're going to be spending a lot of time online: answering e-mail, checking orders, revising your Web site, and marketing your product.

The Podrazas, profiled earlier in this chapter, decided to make a substantial commitment to the success of their online business by investing in a solid hardware system. Dan Podraza says they spent about $6,000 on purchasing and setting up computers to handle orders. They have four computers in their business that are networked together so they can all access the company's database.

Computer-related equipment will probably be your main expense. It pays to shop wisely and get the best setup you can afford up front, so you don't have to purchase upgrades later on. (For more suggestions on buying business hardware and software, see Chapter 3.)

Choosing your software

For the most part, the programs you need in order to operate an online business are the same as the software you use to surf the Internet. You do, however, need to have a wider variety of tools than you would use for simple information gathering.

Because you're going to be in the business of information *providing* now, as well as information gathering, you need programs such as these:

- **A Web page editor:** These programs, which you may also hear called *Web page creation tools* or *Web page authoring tools,* make it easy for you to format text, add images, and design Web pages without having to learn HTML (HyperText Markup Language), the set of instructions that Web browsers use to present those pages the way you want them.

- **Graphics software:** If you decide to create your business Web site yourself, rather than finding someone to do it for you, you need a program that can help you draw or edit images that you want to include on your site.

- **Storefront software:** You can purchase software that leads you through the process of creating a full-fledged online business and getting your pages on the Web.

- **Accounting programs:** To keep track of expenses and income, you can use software that acts as a spreadsheet, helps you with billing, and even calculates sales tax.

The CD-ROM that accompanies this book includes a good selection of easy-to-use software. For this disc, I picked out programs to help you create Web pages, do accounting, download software, and accomplish many other essential online business functions.

Step 5: Find the Support You Need

Conducting online business does involve relatively new technologies, but they aren't impossible to learn. In fact, the technology is becoming more accessible all the time, thanks to more powerful and affordable software.

Keeping track of supplies

As Dan Podraza points out, making sure that you have sufficient inventory to meet demand is important. It's better to have too many items for sale, rather than not enough. "We operated on a low budget in the beginning, and we didn't have the inventory that people wanted," he points out. "People online get impatient if they have to wait for things too long. Make sure you have the goods you advertise. Plan to be successful."

The Collectible Exchange keeps track of its inventory using an Oracle database that's connected to its Web site. When someone orders a product from the Web site, that order is automatically recorded in the database, which then produces an order for replacement stock.

In this kind of arrangement, the database serves as a so-called *back end* or *back office* to the Web-based storefront. This is a sophisticated arrangement that's not for beginners. However, if orders and inventory get to be too much for you to handle yourself, consider hiring a Web developer to set up such a system for you. If you're adventurous and technically oriented, you can link a database to a Web site using a product such as Fusion, which, along with other software included on this book's CD, I describe in the appendix.

Many of the people who start online businesses learn how to create Web pages and promote their companies by reading books, attending classes, or networking with friends and colleagues. Of course, just because you *can* do it all doesn't mean that you have to. Oftentimes, you're better off hiring help, either to advise you in areas where you aren't as strong or simply to help you tackle the growing workload.

Hiring technical consultants

Often, it pays to have professionals point you in the right direction and help you develop an effective Web presence. Many businesspeople who usually work alone (myself included) hire knowledgeable individuals to do design or programming work that they would find impossible to tackle otherwise.

Don't be reluctant to hire professional help in order to get your business online. The Web is full of development firms that perform several related functions: providing customers with Web access, helping to create Web sites, and hosting sites on their servers. The expense for such services may be considerable at first (Dan Podraza estimates that the Collectible Exchange's start-up costs were $12,000, not counting hardware purchases), but they can pay off in the long term.

Another area where you may want to find help is in networking and computer maintenance. As Dan Podraza points out, "along with having the knowledge of your product, you have to know how to keep your computers running. Find out if you have a computer expert in your neighborhood."

The point about finding someone right in your own neighborhood is a good one. In my own case, I work with a graphic designer who lives right around the corner from me, and he uses a consultant who lives across the street from him. Ask around your school or church, as well as other social venues. Your neighbors may be able to help you with various projects, including your online business . . . and your online business just may be able to help them, too.

Businesspeople who provide professional services also commonly recommend other consultants in the course of e-mail communications. Don't work in a vacuum. Participate in mailing lists and discussion groups online. Make contacts and strike up cooperative relationships with individuals who can help you.

If you do find a business partner, make sure that the person's abilities balance your own. If you're great at sales and public relations, for example, find a writer or Web page designer to partner with.

Gathering your team members

Many entrepreneurial businesses are family affairs. For example, a husband-and-wife team started Scaife's Butcher Shop in England, which has a successful Web site. The Collectible Exchange is another example: Besides Dan Podraza, his wife Diana, and their children Bradley and Jennifer, the company employs Grandfather John (bill payments), Grandma Jean (receiving), and son Christopher (straightening up and day-to-day maintenance). (Michael, who is now 12 years old, is too young to be a paid employee.) The Podrazas' next-door neighbor, Roberta, functions as the Collectible Exchange's office manager, performing essential functions like downloading orders and answering e-mail inquiries.

Don't be surprised if you don't feel a need to hire team members early on, when you have plenty of time to do planning. Many people wait to seek help until they have a deadline to meet or are in a financial crunch.

Find people who are reliable and can make a long-term commitment to your project. Because the person you hire will probably work online quite a bit, pick someone who already exhibits high-tech experience. Online hiring practices work pretty much the same as those offline: You should always review a resume, get at least three references, and ask for samples of the candidate's work. Pick someone who responds promptly and courteously and who provides the talents you need. If your only contact is by phone and e-mail, references are even more important.

Step 6: Build a Web Site

A Web site is pretty much indispensable for any online business these days. Fortunately, Web sites are becoming easier to create. You don't have to know a line of HTML in order to create an effective Web page yourself. Chapter 5 walks you through the specific tasks involved in organizing and designing Web pages. Also see Chapter 6 for tips on making your Web pages content-rich and interactive.

Make your business easy to find online. Pick a Web address (otherwise known as a URL or Uniform Resource Locator) that's easy to remember. You can purchase a short domain-name alias, such as `www.company.com`, to replace a longer one like `www.internetprovider.com/~username/companyname/index.html`. See Chapter 9 for more information.

Creating compelling content

Content is the most important part of any Web site. The more useful information you provide, the more visits your site will receive. By *compelling* content, I am talking about words, headings, or images that induce visitors to interact with your site in some way. You can make your content compelling in a number of ways:

- ✔ Provide a call to action (such as "Click Here!" or "Buy Now!").
- ✔ Explain how the reader will benefit by clicking on a link and exploring your site ("Visit our News and Specials page to find out how to win 500 frequent flyer miles").
- ✔ Briefly and concisely summarize your business and its mission.
- ✔ Scan images of your sale items (or of the services you provide) as described in Chapter 5, and post them on a Web page called Products.

Don't forget the personal touch when it comes to connecting with your customers' needs. People who shop online don't get to meet their merchants in person, so anything you can tell about yourself helps to personalize the process and put your visitors at ease. An "About This Company" Web page is often helpful. The Collectible Exchange has just such as page, in which they tell how their business got started. They also have a humorous "Where's Michael?" photo of their son nearly engulfed by Beanies (see Figure 1-1). Let your cybervisitors know that they're dealing with real people, not remote machines and computer programs.

It's only natural to peek in on other businesses' Web sites to pick up ideas and see how they handle similar issues. In cyberspace, you can visit plenty of businesses that are comparable to yours from the comfort of your home office, and the trip takes only minutes.

Establishing a graphic identity

A site with an identity looks a certain way. For example, take a look at Figure 1-2, as well as Figures 1-1 and 1-3, elsewhere in this chapter. All are pages from the Collectible Exchange's Web site. Notice how each has the same white background, the same company logo, and similar heading styles. Using such elements consistently from page to page creates an identity that gives your business credibility and helps viewers find what they're looking for.

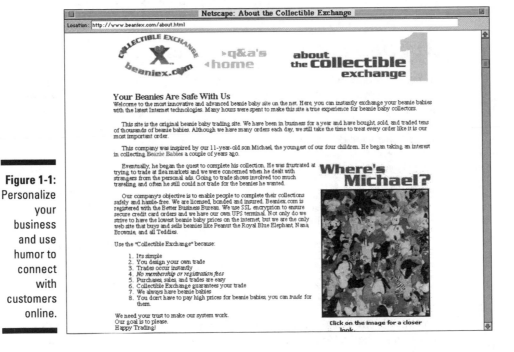

Figure 1-1: Personalize your business and use humor to connect with customers online.

Netscape: BEANIE BABIES – Collectible Exchange – Buy, Sell, Trade Beanie Babies Instantly!

Location: http://www.beaniex.com/index.html

Figure 1-2:
Through careful planning and design, the Collectible Exchange maintains a Web site with a consistent look and feel, or graphic identity, on every page.

The Collectible Exchange's Web pages look simple because they are uncluttered and use a clean white background. But the pages, which are created by their consultant, are actually pretty complex. They use advanced layout options like image maps (images that have been divided into clickable regions), tables, headings that are actually graphic images, and interactive forms. See Chapter 5 for more about such advanced layout options.

Step 7: Set Up Systems for Handling Sales

Many businesses go online and then are surprised by their own success. They don't have systems in place for finalizing sales and tracking finances and inventory.

Early on, the Collectible Exchange found itself in just such a predicament. "We operated on a low budget in the beginning, and we didn't have the inventory that people wanted," Dan Podraza points out. "People online get impatient if they have to wait for things too long. Make sure that you have the goods you advertise. Plan to be successful."

An excellent way to plan for success is to set up ways to track your business finances and to create a secure purchasing environment for your online customers. That way, you can build on your success rather than being surprised by it.

Providing a means for secure transactions

Getting paid is the key to survival as well as success. When your business only exists online, the payment process is not always straightforward. Make your Web site a safe and easy place for customers to pay you. Provide different payment options and build customers' level of trust any way you can.

Although the number of people doing shopping online is increasing steadily, plenty of Web surfers are still squeamish about submitting credit card numbers online. Make them feel at ease by explaining what measures you're taking to ensure that their information is secure. Such measures include signing up for an account with a Web host that provides a *secure server:* a computer that uses software to encrypt data and uses digital documents called certificates to ensure its identity. (See Chapters 8 and 12 for more on Internet security and secure shopping systems.)

Becoming a credit card merchant

The words *electronic commerce* or *e-commerce* bring to mind visions of online forms and credit card data that is transmitted over the Internet. Do you have to provide such service in order to run a successful online business? Of course you don't. Being a credit card merchant makes life easier for your customers, to be sure, but it also adds complications and extra costs to your operation.

To become a credit card merchant, you have to apply to a bank. Small and home-based businesses can have difficulty getting their applications approved. (Some businesses specialize in granting credit card merchant status to small businesses, however; see Chapter 8 for suggestions.)

If you do get the go-ahead to become a credit card merchant, you have to pay the bank a *discount rate,* which is a fee (typically, 2 to 3 percent of each transaction) to the bank. You sometimes have to pay a monthly premium charge of $10 to $25, as well. Besides that, you need special software or hardware to accept credit card payments.

In the early stages of your business, you may find it easier to take orders over the phone. Then, if your business takes off, you can present your sales records to the bank and be more likely to get your merchant application approved. See Chapter 8 for more on electronic commerce options for your business.

To maximize your sales by reaching users who either don't have credit cards or don't want to use them on the Internet, provide low-tech alternatives such as toll-free phone numbers and fax numbers so people can send you their information using more familiar technologies.

One reason the Podrazas' business succeeds is that it inspires the trust and confidence of its customers. The home page of the Collectible Exchange Web site, for example, contains the following messages: "Licensed-Bonded-Insured" and "A Better Business Bureau Program." The site also provides a secure way for people to make electronic purchases by providing online forms, such as the one in Figure 1-3, where people can safely enter credit card and other personal information. The News and Specials page (www.beaniex.com/news.html) contains detailed instructions on how to place orders and check on the status of those orders.

Safeguarding your customers' personal information is important, but you also need to safeguard yourself. Many online businesses get burned by bad guys who submit fraudulent credit card information. If you don't verify the information and submit it to your financial institution for processing, you are liable for the cost. Strongly consider signing up with a service that handles credit card verification for you in order to cut down on lost revenue.

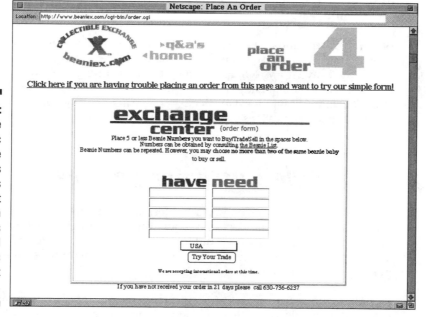

Figure 1-3:
A secure electronic commerce site lets shoppers submit information that is encrypted so criminals can't access it.

Keeping your books straight

What does "keeping your books" mean, anyway? In the simplest sense, it means recording all financial activities that pertain to your business: any expenses you incur, all the income you receive, as well as your equipment and tax deductions. The financial side of running a business also entails creating reports, such as profit-and-loss statements, that banks require if you apply for a loan. Such reports not only help meet financial institutions' needs, but they also provide you with essential information about how your business is really doing at any given time.

You can record all this information the old-fashioned way, by writing it down in ledgers and journals, or you can use accounting software. Because you're making a commitment to using computers on a regular basis by starting an online business, it's only natural for you to use computers to keep your books, too. Accounting software can help you keep track of expenses and provide information that may save you some headaches at tax time.

The Collectible Exchange uses a popular program called QuickBooks to pay the salaries of its employees. However, they do the business's accounting the old-fashioned way: They keep the receipts in a folder and hand everything to their accountant. Other businesses profiled in subsequent chapters use popular programs such as Quicken and Peachtree First Accounting to keep their books.

Before you start looking around the Web for accounting packages to purchase, first check out this book's CD-ROM. It includes Simple Business Invoicing & Inventory to help you keep track of supplies, as well as Simple Business Accounting, EasyAccount, QuickBooks, M.Y.O.B. Accounting Plus, and WhereDidAllMyMoneyGo, all easy-to-use accounting packages that are great for financial novices.

Step 8: Provide Customer Service

The Internet, which runs on wires, cables, and computer chips, may not seem like a place for the personal touch. But technology didn't actually create the Internet and all its content: *People* did that. In fact, the Internet is a great place to provide your clients and customers with outstanding, personal customer service.

By helping your customers get their questions answered and problems resolved, you help yourself, too. You build loyalty as well as credibility among your clientele. For many small businesses, the key to competing effectively with larger competitors is by providing superior customer service. See Chapter 9 for more ideas on how you can do this.

Sharing your expertise

The Podrazas did their homework on Beanie Babies for nearly a year before their business first went online. They could hardly *help* learning about the stuffed animals, which multiplied around the house as Michael accumulated more and more.

Your knowledge and experience are among your most valuable commodities. So you may be surprised when I suggest that you give them away for free. Why? It's a "try before you buy" concept. Helping people for free builds your credibility and makes them more likely to pay for your services down the road.

When your business is online, it's easy for you to communicate what you know about your field and to make your knowledge readily available. One way is to set up a Web page that presents the basics about your company and your field of interest in the form of Frequently Asked Questions (FAQs). Another is to become a virtual publisher/editor and create your own newsletter in which you write about what's new with your company and about topics related to your work. See Chapter 9 for more on communicating your expertise through FAQs, newsletters, and advanced e-mail techniques.

Becoming a resource for customers

Many *ontrepreneurs* (online entrepreneurs) succeed by making their Web sites not only a place for sales and promotion but also an indispensable resource, full of useful hyperlinks and other information, that customers want to visit again and again. For example, the Collectible Exchange, profiled earlier in this chapter, acts as a resource, a meeting place, and a place to do buying and selling.

John Moen, a cartographer, knows the importance of making your site a resource for potential customers. He saw visits to his Graphic Maps business site (`www.graphicmaps.com/graphic_maps.htm`) jump from 30 a day to 1,000 a day after he decided to give away free art (called *clip art*) that he had created. John first took his business, Graphic Maps, online in 1995 for start-up costs of only $300. He now has six employees, receives many custom orders for more than $10,000, and has done business with numerous Fortune 500 companies. To promote his site (shown in Figure 1-4), John gives away free maps for nonprofit organizations, operates a daily geography contest with a $50 prize to the first person with the correct answer, and answers e-mail promptly. "Give visitors more information than they expect, be creative, and take chances," he suggests.

Figure 1-4:
This site
uses free
art, a
mailing list,
and daily
prizes to
drum up
business.

Another way to encourage customers to congregate at your site on a regular basis is to create a discussion area. Chapter 9 shows you how to provide a discussion page right on your own Web site.

Becoming an e-mail expert

E-mail is, in my humble opinion, the single most important marketing tool you can use to boost your online business. Becoming an expert e-mail user increases your contacts and provides you with new sources of support, too.

The two best and easiest e-mail strategies are the following:

- Check your e-mail as often as possible.
- Respond to e-mail inquiries immediately — if not sooner.

Additionally, you can e-mail inquiries about co-marketing opportunities to other Web sites similar to your own. Ask other online business owners if they will provide links to your site in exchange for your providing links to theirs. And always include a signature file with your message that includes the name of your business and a link to your business site. See Chapter 9 for more information on using e-mail effectively to build and maintain relations with your online customers.

Step 9: Advertise Your Business

In order to be successful, small businesses need to get the word out to the people who are likely to purchase what they have to offer. If this group turns out to be only a narrow market, so much the better; the Internet is great for connecting to specialized "niche" markets that share a common interest. (See Chapters 7 and 10 for more on locating your most likely customers on the Internet and figuring out how best to communicate with them.)

The Internet provides many unique and effective ways for small businesses to advertise, including search services, e-mail, newsgroups, electronic mailing lists, and more.

Registering with Internet search services

How, exactly, do you get listed on the search engines such as Yahoo! and Lycos? In many cases, you don't have to do anything; most search engines use special computer programs to index your site automatically.

You can help search services find your site more quickly by including special keywords and site descriptions in the HTML commands for your Web pages. You place these keywords after a special HTML command (or tag) called META, making them invisible to the casual viewer of your site. Turn to Chapter 11 for details.

Reaching the entire Internet

Your Web site may be the cornerstone of your business, but if nobody knows it's out there, it can't help you generate sales. Perhaps the most familiar form of online advertising are *banner ads,* those little electronic billboards that seem to show up on every popular Web page you visit.

But banner advertising can be expensive, and may not be the best way for a small business to advertise online. In fact, the most effective marketing for the Collectible Exchange hasn't been traditional banner advertising or newspaper/magazine placements. Rather, the Podrazas and their Web marketing consultants targeted electronic bulletin boards (such as the one shown in Figure 1-5) and mailing lists where people exchanged inquiries as to where they could find Beanie Babies. When the Podrazas went online, they posted notices on the bulletin boards and sent e-mail messages to the same collectors, notifying them that their trading services were now available.

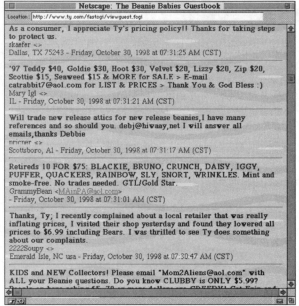

Figure 1-5:
Bulletin
boards
such as
this
provide a
way to
locate
shoppers
who have
already
shown
interest in
what you
have to
sell.

This sort of direct, one-to-one marketing may seem tedious, but it's often the best way to develop a business on the Internet. Reach out to your potential customers and strike up an individual, personal relationship with each one.

Chapter 11 contains everything you need to know about advertising with mailing lists, newsgroups, and even traditional banner ads.

Step 10: Evaluate Your Success and Move On

For any long-term endeavor, you need to establish standards by which you can judge its success or failure — I mean, lack of success. You must decide for yourself what you consider success to be. After a period of time, take stock of where you are and then take steps to do even better.

Taking stock

After 12 months online, the Podrazas took stock. After paying their employees' salaries, they still had over five times their initial investment in the bank. They had provided full-time employment for five people and part-time salaries for two others. That alone was one of their goals. The extra income means that their business was a rousing success.

When all is said and done, your business may do so well that you can reinvest in it by buying new equipment or increasing your services. You may even be in a position to give something back to the community. The Podrazas raised more than $10,000 for the Cystic Fibrosis Foundation by selling ten pairs of collectible Beanie Babies at the Fairmont Hotel in Chicago. Hopefully, you'll have enough money left over to reward yourself, too — as if being able to tell everyone "I own my own online business" weren't reward enough!

Money is only one form of success. Plenty of entrepreneurs are online for reasons other than making money. That said, it *is* important from time to time to evaluate how well you're doing financially. Accounting software such as the programs described in Chapter 14 make it easy to check your revenues on a daily or weekly basis. The key is to establish the goals you want to reach and develop measurements so that you know when and if you reach those goals.

Updating your data

Getting your business online *now,* and then updating your site regularly is better than waiting to unveil the perfect Web site all at once. In fact, seeing your site improve and grow is one of the best things about going online. Over time, you can create contests, strike up cooperative relationships with other businesses, and add more background information about your products and services.

The Collectible Exchange is not about to rest on its laurels. Its resident business genius, Michael Podraza, is now 12 years old and ready to conquer new worlds. At the time of this writing, Michael had just conducted a business meeting with representatives of XNet, their company's Web hosting service, in which he outlined changes he wants to make to the company's Web site.

Michael is also striking up a partnership with the creator of another line of popular dolls, Sally Winey Bears, in order to increase traffic and generate more sales. The company is also planning to advertise in toy-shop magazines and newspapers in major metropolitan areas in Texas and California.

Not all the Collectible Exchange's promotions have been successful. Advertisements in online magazines proved expensive and provided few results, for example. But trial-and-error is the name of the game when it comes to business start-ups. It's better to take a chance and learn from your mistakes than not try in the first place.

Chapter 2

Setting Your Sights on Success

· ·

· ·

Starting your own online business is like restoring a vintage car —
something I undertook back in those long-ago college days when I had
plenty of time on my hands. Both projects involve a series of recognizable
phases:

✔ **The idea phase:** First, you tell people about your great idea. They see
the stars dance in your eyes, nod their heads, and say, "Gee, that
sounds great." It's unusual, it's crazy, it's adventurous, and they don't
know how to react.

✔ **The decision phase:** Undaunted, you begin honing your plan. You read
books, ask questions, and shop around until you find a diamond in the
rough: be it a sketchy business plan or a rusting hulk of an automobile.
Of course, when the project is staring you down in your own workshop,
you may start to panic, asking yourself whether you're really up for the
task.

✔ **The assembly phase:** Still determined to proceed, you forge ahead. You
continue to read books, gather your tools, and go to work. Drills spin,
sparks fly, and metal moves.

✔ **The test-drive phase:** One fine day, out of the smoke and fumes, your
masterpiece emerges. You take it for a spin around the block. All those
who were skeptical before are now full of admiration. You clean and
polish your treasure, tune it up from time to time, and it gives you
enjoyment for years to come.

If the automotive analogy doesn't work for you, think about building a
house, planning a wedding, or devising an adventurous rafting excursion in
Brazil. The point is that starting an online business is no mystery. It's a
project like any other — one that you can understand and accomplish in

stages. Right now, you're at the first stage of launching your new cyber-business. You and your muse are working overtime. You have some rough sketches that only a mother could love.

This chapter helps you get from idea to reality. Your first step is to dream up how you want your business to look and feel. Then you can begin to develop and implement strategies for achieving your dream. With the right combination of inspiration and perspiration, you'll be driving your shiny new online business around the Net for years to come.

Don't let anyone rush you into signing a contract to host your online business before you're ready. I've encountered experienced businesspeople who prepaid for a year's worth of Web hosting and had no idea what to do next. Be sure that you know your options and have a business strategy, no matter how simple, before you sign anything.

Envisioning Your Online Business

How do you get to square one? Start by envisioning the kind of business that is your ultimate goal. Ask yourself: How would my business look if it were humming along like a well-oiled machine and I were totally happy with it? Envisioning your business is an creative way of asking yourself the all-important question: Why do I want to go into business online? What are my goals?

Do you want to make money? Do you want to gain credibility and attention for yourself and your work? Do you just want to have fun and meet new people? Only you can answer these questions and decide whether or not you're doing the right thing. By envisioning the final result you want to achieve, you can determine your online business goals.

Finding inspiration

What's that you say? Your imaginative powers are on the blink, or, in Internet-speak, your bandwidth is a little clogged? Sometimes, just half an hour of surfing the Net can stimulate your own mental network. Find sites with qualities you want to emulate. Throughout this chapter and the rest of this book, I suggest good business sites you can visit to bolster your own inspiration.

Don't be afraid to borrow ideas; ideas can't be copyrighted (although other things can, as Chapter 13 cautions). The important elements to identify are design, graphics, headings, and approaches that you can use to promote your own products and services.

Keep a low-tech pencil and stack of paper handy while you surf for ideas. Draw out ideas that occur to you for logos, Web page designs, snappy slogans, and the like. That way, you won't be scratching your head trying to remember your inspirations later on.

Standing out from the crowd

The Web and other parts of the online world are getting to be crowded places. According to Network Wizards (`www.nw.com`), in July 1998, 36.7 million computers were connected to the Internet, compared with 19.5 million the year before. Most of those computers have Web addresses that end with the commercial (`.com`) designation.

As an *ontrepreneur* (online entrepreneur), your goal is to stand out from the crowd — or to "position yourself in the marketplace," as business consultants like to say. Consider the following tried-and-true suggestions if you want your company to really turn heads:

- **Pursue something you know well.** The more you know about your business, the more valuable the information that you provide will be. In the online world, expertise sells.

- **Make a statement.** On your Web site, include a positioning statement that says what you do, whom you hope to reach, and how you are different from your competitors.

- **Give something away for free.** Giveaways and promotions are sure-fire ways to gain attention and develop a loyal customer base. In fact, there's a whole Web site devoted to providing free stuff online: Free Ride (`www.freeride.com`). The "something" you give away doesn't have to be an actual product; it can be words of wisdom based on your training and experience.

- **Find your niche.** Web space is a great place to pursue niche marketing. In fact, it often seems that the quirkier the item, the better it sells. Don't be afraid to target a narrow audience and direct all your sales efforts to a small group of devoted followers.

- **Do something you love.** Having fun is optional, I suppose. But, given the choice, wouldn't you rather promote something you're passionate about and love to discuss? The more you love your business, the more time and effort you're apt to put into it and, therefore, the more likely it is to be successful. In fact, some of the most successful Web sites capitalize on the love affair — the obsession — people have with something. Such businesses take advantage of the Internet's worldwide reach, which makes it easy for people with the same interests to gather at the same virtual location.

The Collectible Exchange, profiled in Chapter 1, found success by following all these strategies. Operated out of a house in Streamwood, Illinois, the company traded about 50,000 pieces in its first year on the Web and has grown into an operation that involves their entire family. The family sells a desirable product that they love and know well. Their stated mission is to provide a secure and simple means to buy and sell Beanie Babies. They address the niche market of passionate collectors who are looking for particular, often hard-to-find, items.

Sizing up commercial Web sites

Commercial Web sites — those whose Internet addresses end with .com — are the fastest-growing segment of the Net. This is the area you'll be entering, too. But not all commercial Web sites are created equal. They come in many different sizes and levels of complexity. Like Goldilocks, you want to create a Web site that is "just right."

A big company Web site . . . too big

Lots of big companies create Web sites with the primary goal of supplementing a product or business that is already well-known and well-established. Just a few examples are the Ragu Web site (www.ragu.com), the Kotex Web site (www.kotex.com), and the Toyota Web site (www.toyota.com).

True, these commercial Web sites were created by large corporations with many thousands of dollars to throw into Web design, and so they're too big for you to use as a model for your Web site. But you can still look at them to get ideas for your own site.

Always keep this very important fact in the forefront of your consciousness: In the online world, all business sites are new, and they all contain the same basic elements. On the Web, big companies and small communicate with the same tools (Web pages joined by hyperlinks), and they're all listed in the same indexes (such as Yahoo!). So in terms of technology, you compete on a level playing field — even with much larger companies. As a result, you can do what the Big Players do . . . only better. Often, big companies don't use the Web as well as individual entrepreneurs like you.

A mid-size company Web site . . . still too big

The Web is an ideal place for a small business of ten to twelve employees to provide customer service, disseminate information, and post a sales catalog. I describe many of these functions in my book *Small Business Internet For Dummies* (IDG Books Worldwide, Inc.). Yet this sort of online business may also be too extensive and complex to serve as a model for your new endeavor. Chances are that you don't need press releases, messages from the president, employee e-mail accounts, or a firewall for Internet security.

Nevertheless, some features that mid-size companies use, such as a Frequently Asked Questions (FAQ) page or a sales catalog, may be useful to you. Look at the Garden.com site (`www.garden.com`) for a bounty of good ideas.

A home-grown entrepreneurial business . . . just right

Many businesses start entirely on the Web and are run by a single person, couple, or family with little or no prior business experience — in other words, people just like you.

If you're nodding in agreement that the company described in the previous paragraph is "just right" for you, you'll be pleased to know that the story doesn't end there. In fact, the rest of this book is devoted to helping you and your Web site live together happily ever after. This chapter gets you off to a good start by examining the different kinds of businesses you can launch online and some business goals you can set for yourself.

Types of Online Businesses You Can Start

As you comb the Internet for ideas to help you give your online business a definite shape and form, you can easily get confused by the dizzying array of Web sites already out there. Luckily, you can reduce this throng into a few general categories and then hone in on the ones most like your own. Use the following brief descriptions of online businesses to keep your options in mind without getting overwhelmed.

Selling consumer products

Jupiter Communications (`www.jup.com`) predicts that by the year 2002, 55 percent of all U.S. households will be online. If you have products to sell (such as auto parts, antiques, jewelry, or food), the online marketplace is a great place to find customers who are ready to buy. This is especially true if the products you have for sale are unique in some way and attract the narrow, passionately interested audiences that have always gone online. Consider taking your wares online if one or more of the following applies to you:

- ✔ Your products are high in quality.
- ✔ You create your own products; for example, you design jewelry, bake cookies, or prepare gift baskets.

✔ You specialize in some aspects of your product that larger businesses can't achieve. Perhaps you sell regional foods, such as Texas barbecue sauce or New England chowder.

One of my favorite commercial Web sites is Ben and Jerry's (www.benandjerry.com). Years ago, these guys were entrepreneurs, starting out just like you. Their Web site, like the rest of their business, conveys their personality and mission. It focuses on the unique flavors and high quality of their ice cream, as well as their commitment to their employees, their sharcholders, and the communities to which they belong.

The Internet still has plenty of room for talented individuals to set up shop and develop online markets for their wares. The key is to find your niche, as many small-but-successful businesses have done. Believe in what you have to sell and make use of your Web space to express why you love your products (and, by implication, why your customers will love them, too).

Selling your professional services

Chances are that, at one time or another, you've found yourself scratching your head and wondering, "Where do I find the best _____ in the business?" (Fill in the blank with accountant, lawyer, stock broker, insurance agent, health care provider . . . the list goes on and on.)

Simply finding a good professional (or being found, if you're the one hanging out your virtual shingle) is half the battle. Making yourself available in cyberspace, either through a Web site or through listings in indexes and directories, can help people find you.

Offering your professional services online can expand your client base dramatically. It also gives existing clients a new way to contact you: through e-mail. Here are just a few examples of professionals who are offering their services online:

✔ **Attorneys:** Immigration attorney Kevin L. Dixler is based in Chicago. Through his Web site (ourworld.compuserve.com/homepages/ immigrant_Attorney), he can reach individuals around the world who want to come to the United States.

✔ **Psychotherapists:** Carole Killick, a music psychotherapist, has a simple, nicely designed Web site (www.eclipse.co.uk/pens/killick) that explains her work and courses she teaches.

✔ **Physicians:** Dr. Frank Palmer Sweet, a naturopathic physician in Lake Havasu City, Arizona, has a Web site (www.desertstars.com/drsweet) from which he sells a variety of natural nutritional supplements.

✓ **Consultants:** Experts who keep their knowledge up-to-date and are willing to give advice to those with similar interests and needs are always in demand. Consultants in a specialized area often find a great demand for their services on the Internet. Yahoo!'s consulting page (www.yahoo.com/Business_and_Economy/Companies/Consulting) is crowded with fields in which online consultants are available. Here are examples of consultants and experts who have enhanced their professional reputations by creating their own successful businesses in Web-space:

- Dr. Walter Bortz (www.thirdage.com/bortz) writes a regular column for the Third Age Web site, which targets individuals age 50 and older.

- Writing and marketing consultant Herman Holtz supplements his print publications with his Web site (www.bellicose.com/freelance/main.html).

- Publisher and entrepreneur Bill Myers (www.bmyers.com) has a busy Web site that emphasizes his videos and other products.

Tips are a great addition to any publication, online or in print. (You're reading this one, aren't you?) Any tips you can provide your online customers/clients help you build credibility and make visitors feel as though they're getting "something for free." One way you can put forth this professional expertise is by starting your own online newsletter. You get to be editor, writer, and mailing-list manager. Plus, you get to talk as much as you want, network with tons of people who are interested enough in what you have to say to subscribe to your publication, and put your name and your business before lots of people. Nancy Roebke (profiled in Chapter 7) puts out a regular newsletter called Network Ink that supplements her online business site (www.protnet.com), as do Herman Holtz, Dr. Werner Steurenburg, and many of the other online businesspeople I mention in this chapter.

Selling information

The need to share knowledge via computers was the whole reason the Internet was born. And like high-protein baby food, information is the commodity that has fueled cyberspace's rapid growth. As the Internet and commercial online networks continue to expand, information remains key.

Finding valuable information and gathering a particular kind of resource for one location online can be a business in itself. If you've been working in a specific field for some time, you are uniquely qualified to provide information to those interested in that field. For example, if you have a great deal of experience with the college application process, you can sell your expertise to students and parents who need help sorting through the procedures involved and the data required to apply for college. (See educational consultant Cornelia Nicholson's Web site, www.capecod.net/cna, for example.)

Other online businesses provide gathering points or indexes to more specific areas. What kinds of areas? The sky's the limit. Here are just a few examples:

- **Search engines:** Some businesses succeed by connecting cybersurfers with companies, organizations, and individuals that specialize in a given area. Yahoo! (www.yahoo.com) is the most obvious example. Originally started by two college students, Yahoo! has practically become an Internet legend by gathering information in one index so that people can easily find things online.

- **Links pages:** On Beth's Sweepstakes Links page (rapidnet.com/~tiger/sweeps.htm), Beth Venteicher gathers links to current contests along with short descriptions of each one. This is not a for-profit site (Beth says the page is posted only for entertainment purposes), but it has received 80,000 visits in the past year. Although she has received inquiries about advertising, Beth has not accepted them. "I'd feel obligated to keep the site up on a more regular basis, and I wouldn't have fun with it," she says.

- **Electronic magazines (commonly called *e-zines*):** These publications exist only online. One of the most successful is WinFile Update (www.winfiles.com/winfile), a newsletter that is e-mailed to more than 100,000 subscribers each week, and includes up to three advertisements per issue.

- **Online shopping centers:** A freelance consultant named Dave Taylor started the Internet Mall (www.internetmall.com) in 1994. Now it's a Silicon Valley startup company with anticipated revenue in the six digits. It provides Web surfers with a central location where they can find many different kinds of products and services. The Internet Mall doesn't sell products and services itself; rather, it sells information about the location of its member sites and the promotion it provides to those members.

How can information resource sites such as these make money? In some cases, individuals pay to become members; sometimes, businesses pay to be listed on a site; other times, a site attracts so many visitors on a regular basis that other companies pay to post advertising on the site. Big successes like the Internet Mall strike lucrative partnerships with big companies and gain advertising revenue, as well.

Selling technology or computer resources

The online world itself, by the very fact that it exists, has spawned all kinds of business opportunities for entrepreneurs. Just think of all the hardware and software you need to get online.

✔ **Computers:** Some discount computer houses have made a killing by going online and offering equipment for less than conventional retail stores. Being on the Internet means that they save on overhead, employee compensation, and other costs, and they are able to pass those savings on to their customers.

✔ **Internet Service Providers:** These are the businesses that give you a dial-up or direct connection to the Internet. Many ISPs, like Netcom or UUNET, are big concerns. But smaller companies — such as Third Coast Networks (www.thirdcoast.net), based in a small office in Northbrook, Illinois, and owned by Amy Heber — are succeeding, as well.

✔ **Browsers:** The obvious example of a company that made it big by offering its browser (software for viewing the World Wide Web) online is Netscape Communications Corp., which is battling giant Microsoft for the lion's share of the Web browser market.

✔ **Software:** Matt Wright is well-known on the Web for providing free computer scripts that add important functionality to Web sites, such as processing information that visitors submit via online forms. Matt's Script Archive site (scriptarchive.com) now includes an advertisement for a book on scripting that he co-authored, as well as a Web postcard system for sale and an invitation to businesses to take out advertisements on his site.

Selling your creative work

Starving artists, as well as those with a little bit of nourishment in their bellies, need to find wide exposure for little or no money. Where better to turn than the Internet? If you're simply looking for exposure and feedback on your creations, you can put samples of your work online. Consider the following suggestions for virtual creative venues (and revenues):

✔ **Host art galleries.** Thanks to online galleries, artists whose sales were previously only regional can get inquiries from all over the world. Art Xpo (www.artxpo.com) reports thousands of dollars in sales through its Web site and aggressive marketing efforts. Art Quarter (www.art-quarter.com), which is operated by Dr. Werner Steurenburg, is a relatively new site that is receiving worldwide attention (see Figure 2-1). (The upcoming sidebar, "Painting a new business scenario," profiles Steurenburg's site.)

✔ **Sell your art.** Tony Barker is an Australian graphic designer. His company, Moving Pixels, sells a computer drawing program called Art for Kids from its Web site (www.bigearth.com.au).

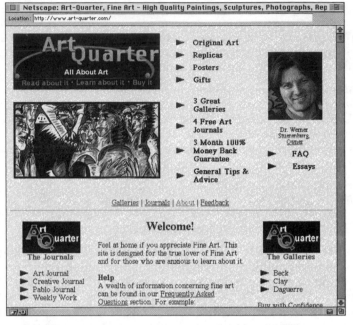

Figure 2-1:
This Web-based business enables artists to gain recognition and sell their creative work.

✔ **Publish your writing.** You can find many literary publications online at `www.meer.net/~johnl/e-zine-lit/keywords/literary.html`. Several of these journals, such as *American Literary Review* (`www.engl.unt.edu/alr`) and *BeeHive* (`www.temporalimage.com/behive/index.html`), provide forums for writers.

✔ **Sell your music.** Joel Fisher composes and records music for film, video, CD-ROM, and the Internet. He provides samples of his work on his Joel Fisher Music Services Web site (`www.ccnet.com/~score`).

One-to-One Marketing Strategies

After you review your options and check out any Web sites that already conduct the sorts of business ventures that you hope to tackle yourself, it's time to put your goals into action. You do so by developing marketing strategies that are well-suited to expressing your unique talents and services and by encouraging customers to explore your business and place orders with you.

The most effective online marketing strategies are those that run counter to the widespread image of cyberspace as a place where millions of lonely, disconnected people interact, without really getting to know one another.

Painting a new business scenario

Dr. Werner Steurenburg is the owner of Art Quarter (www.art-quarter.com), a Web site devoted to teaching, displaying, and selling works of art. He decided to start his Web site after encountering many ups and downs in his personal life and previous business enterprises. He first went online in February 1998, and now spends virtually all his time working — sometimes 20 hours a day, 7 days a week — on his Web site, e-zines, and related activities.

Q. What were your start-up costs?

A. Well, I already had a PC with ISDN card, an ISDN telephone connection, a scanner, and a printer, all left over from my previous business. After starting out with America Online and CompuServe, I switched to an Internet Service Provider that charges a flat rate of $20 per month. My telephone costs are about $150 to $200 per month. I spent some money on FtpVoyager software and Pretty Good Privacy. I bought a book on the Internet and took a course on creating Web pages. I guess it all adds up to less than $700. (See Chapter 3 for suggestions on hardware and software for your online business.)

Q. What would you describe as the primary goals of your online business?

A. To market my own art and to market the work of fellow artists, maintaining a high quality level.

Q. Has your online business been profitable financially?

A. Not yet. Sales happen now and then, but are still scarce.

Q. How do you promote your site?

A. To attract prospects, I set up five e-zines. After eight weeks of promotion, I got some 100 subscribers for each of them. All the feedback I have received is highly positive. I think this is a success. Also, I hit upon some business mailing lists recently that are highly supportive, and posting to them has brought huge feedback. I think this is a big success, being accepted by biz gurus after such a short time on the Net. The help I got proved to me that those people cared about me, and that's a big success indeed.

Q. Do you create your Web pages yourself or do you work with someone to do that?

A. I used to do it all by myself. First, I used frames and sound, but soon I learned the KISS rule (Keep It Simple, Stupid). But I saw that I missed something. The design was dull. Then came Steve. He is one of the list partners. Being on a tight budget, I could not afford paying someone to design a big site like this (my first had 900 files, my second 1100, and this one has 700).

Q. What advice would you give to someone starting an online business?

A. Ask yourself: What is your thing? What are you good in? Don't try marketing just anything online. If you can't think of anything to sell, ask yourself: What do I need that I don't have? Where is a need others have that I detect?

Quite the contrary: Online communities are often close-knit, long-standing groups of people who get to be great friends. The best way to promote your business is to reach out to people and help them, to communicate with them as individuals. The Web, newsgroups, and e-mail let you accomplish this goal in ways that other media can't match.

Get to know your audience

Remember the days of the corner drugstore and the local market whose proprietors knew each of their customers by name and did their best to provide them with personal service? Are those days really gone? Well, of course, to a large extent, they are. But old-fashioned business practices are alive and well in cyberspace. Your number one business strategy, when it comes to starting your business online, sounds simple: *Know your audience.*

What's not so simple about this little maxim is that, in cyberspace, it takes some work to get to know exactly who your customers are. Web surfers don't leave their names, addresses, or even a random e-mail address when they visit your site. Instead, when you check the records (or *logs*) of the visitors who have connected to you, you see pages and pages of what appears to be computer gobbledygook.

The surprising thing is this: You *can* get to know the individuals who come to your Web site. You can develop long-standing relationships in which your customers come to trust you and return to your site on a regular basis.

How do you do this?

- ✔ **Get your visitors to identify themselves.** Have them send you e-mail messages, place orders, enter contests, or provide you with feedback. (For more specific suggestions, see Chapter 6.)

- ✔ **Become an online researcher.** Find existing users who already purchase goods and services online that are similar to what you offer. (I describe this process in detail in Chapter 10.)

- ✔ **Keep track of your visitors.** Count the visitors who come to your site and, more importantly, the ones who make purchases or seek out your services.

- ✔ **Help your visitors get to know you.** Web space is virtually unlimited. Don't be reluctant to tell people about aspects of your life that don't relate directly to how you hope to make money. Consider Judy Vorfeld, who does Internet research, Web design, and office support. Her Web site (www.ossweb.com) includes the usual lists of clients and services; however, it also includes a page about her family and one that describes her community service work (see Figure 2-2).

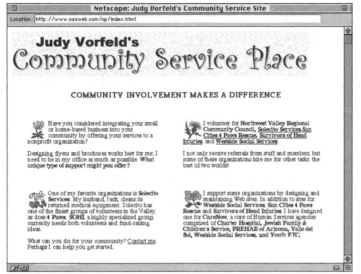

Figure 2-2:
Telling
potential
customers
about
yourself
makes them
more
comfortable
telling you
about
themselves.

I recommend doing your own Internet research so you can learn more about the culture of the online world: how the most successful Web sites look and feel, and how many Web sites use a hip, techno-savvy tone when presenting information. But if you don't have scads of time to spend online, you can hire researchers to do the job for you. A site called HumanSearch (www. humansearch.com) claims that it will answer any question for you for $8.

The more clearly you *target* your market and focus your sales pitches, the more successful your online business will be.

Catch a wave: Grab Web surfers' attention

Imagine yourself standing in the front door of your store on Main Street, arms folded, watching cars zoom by. How do you stop traffic so that people will at least look at you?

On the Web, people move quickly, jumping from site to site. Job number two in your marketing strategy is to catch their attention: You have two ways to do this:

 ✔ **Make yourself visible.** In Web-space, the problem isn't so much that potential customers are surfing right past your site. Rather, your task is simply making them aware that you exist at all. You do this by getting yourself included in as many indexes, search sites, and business listings as possible; Chapter 11 outlines some strategies for doing so. You can also do a bit of self-promotion in your own online communications: John

Counsel of the Profit Clinic (www.profitclinic.com) appends this interesting teaser, followed by a link to his Web site, to his e-mail messages:

```
"90% of all small business owners are PRE-PROGRAMMED to
        FAIL. Are you one? Check out the Small Biz Quick
        Quiz and see for yourself."
```

✔ **Make your site an eye-catcher.** Getting people to come to you is only half the battle. The other half is getting them to do some shopping or investigation once they are there. You encourage this participation by combining striking images with promotions, useful information, and ways for them to interact with you. (See Chapters 5 and 6 for details.)

Promote your expertise

You know just how knowledgeable you are in your area of business. You may have been selling insurance, plumbing, painting, or trading collectibles for many years. Even if you are just starting out, you're still an expert, right?

Marketing task number three is to transfer your confidence and sense of authority about what you do to anyone who visits you online. Make them believe that you are an expert and a good person with whom to do business.

The Web has only been around since the mid '90s. Everyone is a relative newcomer to online commerce. Many individuals pretend to be experts, making it difficult to know for sure who's reliable and worth visiting.

Here, too, you can do a quick two-step in order to market your expertise:

Show your credentials

List any honors, awards, or professional affiliations you have that relate to your online work. If you are providing professional or consulting services online, you might even make a link to your online resume. Tell people how long you've been in your field and how you got to know what you know about your business.

Of course, if you're just starting to sell pet supplies or homemade pottery, you won't have this sort of information available; in that case, move to the all-important technique described next.

Convince with authoritative information

Providing useful, practical information about a topic is one of the best ways to market yourself online. One of the great things about starting an online business is that you don't have to incur the design and printing charges to get a brochure or flyer printed. You have plenty of space on your online business site to talk about your sales items or services in as great detail as your want.

Most Internet Service Providers give you 10 to 20MB (megabytes, that is) of space for your Web pages and associated files. Because the average Web page only occupies 5 to 10K (that's kilobytes) of space, it'll take a long time before you begin to run out of room.

What, exactly, can you talk about on your site? I'm glad you asked. Here are some ideas:

✔ Provide detailed descriptions and photos of your sale items.

✔ Include a full list of clients you have worked for previously.

✔ Publish a page of testimonials from satisfied customers.

✔ Give your visitors a list of links to Web pages and other sites where people can find out more about your area of business.

✔ Toot your own horn: Tell why you love what you do and why you're so good at it.

When the job is done, be sure to get someone to give you a good testimonial. Ask them for a sentence or two you can use on your Web site.

A site that is chock-full of compelling, entertaining content will become a resource that online visitors bookmark and return to on a regular basis — and that, of course, is any online business owner's dream.

Encourage potential customers to interact

A 16-year-old cartoonist named Gabe Martin put out his cartoons on his Web site, called The Borderline (`www.the-borderline.com`). Virtually nothing happened. But when his dad put up some money for a contest, young Gabe started getting hundreds of visits and inquiries.

Cybersurfers are used to getting things for free online. They regularly download shareware or freeware programs. They get free advice from newsgroups, and they find free companionship from chat rooms and online forums. Having already paid for network access and computer equipment, they actually *expect* to get something for free.

Help meet your customers' expectations by devising as many promotions, giveaways, or sales as possible. You can also get people to interact through online forums or other tools, as described in Chapter 6.

In online business terms, anything that gets your visitors to click on links and enter your site is good. Provide as many links to the rest of your site as you can on your home page. Many interactions that don't seem like sales do lead to sales or help your fledgling business in some way.

See Chapters 5 and 6 for instructions on how to create hyperlinks and add interactivity to your Web site. For more about creating Web sites, check out *Creating Web Pages For Dummies,* 4th Edition by Bud Smith and Arthur Bebak, published by IDG Books Worldwide, Inc.

Be a joiner

You may be physically alone, tapping away at your keyboard or peering at your monitor in your home office, but that doesn't mean that you really *are* alone. Thousands of home office workers and entrepreneurs just like you connect to the Net every day and share many of the same concerns, challenges, and ups and downs as you.

Starting an online business isn't only a matter of creating Web pages, scanning photos, and taking orders. Marketing and networking are essential to making sure that you meet your goals. Participate in groups that are related either to your particular business or to online business in general. Here are some ways you can make the right connections and get support and encouragement at the same time:

Be a newsgroupie

Newsgroups are discussion groups that occupy an extensive and popular part of the Internet called Usenet, as well as appearing on America Online and other online services. Many large organizations such as universities and corporations run their own internal newsgroups, too.

Businesspeople tend to overlook newsgroups because of admonitions about spam (unsolicited messages sent by people trying to sell something to newsgroup participants who don't want it) and other violations of *Netiquette,* the set of rules that govern newsgroup communications. However, when used correctly, newsgroups can be a wonderful resource for businesspeople. They attract knowledgeable consumers who are strongly interested in a topic: just the sorts of people who make great customers.

A few newsgroups (in particular, the ones with `biz` at the beginning of their names) are especially intended to discuss small business issues and sales. Here are a few suggestions:

- ✔ misc.entrepreneurs
- ✔ biz.marketplace.discussion
- ✔ biz.marketplace.international.discussion
- ✔ biz.marketplace.services.discussion
- ✔ alt.business.home
- ✔ alt.business.consulting
- ✔ alt.business.franchising
- ✔ aol.business.general

The easiest way to access newsgroups is to use the newsgroup software that comes built into the two most popular Web browser packages, Netscape Communicator and Microsoft Internet Explorer. (Netscape's newsgroup software is called Collabra.) Each browser or newsgroup program has its own set of steps for enabling you to access Usenet. Use your browser's online help system to find out how you can access newsgroups.

Be sure to read the group's FAQs (frequently asked questions) before you start posting. It's a good idea to *lurk before you post* — that is, simply read messages being posted to the group in order to find out about members' concerns before posting a message yourself. Stay away from groups that are full of get-rich-quick schemes or other scams. When you do post a message, be sure to keep your comments relevant to the conversation and give as much helpful advice as you can.

The most important business technique in communicating by either e-mail or newsgroup postings is to include a signature file at the end of your message. A *signature file* is a simple text message that newsgroup and mail software programs automatically add to your messages. A typical one includes your name, title, and the name of your company. You can also include a link to your business's home page. A good example is Judy Vorfelds' signature file, shown in Figure 2-3. (Chapter 9 tells how to create your own signature file.)

Figure 2-3:
The signature on your messages serves as an instant business advertisement.

~~~~~~
Judy Vorfeld aka Webgrammar
Great documents & Web sites always have great grammar & style!
Typing, Editing, Internet Research, Web Design & Analysis
mailto:oss@ossweb.com   •   URL: http://www.ossweb.com
Memb. ABSSI http://www.abssi.org Memb. AEIP http://www.aeip.com
~~~~~~

Be a mailing list-ener

A *mailing list* is a discussion group that communicates by exchanging e-mail messages between members who share a common interest and who have subscribed to join the list. Each e-mail message sent to the list is distributed to all of the list's members. Any of those members can, in turn, respond by sending e-mail replies. The series of back-and-forth messages develops into discussions.

The nice thing about mailing lists is that they consist only of people who have subscribed, which means that they really want to be involved and participate.

An excellent mailing list to check out is the Small and Home-Based Business Discussion List (`www.talkbiz.com/bizlist/index.html`). This list is *moderated,* meaning that someone reads through all postings before they go online and filters out any comments that are inappropriate or off-topic. Also, try searching the Liszt mailing-list directory (`www.liszt.com`).

The number of groups you join and how often you participate in them is up to you. The important thing is to regard every one-to-one-personal contact as a seed that may sprout into a sale, a referral, an order, a contract, a bit of useful advice, or another profitable business blossom.

Find more than one way to sell

Many successful online businesses combine more than one concept of what constitutes electronic commerce. Chapter 8 discusses ways to sell your goods and services on your Web site, but the Internet offers other venues for promoting and selling your wares, too.

Selling through online classifieds

If you're looking for a quick and simple way to sell products or promote your services online without having to pay high overhead costs, it's hard to beat taking out a classified ad in an online publication or other site.

The classifieds work the same way online as they do in print publications: You pay a fee and write a short description along with contact information, and the publisher makes the ad available to potential customers. However, online classifieds have a number of big advantages over their print equivalents:

  ✔ **Audience:** Instead of hundreds or thousands who might view your ad in a print publication, tens of thousands or perhaps even millions can see it online.

> ✔ **Searchability:** Online classifieds are often indexed so customers can search for particular items with their Web browser. This makes it easier for shoppers to find exactly what they want, whether it's a three-bedroom house or a Betty Boop cookie jar.
>
> ✔ **Time:** Your ad in a daily newspaper may be in print for only a day or a week, depending on how much you pay for it. On the Net, ads are often online for a month or more.
>
> ✔ **Cost:** Some sites, such as Yahoo! (`classifieds.yahoo.com`) and Classfieds2000 (`www.classifieds2000.com`) let you post classified ads for free.

On the downside, classifieds are often buried at the back of online magazines or Web sites, just as they are in print, so they are hardly well-traveled areas. Also, most classifieds don't make use of the graphics that help sell and promote goods and services so effectively throughout Web-space.

Use classifieds if you are short on time or money. Otherwise, stick with traditional media or your own online business site where you can provide more details to customers and possibly save money.

Selling via online auctions

Many small businesses, such as antique dealerships or jewelry stores, sell individual merchandise through online auctions. Increasingly popular auction sites provide effective ways to target sales items at highly motivated collectors who are likely to pay top dollar for especially scarce or desirable goodies.

Sellers often make far more money on desirable single items through auctions than they could by putting the items on a garage-sale table or even in a consignment shop. Why? Auctions attract buyers from all over the world rather than from around the neighborhood. Auctions also attract buyers who are passionate about a particular kind of item and who know its value.

Know what you're selling. Pick out the antiques or collectibles from the junk when you go to a garage sale. Research them so you know roughly what they're worth. Chances are the people who will be bidding on your items know as much as (or more than) you do. The more knowledge you display about an item, the more interest you'll get and the better the chances that the bids will go higher, as well.

The best way to discover what you can sell and how much a particular goodie might fetch is to visit the auction yourself. Keep track of prices and look at the photos and descriptions to see which items are likely to attract the next bidder. Here are some places you can visit:

- ✔ **Yahoo!Auction (**`auctions.yahoo.com`**):** A sure sign of the rising profitability of online auctions is the fact that Yahoo! recently started its own service.

- ✔ **eBay (**`www.ebay.com`**):** This is one of the best-known auction companies on the Web, dealing in all sorts of items.

- ✔ **Onsale Inc. (**`www.onsale.com`**):** This site specializes in auctioning off computer equipment.

Each auction house works differently, but the basic elements have been part of the online world for years: trust, honesty, and courtesy. The buyer trusts you to put out an honest description, you trust the buyer to send in the payment, and the auction house trusts you to pay your share and treat people well. Infractions are documented in reports that can ruin your reputation and prevent you from selling again. On the other hand, those who make lots of successful transactions get gold stars by their names that attract more customers.

Typically, you sign up with the auction house and agree to pay a fee for each item sold. You either put the item online and let the marketplace determine how much it's worth or, if you want to protect your investment, you specify a "reserve" amount that covers how much you paid for it. If your reserve is not met, you don't have to sell. On the other hand, if the reserve is met, you are obligated to sell. You also specify how long the item is to be offered for sale — usually a few days or a week. You also tell people how you want to be paid — postal money orders are common, although some sellers accept credit cards or personal checks.

Chapter 3

Your Online Business Equipment List

● ●

● ●

*O*ne of the many exciting aspects of launching a business online is the absence of something: You don't have to encounter much *overhead* (that is, operating expenses). Many non-cyberspace businesses must take out loans, pay rent, remodel their storefronts, pay license fees, and purchase store fixtures. Only then can they stock the shelves, hire employees, and open for business.

When you start a business online, many (though not all) of these tasks are unnecessary. Instead of patching plaster and painting walls, you pick colors and add graphics to your Web pages. Rather than writing checks to a landlord, you (sometimes, though not always) pay Web hosting and registration fees.

The primary overhead for an online business is computer hardware and software. Although it's great if you can afford top-of-the-line equipment, you'll be happy to know that the latest bells and whistles are not absolutely necessary in order to get a business site online and maintain it effectively.

As a lone entrepreneur, you're probably on a limited budget. If you already have an Internet connection and enough equipment to surf the Web, you're probably asking yourself: "Do I have to spend thousands of dollars on upgrading my equipment and purchasing slick new software to start an online business?"

Short answer: Nope!

Long answer: No, but to streamline the technical aspects of connecting to the online world and creating a business Web site, some investment may be a wise and profitable idea. Read on for more details.

Hardware and Software Rules to Live By

Some general principles apply when assembling machinery and programs for an online endeavor. First and foremost, look on the Internet for what you need. You can find just about everything you want to get you started.

If you're looking for hardware and software that's tailored to the needs of a small business or home office, I strongly recommend checking out the Tech Tips and Reviews section of the Smalloffice.com Web site (www. smalloffice.com/expert). This site includes ample links to shareware and freeware programs, reviews of computer equipment, and articles about subjects like telecommuting.

Be sure to pry before you buy! Don't pull out that credit card until you get the facts on what warranty and technical support your hardware or software vendor provides. Make sure that your vendor provides phone support 24 hours a day, seven days a week. Also ask how long the typical turnaround time is in case your equipment needs to be serviced.

If you purchase lots of new hardware and software, remember to update your insurance by sending your insurer a list of your new equipment. Also consider purchasing insurance specifically for your computer-related items from a company such as Safeware (www.safeware.com).

Easyware (Not Hardware) for Your Business

Sure, you have a computer. You dial up the Net. You surf the Web. Isn't that the end of the story?

Indeed, your existing hardware setup may work just fine for you as a consumer. But becoming an information provider on the Internet places an additional burden on your computer and peripheral equipment, such as your modem. When you're "in it for the money," you may very well start to go online everyday, and perhaps several times a day. The better your computer setup, the more e-mail messages you can download, the more catalog items you can store, and so on. This section introduces you to any upgrades you may need to make to your existing hardware configuration.

The right computer for your online business

You very well may already have an existing computer setup that's adequate to get your business online and start the ball rolling. Or you may be starting from scratch and looking to purchase a computer for personal and/or business use. In either case, it pays to know what all the technical terms and specifications mean. That way, when you go to the computer store (either online or down the street), the spec sheets and manuals won't seem like so much alphabet soup to you. Here are some general terms you need to understand:

- **Megahertz (MHz):** This unit of measure indicates how quickly a computer's processor can perform functions. The *central processing unit,* or CPU, of a computer is where the computing work gets done. In general, the higher the processor's internal clock rate, expressed in megahertz, the faster the computer. Taking other variables (such as available memory, the programs you're running, and your Internet connection) into account, a 266 MHz processor operates roughly twice as fast as one that has a clock rate of 133 MHz.

- **Random Access Memory (RAM):** This is the memory — usually expressed in millions of bytes, or *megabytes* (MB), of information — that your computer uses to temporarily store information needed to operate programs. The more RAM you have, the more programs you can run at once. If you don't have enough RAM to operate all the programs you have open at any one time, your computer slows to a crawl.

- **EDO RAM:** *Extended data output RAM* is a high-speed type of RAM that provides the best benefits with faster microprocessors, such as the Intel Pentium.

- **SDRAM:** Many ultra-fast computers use some form of *synchronous DRAM (SDRAM),* which is synchronized with a particular clock rate of a CPU so a processor can perform more instructions in a given time.

- **Auxiliary Memory:** This term refers to physical data-storage space on a hard disk, cartridge, CD-ROM, or other device.

- **Virtual Memory:** Memory on your hard disk that your computer can "borrow" to serve as extra RAM.

- **Network Interface Card (NIC):** You only need this hardware add-on if you expect to connect your computer to others on a network. Having a NIC usually provides you with Ethernet (a network technology that permits you to send and receive data at very fast speeds) data transfer to the other computers.

The Internet is teeming with places where you can find good deals on hardware. A great place to start is CNET's Shopper.com Web site (www.shopper.com). Also visit the Inter-Mart Computer Store (www.buysoftware.com/intermart). And if you're looking for bargains on used hardware, don't forget the newsgroups devoted to equipment for sale, such as comp.sys.mac.forsale and comp.sys.sgi.marketplace.

Processor speed: Don't be dazzled

Computer processors are getting faster all the time. Every month, it seems, some manufacturer comes out with a faster chip that is supposed to make games leap off the screen, perform all your functions in half the time, and wax the kitchen floor, besides.

Don't be overly impressed by a computer's clock speed (measured in megahertz). Sure, it's wise to purchase the fastest computer you can afford, but don't obsess about getting the latest and fastest processor on the block. By the time you get your computer home, another, faster chip will have been released.

A superfast Pentium chip primarily helps if you have to perform scads of calculations, fill out spreadsheets, and deal with other number-crunching tasks. For basic business needs, Web surfing, and viewing graphics, concentrate on getting lots of memory — not speed — for your computer.

A Pentium chip is a popular processor introduced in the early 1990s by the Intel Corporation to replace its own 486 processor. Faster versions of the original Pentium — the Pentium Pro and Pentium II chips — are now available. Pentium processors are great, no doubt about it. But in my experience, you can still surf the Web, exchange e-mail messages, and update Web pages with a 486 processor in your computer. When should you upgrade to a Pentium? If your computer already has 32 to 48MB of RAM installed, you have a 56 Kbps modem, and you're still crawling slowly from one Web page to another, consider taking your machine to a computer service center and having your 486 upgraded to a Pentium chip, which is becoming more practical and reasonable in cost as time goes on.

Hello, Computer Central? Get me more RAM!

The single most important item on your business-equipment shopping list is memory. Once you go online and start assembling a Web site, your memory requirements go up dramatically. Think about the memory required to run the types of applications shown in Table 3-1. (Note that these are only estimates based on the Windows versions of these products that were available at the time of this writing.)

Table 3-1	Memory Requirements	
Type of Application	*Example*	*Amount of RAM Recommended*
Web browser	Netscape Communicator	24MB
Web page editor	Macromedia Dreamweaver	16MB
Word processor	Microsoft Word	16MB
Graphics program	Paint Shop Pro	16MB
Accounting software	Microsoft Excel	16MB
Animation/Presentation	Macromedia Director	8MB

The sample applications in Table 3-1 add up to a whopping 96MB of RAM. And it doesn't stop there. As long as the number of Web pages you view and graphics you download increase, your RAM requirements also go up. The About This Macintosh window provided by the Macintosh operating system illustrates the memory consumption problem graphically (see Figure 3-1).

Figure 3-1:
A few
Internet
applications
can quickly
consume
your
computer's
available
RAM.

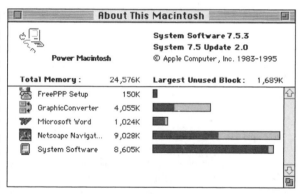

The applications shown in Figure 3-1 have already consumed all of my Power Mac's meager 24MB of RAM. (Sharp eyes will notice that I'm running early versions of Microsoft Word and Netscape Navigator. More recent versions require even more RAM.) If I try to start a Web page editor or other program, I get the dialog box shown in Figure 3-2.

Virtual Memory (VM) may seem like a good solution, but it's not a long-term substitute for "real" RAM that you or a service person physically adds to your computer in the form of memory chips. The problem is that VM only *simulates* more memory than your computer actually has. It breaks a program into small sections, called *pages,* and in some instances, widely separates these pages on your computer disk. As a result, the program needs to thrash back and forth to your disk in order to run, which slows down your general computer operation.

Figure 3-2:
24MB of
RAM is
insufficient
to run
several
Internet
programs at
once; go
with a
minimum of
32MB.

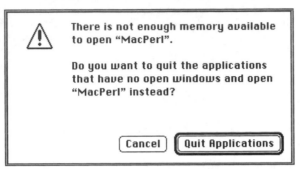

There is not enough memory available
to open "MacPerl".

Do you want to quit the applications
that have no open windows and open
"MacPerl" instead?

[Cancel] [**Quit Applications**]

If you plan to work online on a regular basis, be sure to get at least 32MB of
RAM — more, if you can swing it. Don't believe the Windows 98 box that
says you can get along with 16MB of RAM. Windows 98 is a hungry beast
that consumes lots of food. Your author, who has 32MB of RAM, is poking
along with Windows 98. Get a minimum of 64MB of RAM if you can afford it.
(Remember, you can record all these purchases as expenses on your tax
returns.)

Don't try to perform memory upgrades yourself unless you've done it
before. You can easily cause serious damage to your computer through
static electricity discharge. Take the machine to a service center at a
computer or electronics store and pay the nominal service fee to get more
memory installed.

Hard disk storage

Random Access Memory is only one type of memory your computer uses;
the other kind, *hard disk,* stores information: text files, audio files, programs,
and the many essential files that your computer's operating system needs in
order to boot up and function the way you want.

Most of the new computers on the market come with hard disk drives that
store one or more GB (that's *gigabytes*; a gigabyte is a thousand megabytes)
of data. Any hard disk of a gigabyte or more should be fine for your business
needs. (Many new computers come with hard disks of 3, 6, or more GB in
size.) If you're buying a used computer, beware. Don't consider coming
home with anything that has less than a gigabyte of storage space, or you'll
run out of room before you know it.

If you want to ensure that you *never* run out of disk space, purchase a
removable disk drive for your computer. The most popular such devices are
made by Iomega Systems. The Iomega Zip disk holds a cartridge that gives
you about 100MB of storage; the Jaz drive provides 1.6GB per cartridge.
Other such devices are on the market, but there's an advantage in going

with the ones that are popular: Printers and service bureaus are likely to have their own Zip and Jaz drives that you can use to transmit graphics and other files.

CD-ROM drive

Although a CD-ROM drive may not be the most important part of your computer for business use, it can perform essential installation, storage, and data communications functions:

- ✔ A CD-ROM drive is pretty much a must-have item for installing sophisticated Internet software of the sort that I describe throughout this book. A wide range of entertainment software is available only on CD, and so are general reference materials, such as online encyclopedias, that can help you prepare documentation for your products.

- ✔ Some newer CD-ROM drives let you record data yourself onto disc. In terms of storage, a writeable CD lets you store 650MB or more of data on a single disc.

- ✔ As a mode of data communications, CDs are lightweight and easy to ship. If you work in music or multimedia, writeable CDs can be a terrific way to present a digitized copy of your work to your customers. CDs are also a great way to deliver your product to customers if you work in the software industry.

The *speed* of a CD-ROM drive is a measurement of how fast the drive can transfer data to or from a CD. The earliest CD-ROM drives transferred data at 150KB per second. A double (or 2X) drive works twice that fast, a 4X drive works four times as fast, and so on. These days, 40X drives are common. Usually, the speed of the drive is printed right on the front of your computer.

Every computer comes with a CD-ROM drive these days; the current ones are rated at a speed of 16X or 24X. 16X is the minimum that your machine should have. If your drive works more slowly than you want, you can upgrade it at the same service center where you obtain a memory upgrade.

A growing number of machines are now being made available with a drive that operates a new type of CD called a DVD (Digital Video Disc). These discs can hold many gigabytes of information, compared with the 600MB or so that a conventional CD-ROM can handle. If you can find a new computer that includes a DVD drive at an additional cost that you can afford, by all means go for it. You'll be able to view an entire motion picture on your computer's CD, for example.

Another attractive option is a writeable CD — a CD-ROM on which you can write or record data. Your computer needs a special CD-R drive in order to use writeable CDs. Writeable CDs provide you with loads of storage space, but the downside is that the information on a writeable CD cannot be changed after it's written. You can only add more data to the disc. Unless you're a musician and want to create your own music CDs, stick with a removable cartridge to fulfill your storage needs.

Safety devices

You can spend all the money you want to on top-notch computer equipment, but if you plug your expensive machines into a substandard electrical system, your investment can (almost literally) go up in smoke.

Be sure to protect your equipment against electrical problems that can result in loss of data or substantial repair bills. What kinds of problems? A power surge or spike is a sudden increase in voltage that can damage your equipment. Electrical storms can damage ungrounded equipment, and blackouts can put you offline and prevent you from getting work done, which can hit you in your pocketbook.

At the very least, make sure that your home office has grounded three-prong outlets. (Even if the rest of your house has the old-fashioned outlets, it's worth paying an electrician to upgrade the line to your office.) Upgrading doesn't just mean changing the outlets themselves, however; it means that you use a three-wire cable to bring electricity to the outlet. The third wire, the ground wire, should literally connect to the ground. Usually, electricians do this by burying a copper spike in the ground near your house. This causes shorts or lightning strikes go into the ground, rather than into your computer equipment.

Another must-have is a *surge suppresser,* a device which guards your equipment against power surges and other electrical problems. A common variety is a five- or six-outlet strip that has a protection device built in. You can find surge suppressers at your neighborhood hardware store.

Also consider the option of an uninterruptible power supply (UPS). These hardware add-ons can get expensive, but one affordable variety is the PowerCard by Guardian On Board. It costs $199 and fits in one of your computer card slots. A UPS keeps devices from shutting off immediately in the event of blackouts or on/off flickering that frequently occurs during electrical storms. You get a few extra minutes of operation during which you can save your data and shut down programs.

Multimedia add-ons

If multimedia is important to your business, be sure that you have a sound card, speakers, and a microphone. Usually, these features are included with computers that you purchase in retail outlets.

If you aren't sure whether your computer is equipped with these devices, here's how to check:

- ✔ **Windows 95 (or higher) users:** Choose Start⇨Settings⇨Control Panel. When the Control Panel window appears, double-click on System. The System Properties dialog box appears. Click on the Device Manager tab to bring it to the front. The Device Manager dialog box presents a list of the hardware available on your computer, arranged by the type of device. For example, to see whether your computer has a built-in sound card, click on the plus sign (+) next to the Sound, video and game controllers category. If your system already has a sound card, it will be listed beneath the category name, along with other sound, video, or game hardware you have.

- ✔ **Macintosh users:** Many Macs don't come with a built-in mike, although virtually all have built-in speakers and sound cards. System software called *extensions* enable the Mac to record audio and play and video files. To find out what extensions you have, from the Apple menu, choose Control Panel⇨Extensions Manager. Your currently available extensions appear under the Extensions heading, and those that are currently enabled have a check mark. To see whether you have a microphone, from the Apple menu, choose Control Panel⇨Sound. Make sure that the Mute check box is unchecked in the Volumes Sound options, and then select Sound In from the drop-down menu near the top of the Sound dialog box. If you have a built-in microphone, you see a Macintosh computer icon with the words Built-in beneath it.

If you know exactly what type of device you need to buy and are only looking for the best price, check one of the online auction services that specialize in computer equipment, such as Onsale.com (`www.onsale.com`). If you don't know what you need, talk to a consultant at a computer store or check out a computer buying guide at a newsstand.

You probably don't need to worry about purchasing special sound cards, external speakers, or adding audio-video goodies when you're first starting out. At a later stage, when your online business site becomes more sophisticated, you may want to try Web browser add-ons that require you to be able to listen to audio and conduct voice communications online, such as the conferencing and whiteboard technologies that are built into the major browser packages: Netscape Communicator and Microsoft Internet Explorer. (Conferencing lets you communicate by voice with other Internet users in real time, almost as though you are using your computer to make an online phone call.)

Monitor

In terms of your online business, the quality of your monitor doesn't affect the quality of your Web site directly. Even if you have a poor-quality monitor, you can create a Web site that looks great to those who visit you. The problem is that you won't know how good your site really looks to those customers who have high-quality monitors. It's a good idea to view your Web site on several different kinds of monitors to see how it will look to people with small, poor-quality monitors and to those with bigger, high-quality ones.

The quality of a monitor depends on several factors:

- **Resolution:** The resolution of a computer monitor refers to the number of pixels it can display horizontally and vertically. A resolution of 640 x 480 means that the monitor can display 640 pixels across the page and 480 pixels down the page. Higher resolutions, such as 800 x 600 or 1,024 x 768, make images look sharper but require more RAM in your computer. Anything less than 640 x 480 is unusable these days.

- **Size:** Monitor size is measured diagonally, as with TVs. Sizes such as 14 inches, 15 inches, and up to 21 inches are available. (Look for a 15-inch or 17-inch monitor, which can display most Web pages fully.)

- **Refresh rate:** This is the number of times per second that a video card redraws an image on-screen. Look for a monitor with a refresh rate of at least 60 Hz (hertz).

It's tempting to scrimp on computer monitors, especially for bargain hunters like me. You can find cheap monitors for $100, or even less if you want to go with a used device. I've been known to buy recycled 14-inch monitors myself. But if I had to do it over again, I'd probably get at least a 15- or 17-inch monitor instead of the smaller variety. Even an extra inch makes a huge difference in terms of viewing word processing documents and Web pages. Figure 3-3 gives you an idea of how to do the job right.

Lots of Web pages seem to have been designed with 17-inch or 21-inch monitors in mind. It's annoying when you can't even read an entire line of type, but instead have to scroll to the right just to finish reading or to see an extra column full of hyperlinks. Besides making your Web surfing more difficult, a small monitor can slow down the process of viewing Web pages that you have created and want to view, either before or after you put them online.

Computer monitors display graphic information that consists of little units called *pixels*. Each pixel appears on-screen as a small dot — so small that it's hard to perceive with the naked eye, unless you magnify an image to look at details close up. Together, the patterns of pixels create different intensities of light in an image, as well as ranges of color. A pixel can contain one or more bytes of binary information. The more pixels per inch (ppi), the higher

Figure 3-3:
The
smalloffice.
com site
fits exactly
into a 14-
inch
monitor's
display
space.

a monitor's potential resolution. The higher the resolution, the closer the image appears to a continuous-tone image such as a photo. When you see a monitor's resolution described as 1,280 x 1,024, for example, that refers to the number of pixels per inch that the monitor can display. *Dot pitch* refers to the distance between any two of the three pixels (one red, one green, and one blue) that a monitor uses to display color. The lower the dot pitch, the better image resolution you obtain. A dot pitch of .28 mm is a good measurement for a 17-inch monitor.

Modem

A *modem* is a hardware device that translates your computer's digital data to the analog signals carried over ordinary telephone lines. Modems can do more than just connect computers on the Internet; *fax modems* can also send and receive fax transmissions with other computers or fax machines. Fax modems also let you exchange programs and data files with other computers that are equipped with fax modems.

If you already have a modem that you use to connect your computer to the Internet, you don't necessarily need to purchase a new and faster one just because you're starting an online business. I recommend that you keep your existing device and try it for a while. If you find that it takes too long to download your e-mail messages or transmit files, by all means upgrade to a faster device that provides you with more bandwidth.

Bandwidth refers to the amount of data that you can transmit through an Internet connection. This amount is usually measured in bits per second (bps). Different kinds of modems provide varying amounts of bandwidth:

- **Analog modems:** These devices, either external or built into your computer, are used for dial-up connections to the Internet. Modems that transmit 56 Kbps (kilobits per second) of data are common at this writing, though you can probably get by with a 36.6 Kbps or even a 28.8 Kbps modem.

- **ISDN modems:** You use a digital ISDN modem if you have an ISDN line installed to your home or business. (I discuss the benefits and downsides of ISDN lines later in this chapter, under "Internet Connection Options.") ISDN modems can deliver 56 Kbps or 128 Kbps of data.

- **Cable modems:** These modems can receive data from the Internet through a cable TV company's existing underground fiber-optic cable. They are an extremely fast, attractive option — if they are available in your area. (See the section entitled "Cable modem," later in this chapter.)

- **ADSL modems:** Asymmetrical Digital Subscriber Line (ADSL) modems let conventional telephone lines transfer data at very high rates and are becoming common in many areas. (See the section entitled "ADSL," later in this chapter.)

Fax equipment

Fax (short for FACSimile) technology permits the transmission of data between devices in remote locations. A fax machine is an essential part of many home offices. If you don't have the funds available for a standalone machine, you can install software that helps your computer send and receive faxes.

You have two options for fax communications via your computer:

- You can install a fax modem, a hardware device that usually works with fax software. The fax modem can either be an internal or external device.

- You can use your regular modem, but install software that enables your computer to exchange faxes with someone else's computer or fax machine.

In particular, look into WinFax by Symantec (`www.symantec.com/winfax/index.html`), which is included on this book's CD-ROM. I found the program easy to set up, and software reviewers frequently recommend it. Your Windows computer needs to be equipped with a modem in order to send or receive faxes with WinFax.

After you configure your computer to handle faxes, it can do just about anything that a real fax machine can do. For example, you can broadcast faxes to multiple destinations. You can also print faxes to your regular laser printer, thus avoiding the flimsy fax paper that many machines use.

Another option is to purchase a multifunction machine, which acts as a fax machine, printer, and photocopier, among other things. (See the upcoming section, "Scanners," for more information on multifunction machines.)

 If you plan to do fax transmissions and access the Internet from your home office, you really should get a second phone line. That way, people won't get a busy signal when they're trying to phone or fax you, in case you're already on the phone or the Internet.

Image capture devices

When you're ready to move beyond the basic hardware and on to a frill, think about obtaining a tool for capturing photographic images. (By "capturing," I mean *digitizing,* which refers to the process of saving a continuous-tone image such as a photographic print in computerized, digital format.) Photos are often essential elements of business Web pages: They attract a customer's attention, they illustrate items for sale in a catalog, and they can provide before-and-after samples of your work. If you're an artist or designer, having photographic representations of your work is especially important.

Most marketing gurus agree that a picture is worth a thousand megabytes of information, in online terms. Including a clear, sharp image on your Web site greatly increases your chances of selling your product or service. You have two choices for digitizing:

- ✔ Taking photos with a conventional camera and then processing the prints with a scanner
- ✔ Taking photos with a digital camera and saving the image files on your computer

The choice depends on your budget and your needs; the following sections discuss the advantages and disadvantages of each.

Digital camera

The advantage of using a digital camera instead of a scanner to capture images for your Web site is that it's portable and convenient. A digital camera connects directly to your computer, so you can save images right to disk. You can get photos online in a matter of minutes, without spending money or time having them processed and printed conventionally and then scanning them in.

Not so long ago, digital cameras cost thousands of dollars. These days, you can find a good digital camera made by a reputable manufacturer like Nikon, Fuji, Canon, Olympus, or Kodak in the $300 to $700 range. You have to make an investment up front, but this particular tool can pay off for you in the long run. Not only can you use the camera for your business but, with the addition of a color printer, you can even print your own photos, which could save you a pile in photo lab costs.

Don't hesitate to fork over the extra dough to get a camera that gives you good resolution. It doesn't pay to cut corners and end up with images that look fuzzy. Most low-cost devices have a resolution of 640 x 480 pixels, at best. Try one like the Epson PhotoPC 600, which costs about $500 and has a top resolution of 1,024 x 768 pixels. Others, such as the Fuji MX-700 or Agfa ePhoto 1280, can take photos at a resolution of 1,280 x 1,024 pixels, and the Kodak Digital Science DC260 can reach 1,536 x 1,024. But keep in mind that the higher the resolution, the fewer photos your camera will be able to store at any one time, because each image file requires more memory.

On the other hand, having super-high resolution images isn't critical when it comes to Web pages. That's because online material is primarily intended to be displayed on computer monitors, which have limited resolution. Besides, in order to be displayed by Web browsers, images must first be compressed using the GIF or JPEG formats (see Chapter 6). Also, smaller and simpler images (as opposed to large, high-resolution graphics) generally appear more quickly on the viewer's screen. If you make your customers wait too long to see any given image, they are apt to get bored and go to someone else's online store.

When shopping for a digital camera, look for the following features:

- ✔ The ability to download images to your computer via a serial port
- ✔ Bundled image processing software
- ✔ The ability to download image files directly to a floppy disk
- ✔ An included LCD screen that lets you see your images as soon as you take them

On the downside, photos taken with digital cameras tend to be less sharp than conventional 35mm photos, due to optical filtering that is intended to reduce *color artifacts* — distortions of the image caused by limitations in hardware. You can correct this problem in a graphics program, but that can be time-consuming. If you want high-quality close-ups and your budget is limited, try a scanner instead.

Scanners

Scanning is the process of turning the colors and shapes contained in a photographic print or slide into digital information (that is, bytes of data) that a computer can understand. You place the image in a position where the scanner's camera can pass over it, and the scanner turns the image into a computer document that consists of tiny bits of information called _pixels_.

The best news about scanners is that they've been around for a while, which, in the world of computing, means that prices are going down at the same time quality is on the rise. The bargain models are well under $200, and I've even seen a couple (including the Microtek ScanMaker E3) priced under $135.

Scanners come in many different types. Some devices scan slides, but most accept photographic prints. The one that I find easiest to use is a flatbed scanner. You place the photo or other image on a flat glass bed, just like you find on a photocopier. An optical device moves under the bed and scans the photo.

A type of scanner that has lots of benefits for small or home-based businesses is a multifunction device. You can find these units, along with conventional printers and scanners, at computer outlets. I have one a multifunction device myself, in my home office. It sends and receives faxes, scans images, acts as a laser printer, and makes copies — plus it includes a telephone and answering machine. Now, if it could just make a good cup of espresso. . . .

Video capture devices

If you already have a video camera for home use and you need a way to get images on the Web, consider a neat little device called Snappy Video Snapshot, which lets you select still images from your videotapes and save them in digital format so that you can show them on your Web pages.

Snappy, by Play Incorporated (www.play.com), is a software and hardware package that works only with PCs, not Macs. You plug the hardware module into your printer port, install the software, and then plug your camcorder into the hardware module using the cables that come with the product. The taped images appear on your computer screen through the Snappy software window. When you find the image you want, you can adjust contrast and brightness and then save it as a computer file.

A low-budget alternative

If you only want to get a computerized version of your smiling face on your Web site, and you don't want to invest in any of the hardware mentioned here, not to worry. Just call your local photo shop or copy center. Many Kinko's Copies outlets, for example, provide computer services that include scanning photos.

Wherever you go, be sure to tell the technician that you want the image to appear on the Web, so it should be saved in GIF or JPEG format. Also, if you have an idea of how big you want the final image to be when it appears online, tell that to the technician, too. The person can save the image in the size you want, so you don't have to resize it later on in a graphics program.

Internet Connection Options

After you purchase the computer hardware you need, telephone bills are likely to be the biggest monthly expense you'll encounter in connection with your online business. It pays to choose your telco (telephone company) connection wisely.

A second phone line

First and foremost, you should strongly consider obtaining a second phone line for your office. Having a second line is pretty much a given if you plan to do business online regularly — or if your children and significant other use your existing phone line even on a semi-regular basis. (The digital modem that you need when you install an ISDN line comes with extra analog phone lines — that is, the kind you use for normal voice and dial-up modem connections. See the section called "ISDN," later in this chapter.)

Because you'll be using your modem to dial the same one or two access numbers provided by your Internet Service Provider, confirm with your telco that your Internet access number is truly local — not a number for which you are required to pay any kind of a toll fee.

Ask your telco whether a call pack is available. Call packs allow you to make a large number of calls to the same number for the same rate: 100 calls per month for a flat $10 fee, for example.

Beyond modems

Most people on a budget use a regular dial-up modem connection. This is the simplest and most straightforward way to connect to the Net — though it's also the slowest. A far better way to connect to the Internet is through a *direct line,* which means that, rather than being connected to the Net for the length of your modem's phone call, you are connected all the time. Besides freeing up a phone line, a direct connection is typically light-years faster than a dial-up modem connection.

If you have a modem and a dial-up connection already, fine; go ahead and use it. But when your e-mail messages begin to mount and you start surfing the Web more often to market your online business, you may find your old connection to be slow and cumbersome. In that case, consider upgrading to a direct connection. But if you haven't signed up with a provider, look around to see whether these other attractive options are available, first.

Cable modem

Cable modem connections are relatively new, but I wouldn't let that stop me. I'm still convinced that they are going to take off, because they offer a really attractive way to get a high-speed connection to cyberspace. So go ahead and ask your local cable TV providers if they provide this service.

In my neighborhood in Chicago, a company called 21st Century (www.21stcentury.com) offers basic cable TV service for $29.45 a month and Internet access for an additional $44.95 per month, plus a $125 installation fee that includes the cable modem device itself.

The advantages of having a cable modem connection are many: It's a direct connection, it frees up a phone line, and it's super fast. Cable modems have the capacity to deliver 4 or 5MB of data per second. In reality, of course, the speed is going to be less than this, because you're sharing access with other users. But a cable modem is still almost certainly going to be far faster than your dial-up connection.

ADSL

Wouldn't it be great if you could use conventional telephone lines to connect to the Net all the time? Wouldn't it be even better if the connection were really fast — say, 100 times as fast as a 56 Kbps dial-up modem?

If your telephone company offers its customers Asymmetric Digital Subscriber Line (ADSL) connections, these aren't just pie-in-the-sky questions. ADSLs "borrow" the part of your phone line that your voice doesn't use, the part that transmits signals of 3,000 Hz (hertz) or higher. ADSLs can *upload* (send) data to another location on the Net at 1.088 Mbps (megabits per second), and *download* (receive) data at more than twice that rate: 2.560 Mbps.

Of course, you can't just use your existing telephone to connect via ADSL. ADSL requires you to buy and install special hardware at your end of the telephone line. The telephone company needs to have the same piece of ADSL hardware at its end. Where you live also makes a difference: You must be located relatively close to a telephone switch that supports ADSL technology.

A similar technology, Symmetrical Digital Subscriber Line (SDSL) transmits information at the same speed in both directions. Both ADSL and SDSL are cost-effective "starter" types of direct connections to the Net, making them good alternatives for small businesses.

WebTV

I'm not terribly enthusiastic about WebTV, but I mention it as an option that a home-based entrepreneur might consider as an alternative to owning two computers. With WebTV, you purchase a set-top box, a hand-held controller, and a keyboard. You sign up with the WebTV network and pay a monthly fee for access. You may also need to install another phone line, because WebTV uses a regular telephone jack.

The advantage of WebTV is that it gives you a way to surf the Web and use Internet software without having to purchase a computer. It frees up your regular computer so someone else in the family can do homework — or you can work on your business site — while someone else surfs the Web.

ISDN

ISDN (short for Integrated Services Digital Network) service is a practical alternative for many small businesses that need a connection to the Internet that's somewhat faster than that provided by conventional dial-up modems, and that's still affordable. ISDN enables your computer to connect to the Net at 64 or 128 Kbps by means of a special phone line and line-switching equipment that your phone company must install. You have to check with your phone company to find out whether they provide ISDN service.

Basic Rate Interface, or BRI, is the most common type of ISDN connection. A BRI connection divides the two copper wires used for a standard telephone connection into three channels. Your computer connects to the line by means of an ISDN terminal adapter. With a BRI connection, your computer can communicate at 128 Kbps (or, if you use multiple BRI connections together, up to 384 Kbps). Primary Rate Interface (PRI) ISDN is a dedicated connection that can communicate at 1.544 Mbps, but is much more expensive than BRI ISDN.

If you're thinking about installing an ISDN line, consider the following pros and cons:

Pro: ISDN gives you a digital line, which is clearer and more reliable than traditional analog phone lines.

Con: ISDN is more expensive than a simple dial-up modem connection; you pay an installation fee, you buy the terminal adapter, and then you pay monthly charges to both your telephone company and your Internet Service Provider.

Pro: You get new phone lines with ISDN.

Con: The new phone lines can go down like any others. When your ISDN connection goes down, the analog phone lines on your ISDN terminal adapter also go down.

Pro: ISDN frees up your regular home phone line.

Con: ISDN isn't necessarily faster than a 56 Kbps analog modem.

I have an ISDN line in my own home office. My setup costs were as follows:

- $353 for the ISDN terminal adapter
- About $100 for a technician to install the ISDN line and hook up the adapter
- $31 per month to the phone company
- About $10 a month to my ISP (Internet Service Provider), in addition to my regular monthly ISP charges

In my opinion, the best thing about the ISDN setup is that the terminal adapter comes with two POTS (Plain Old Telephone Service lines), which I use for my fax machine and extra modem connection. I rarely use the 128 Kbps option (for which my ISP charges a higher rate). If I had to do it over again, I'd probably purchase a 56 Kbps modem and an extra phone line, rather than an ISDN.

Internet and Other Software

One of the great things about starting an Internet business is that you get to use Internet software. As you probably know, the programs you use online are inexpensive (sometimes free), easy to use and install, and continually being updated.

Although you probably already have a basic selection of software to help you find information and communicate with others in cyberspace, the following sections describe some programs you may not have as yet, and that will come in handy when you create your online business.

Web browser

A *Web browser* is software that serves as a visual interface to the images, colors, links, and other content contained on the Web. The two most popular such programs are Microsoft Internet Explorer and Netscape Navigator (part of the Communicator suite).

Your Web browser is your primary tool for conducting business online, just as it is for everyday personal use. When it comes to running a virtual store or consulting business, though, you have to run your software through a few more paces than usual. You need your browser to

- Preview the Web pages you create
- Display frames, animations, movie clips, and other goodies you plan to add online
- Support some level of Internet security, such as Secure Sockets Layer (SSL), if you plan to conduct secure transactions on your site

In addition to having an up-to-date browser with the latest features, it's a good idea to have more than one kind of browser installed on your computer. For example, if you use Microsoft Internet Explorer because that's what came with your operating system, be sure to download the latest copy of Netscape Communicator, as well. That way, you can test out your site to make sure that it looks good to all your visitors.

Web page editor

HyperText Markup Language (HTML) is a set of instructions used to format text, images, and other Web page elements so that Web browsers can correctly display them. But you don't have to learn HTML in order to create your own Web pages. Plenty of programs called *Web page editors* are available to help you format text, add images, make hyperlinks, and do all the fun assembly steps necessary to make your Web site a winner.

In many cases, Web page editors come with electronic storefront packages; QuickSite, which I discuss in Chapter 4, comes with Microsoft FrontPage Express. Sometimes, programs that you use for one purpose can also help you create Web documents: Microsoft Word has an add-on called Internet Assistant that lets you save text documents as HTML Web pages, and Office 98 enables you to export files in Web page format automatically.

Taking e-mail a step higher

You're probably very familiar with sending and receiving e-mail messages. But when you start an online business, you should make sure that e-mail software has some advanced features:

- **Autoresponders:** Some programs automatically respond to e-mail requests with a form letter or document of your choice.

- **Mailing lists:** With a well-organized address book (a feature that comes with some e-mail programs), you can collect the e-mail addresses of visitors or subscribers and send them a regular update of your business activities or, better yet, an e-mail newsletter.

- **Quoting:** Almost all e-mail programs let you quote from a message to which you are replying, so you can respond easily to a series of questions.

- **Attaching:** Attaching a file to an e-mail message is a quick and convenient way to transmit information from one person to another.

- **Signature files:** Make sure that your e-mail software automatically includes a simple electronic signature at the end. Use this space to list your company name, your title, and Web site URL.

Both Outlook Express, the e-mail component of Microsoft Internet Explorer, and Netscape Messenger, part of the Netscape Communicator suite of programs, include most or all of these features. Because these functions are all essential aspects of providing good customer service, I discuss them in more detail in Chapter 9.

Discussion group software

A *newsgroup* is a collection of messages about a particular subject. Newsgroups are part of Usenet, an extensive and popular part of the Internet. In order to read and post messages to Usenet discussion groups, you need newsgroup software, which is built into Netscape Communicator and Microsoft Internet Explorer.

However, when your business site is up and running, consider taking it a step further by creating your own discussion area right on your Web site. This sort of discussion area isn't a newsgroup as such; it doesn't exist in Usenet, and you don't need newsgroup software to read and post messages. Rather, it's a Web-based discussion area where your visitors can compare notes and share their passion for the products you sell or the area of service you provide.

Programs such as Microsoft FrontPage enable you to set up a discussion area on your Web site. See Chapter 9 for more information.

FTP software

FTP (File Transfer Protocol) is one of those acronyms you see time and time again as you move around the Internet. You may even have an FTP program that your Internet Service Provider gave you when you obtained your Internet account. But chances are you don't use it that often.

In case you haven't used FTP yet, start dusting it off. When you create your own Web pages, a simple, no-nonsense FTP program is the easiest way to transfer them from your computer at home to your Web host. If you need to correct and update your Web pages quickly (and you will), you'll benefit by having your FTP software ready and set up with your Web site address, username, and password so you can transfer files right away. See Chapter 4 for more on using File Transfer Protocol.

Image editors

You need a graphics editing program either to create original artwork for your Web pages or to crop and adjust your scanned/digitally photographed images. In the case of adjusting or cropping photographic image files, the software you need almost always comes bundled with the scanner or digital camera, so you don't need to buy separate software for that.

In the case of graphic images, the first question to ask yourself is: "Am I really qualified to draw and make my own graphics?" If the answer is yes, think shareware first. Two programs I like are LView Pro, by Leonardo Haddad Loureiro (www.lview.com) and Paint Shop Pro by Jasc, Inc. (www.jasc.com). You can download both of these programs from the Web to use on a trial basis. After the trial period is over, you are asked to pay a small fee to the developer in order to register and keep the program. LViewPro costs $40; Paint Shop Pro costs $69 for version 3.01, shown in Figure 3-4, or $99 for version 5.01.

The ability to download and use free (and almost free) software from shareware archives and many other sites is one of the nicest things about the Internet. Keep the system working by remembering to pay the shareware fees to the nice folks who make their software available to individuals like you and me.

Internet Relay Chat

Internet Relay Chat is a form of real-time computer conferencing between Internet users. Users communicate by typing messages and submitting them to a central computer, called a *chat server,* using special chat software.

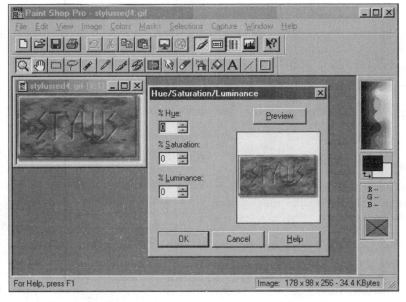

Figure 3-4:
Paint Shop
Pro lets you
crop, resize,
re-color,
and save
images for
the Web.

Chances are you don't have to download a special chat program, because chat functionality is integrated into the latest versions of Microsoft Internet Explorer and Netscape Communicator. The difference between Internet Relay Chat and newsgroups is that participants in a chat room can read messages and respond with their own within a matter of seconds.

Chatting is one of the most popular features of the Internet and a great source of fun and recreation. But it's not just a way for teenagers to share their angst. Some ways that you can use chat for business include conducting an online meeting with a group of customers or clients, or connecting with people who are interested in your area of expertise.

Internet Phone

Some businesspeople regularly use Internet Phone to communicate in real-time with colleagues and customers across the country and around the world. You can use Conference, one of the Netscape Communicator suite of applications, or NetMeeting, which comes with Microsoft Internet Explorer, to make Internet phone calls.

Building an online presence takes time

Judy Vorfeld, who goes by the *nom de Net* Webgrammar, started the online version of her business Office Support Services (www.ossweb.com) from her home in Arizona in early 1998. She does typing and document preparation as a virtual office employee.

As far as equipment, Judy estimates that she spent about $1,500 on computer hardware and $350 on software related to her business. Her computer has a Pentium II processor with 32MB of RAM and a 2GB hard drive. She uses a 28.8 Kbps modem to connect to the Net and has a scanner and 17-inch monitor. As far as software, she uses the Web page editor Allaire HomeSite to create Web pages and Paint Shop Pro to work with graphics.

Q. What would you describe as the primary goal of your online business?

A. To obtain work as a virtual secretary and document analyst.

Q. How many hours a week do you work on your site?

A. Six to ten hours, minimum.

Q. How do you promote your site?

A. Letterhead, biz cards, fax cover sheets, press releases, client newsletters, signature lines on e-mail, online discussion groups, search engine and directory submissions, creating free sites for nonprofit 501 (c)(3) groups, and anything else creative that comes to mind.

Q. Has your online business been profitable financially?

A. It's not yet profitable, but it's moving in that direction. Many visitors want or need only advice. Others have needs that I cannot fill (such as knowledge of esoteric databases), so I refer them to trusted, respected colleagues.

I am in it for the money, but I understand that building an Internet presence takes time and effort. My local business is supporting my online business for now.

Q. Who creates your business's Web pages?

A. I create them myself. I tried having others do it, but I wanted the ability to make extensive and frequent changes in text and design. The solution: get some training. It was time-consuming, but rewarding.

Q. What advice would you give to someone starting an online business?

A. I have a bunch of suggestions to give, based on my own experience:

- **Network with others in your profession.** Visit lots of Web sites and, when you see work that you admire, contact the owners of those sites. Explain the areas in which you function best and offer to send referrals when visitors come to you asking for help that's out of your immediate area of expertise. After you get to know some professionals, make links to their sites. It's important to think of these people as colleagues rather than competitors. Also, network by joining credible associations and mentioning on your site that you are a member. Link to these associations and offer to help the owners and operators.

- **Join newsgroups.** Lurk until you can adequately answer a question or make a comment. Also, keep on the lookout for someone with whom you can build up a relationship, someone who might mentor you and be willing to occasionally scrutinize your site, a news release, and so on. This person must be brutally honest.

- ✔ **Learn Web design and the culture.** Even if you don't do the actual design, you have to make decisions on all the offers you receive regarding how to make money via affiliate programs, link exchanges, and so on. It's vital that you keep active online and make those judgments yourself, unless you thoroughly trust your Webmaster. Find a pragmatic "devil's advocate" who is knowledgeable in the field of affiliates and link exchanges, until you are in a position to make your own decisions.

- ✔ **Include a Web page that shows your business biography or profile.** Mention any volunteer work you do, groups to which you belong, and anything else you do in and for the community. You need to paint as clear a picture as possible in just a few words. Avoid showcasing your talents and hobbies on a business site unless they are directly related to your business.

- ✔ **In *everything* you write, use the word "you" as much as possible.** Avoid the words "I," "we," and "us." You, as a businessperson, are there to connect with your visitors. You can't give them eye contact, but you can let them know that they matter, that they are (in a sense) the reason for your being there.

- ✔ **Become known as a specialist in a given field.** Be someone who can always answer a question or go out and find the answer. Hits are important to some businesses, but if you're a consultant offering a service, forget hits and concentrate on being so effective that your visitors will respond, remember, or refer you to others.

Other Business Software

Besides the software that lets you navigate and communicate online, your business can also benefit from programs that help you keep track of accounts, solve technical problems, and get your words online. The following sections briefly present some suggestions for business software you can use.

Voice recognition software

Personally, I like to type. It gives my hands something to do while thoughts are cooking inside my brain. But I realize that, for lots of other people, typing is akin to sitting in the dentist's chair listening to the drill whine. Many small-business people are interested in voice recognition software that automatically turns their spoken words into typed computer text. Here are two suggestions:

✔ **Dragon Naturally Speaking:** This program, by Dragon Systems, Inc. (www.dragonsys.com), won a handful of awards at the RetailVision show in 1998. The Standard version costs $109 and requires a 133 MHz or higher Pentium processor, 64MB of RAM, and 240MB of hard disk space.

✔ **IBM ViaVoice 98, Home Edition:** This program, which costs only $42.95, lets you dictate directly into a Microsoft Word document. To use this program, IBM recommends that you have 64MB of RAM and 180MB of hard disk space. Spanish-language versions are also available. Find out more at www.software.ibm.com/speech/index.html.

Antivirus and troubleshooting software

Lots of good things can come to you from cyberspace, but, unfortunately, some bad things can invade your computer space, as well. These include harmful programs called *viruses,* destructive *macros,* or *Trojan Horses,* each of which can rob you of data or disable your computer in some way.

Every computer that is connected regularly to the Internet needs to be equipped with some sort of virus protection software. Such programs have the ability to detect a virus if it is downloaded to your machine from the Net. Usually, the software notifies you when it detects a virus and disables the virus, as well.

Because new viruses keep cropping up, it's important to buy a program that provides you with free upgrades to catch the latest harmful things that could invade your computer. Here are some good bets:

✔ **VirusScan** by Network Associates, Inc. (www.mcafee.com/products/virusscan/virusscan.asp)

✔ **Dr. Solomon's Anti-Virus** (www.drsolomon.com/index_new.cfm)

✔ **Backup Exec** by Seagate Software (www.seagatesoftware.com)

One way to deal with computer trouble, in case you do encounter it, is to record serial numbers and make/model information for all of your equipment. This is not only important for insurance purposes, in case something is lost or stolen, but it helps if your computer is down and you need to talk to service people about exactly how much memory and what kind of peripheral hardware you have attached to the machine.

If you need help . . .

Your wires are crossed, your computers aren't speaking to one another on your network, and your browser is freezing up. Don't suffer in silence.

For free help, there's no better place to look than the Internet itself. After you restart, try to connect to the Net and consult newsgroups. If you can't get your computer to work, use another computer; you may have to visit your local library to use a public computer that can access the Internet. Turn to any newsgroup that relates to the problem you're having.

Check out the `comp.infosystems` hierarchy for computer issues. Groups in the `rec.software` category address software problems.

When all else fails, find out whether the computer store where you purchased your equipment will help you. They may charge a fee, but, in the long run, the expense may be worthwhile, especially if a qualified technician can get your computer to run faster or your browser to operate better every time you go online.

Backup software

Losing copies of your personal documents is one thing, but losing files related to your business can hit you hard in the pocketbook. That makes it even more important to make backups of your online business computer files.

Iomega Zip or Jaz drives come with software that lets you automatically make backups of your files. If you don't own one of these programs, I recommend you get really familiar with the backup program included with Windows 95 and 98.

Internet storefront software

If you plan to present lots of catalog items for sale on the Web, and you envision a full-fledged online business that includes customer service options and online purchases, you may want to look into software that guides you through the process of creating an online store.

Electronic storefront programs take much of the work out of designing Web pages and putting them online. These programs often provide you with pre-designed Web pages, called *templates,* that you can customize with your own content. They usually also provide space on a Web server that will host your site, and they lead you through the process of transferring your files from your computer to the server.

Chapter 4 examines some of the more affordable storefront programs, but if you're curious, check out some Web sites that also let you create a storefront online:

✔ **iCat** (www.icat.com): Provides Web visitors with easy-to-use forms that you can fill out in order to create your own business site, which iCat then hosts.

✔ **MiniVend** (www.minivend.com): Try a demo of this complete online storefront created by Internet Robotics.

Accounting software

Because you are essentially creating and operating your online business through your computer, it only makes sense to keep track of your finances on your computer, as well.

You don't necessarily have to purchase special accounting software to do this. You can set up a table in Word or Word Perfect, or use Microsoft Works or Excel. But with luck, you'll need to keep track of lots of orders and will want a more powerful financial software package. For something more elaborate, try programs like QuickBooks, Quicken, Peachtree Accounting, or one of the other popular software packages described in Chapter 14.

Part II
Putting Your Web Site to Work

The 5th Wave   By Rich Tennant

"Games are an important part of my Web site. They cause eye strain."

In this part . . .

*J*ust as business owners in the real world have to rent or buy a facility and fix it up to conduct their business, you have to develop a storefront online to conduct your online business. This part explains how to put a virtual roof over your store and light a cyberfire to welcome your customers. In other words, it focuses on the nuts and bolts of your Web site itself.

The World Wide Web is the most exciting and popular place to open an online store. But merely creating a set of Web pages isn't enough to succeed online. Your site needs to be compelling — even irresistible. This part shows you how to organize your site and fill it with useful content that attracts customers in the first place and encourages them to stay to browse. This part also shows you ways to open your Web site to an international audience, and to equip your site (and yourself) to handle many different kinds of electronic purchases.

Chapter 4

Choosing Your Web Host and Design Tools

- -

In This Chapter

▶ Finding a program to create and edit your Web pages

▶ Taking the template shortcut

▶ Coming up with compelling content that attracts customers

▶ Selecting a hosting service for your Web site

▶ Transferring your Web site files to your hosting service

- -

Although you can sell items online without having a Web site, doing real online business without one is pretty much impossible. The vast majority of online commercial concerns use their Web sites as the primary way to attract customers, convey their message, and make sales.

Two of the most important factors in determining a Web site's success are where it's hosted and how it's designed. These factors affect how easily you can create and update your Web pages, what special features such as multimedia or interactive forms you can have on your site and even how your site looks. Some hosting services provide Web page creation tools that are easy to use but that limit how your pages look. Others leave the creation and design up to you. This chapter provides an overview of your Web hosting options and different design approaches you can implement.

A growing number of Web sites and CD-ROMs say that they can have your Web site up and running online "in a matter of minutes" using a "seamless" process. The actual construction may indeed be quick and smooth — as long as you've done all your preparation work beforehand. This preparation work includes identifying your goals for going online, deciding on the market you want to reach, deciding what products you want to sell, writing descriptions and capturing images of those products, and so on. Before you jump over to Yahoo! Store or iCat and start assembling your site, be sure that you've done all the groundwork mentioned in Chapters 2 and 3.

Finding a Host with the Most

An Internet connection and a Web browser are all you need if you're simply intending to surf through cyberspace, consuming information and shopping for online goodies. But when you're starting an online business, you're no longer just a consumer; you're going to become a producer of information and consumable goods. Along with a way to connect to the Net, you need to find a hosting service that will make your online business available to your prospective customers.

A *Web hosting service* is the online world's equivalent of a landlord. Just as the owner of a building gives you office space or room for a storefront where you can hang your shingle, a hosting service provides you with space online where you can set up shop.

A Web host provides space on special computers called Web servers that are connected to the Internet all the time and equipped with software that makes your Web pages visible to people who connect to them using a Web browser. The process of using a Web hosting service for your online business works roughly like this:

1. **You decide where you want your site to appear on the Internet.**

   Do you want it to be part of a virtual shopping mall that includes many other businesses? Or do you want a standalone site that has its own Web address and doesn't appear to be affiliated with any other organization?

2. **You sign up with a Web host.**

   Sometimes you pay a fee; sometimes no fee is required. In all cases, you are assigned space on a server. Your Web site gets an address, or URL, that people can enter to view your pages.

3. **You create your Web pages.**

   Usually, you use a Web page editor to do this.

4. **After creating content, adding images, and making your site look just right, you transfer your Web page files (HTML documents, images, and so on) from your computer to the host's Web server.**

   You generally need special File Transfer Protocol (FTP) software to do the transferring.

5. **You access your own site with your Web browser and check the contents to make sure that all the images appear and that any hypertext links you created go to the intended destinations.**

   At this point, you're open for business — visitors can view your Web pages by entering your Web address in their Web browser's Go to field.

6. **You market and promote your site to attract potential clients or customers.**

The choice of Web host is important because it has a bearing on which software you'll use to create your Web pages and get them online. It also affects the way your site looks, and it may determine the complexity of your Web address. (See the sidebar "What's in a name?," later in this chapter, for details.)

If you have a direct connection to the Internet and are really good with computers (or if you have access to someone who is), you can host your own site on the Web. However, turning your own computer into a Web server is a lot more complicated than signing up with a hosting service. You need to install server software and set up a domain name for your computer. You may even have to purchase an IP address for your machine. (An *IP address* is a number that identifies every computer that's connected to the Internet, and that consists of four numerals separated by dots, such as 206.207.99.1.) If you're just starting a simple home-based or part-time business, hosting your own Web site is probably more trouble than you care to handle, but it is an option to be aware of.

Shopping for a Web Server to Call Home

Hi! I'm your friendly World Wide Web real estate agent. Call me Virtual Larry. You say you're not sure exactly what kind of Web site is right for you, and you want to see all the options, from a tiny storefront in a strip mall to your own landscaped corporate park? Your wish is my command. Just hop into my 1998-model Internet Explorer, buckle your seat belt, and I'll show you around the many different business properties available in cyberspace.

Here's a road map of our tour:

- ✔ Online Web-host-and-design-kit combos, including Yahoo! Store, GeoCities, and iCat
- ✔ America Online: My Place and Hometown AOL
- ✔ Electronic merchant CD-ROMs, including QuickSite and Online Merchant
- ✔ A space in an online shopping mall
- ✔ Your current Internet Service Provider (ISP)
- ✔ Companies devoted to hosting Web sites full-time

The first three options combine Web hosting with Web page creation kits. Whether you buy these services or get to use them on the Web for free, you simply follow the manufacturer's instructions. Most of these hosting services enable you to create your Web pages by filling in forms; you never have to see a line of HTML code if you don't want to. Depending on which service you choose, you have varying degrees of control over how your site ultimately looks.

The last three options (ISPs, online malls, and full-time Web hosts) tend to be do-it-yourself projects: You sign up with the host, you choose the software, and you create your own site. However, the distinction between this category and the others is blurry. As competition between Web hosts grows keener, more and more companies are providing ready-made solutions that streamline the process of Web site creation for their customers. For you, the end user, this is a good thing: You have plenty of control over how your site comes into being and how it grows over time.

If you simply need a basic Web site and don't want a lot of choices, go with one of the kits. Your site may look like everyone else's and seem a little generic, but setup is easy and you can concentrate on marketing and running your business.

But if you're the independent type who wants to control your site and have lots of room to grow, consider taking on a do-it-yourself project. The sky's the limit as far as the degree of creativity you can exercise and the amount of sweat equity you can put in. The more work you do, the greater your chances of seeing your business prosper.

Using online Web site creation and hosting kits

A new class of Web sites has caught on to the concept of making things easy and affordable for would-be *ontrepreneurs* (online entrepreneurs). These sites act as both a Web host and a Web page creation tool. You connect to the site, sign up for service, and fill out a series of forms. Submitting the completed forms activates a script on the host site that automatically generates your Web pages based on the data you entered.

In this section, I show you how to set up a business Web site using Yahoo! Store, a popular "kit" service. Many such sites are available, and it never hurts to investigate all your options. Some other Web site creation packages are available at the following sites:

- **GeoCities** (www.geocities.com): GeoCities is a popular spot for individuals who want to create home pages and full-fledged personal and business Web sites for free.

- **iCat** (www.icat.com): For lower volume businesses, hosting with iCat Commerce Online Store is less expensive than with Yahoo! Store. The first 30 days are free. After that, a site that sells 50 items or less is charged $50 per month. Yahoo! Store charges $100 per month for a site that sells less than 300 items.

✔ **Hometown AOL (**hometown.aol.com**):** America Online hosts this Web site where individuals can create their own Web pages for business or personal use. A "neighborhood" within Hometown AOL, called Business Park, is set aside for commercial sites, and an area within *that* area hosts home-based businesses. (See the upcoming section, "Setting up shop with America Online," for more information.)

Yahoo! Store (which, by the way, was called Viaweb Mall from its beginnings in 1994 until it was purchased by Yahoo! in June 1998) makes setting up an online business easy. The hard part is deciding what you want to sell, how best to describe your sales items, and how to promote your site. Getting your words and images online is remarkably straightforward:

1. **Connect to the Internet, start up your Web browser, and go to the following URL:** store.yahoo.com.

   The Yahoo! Store home page appears in your browser window.

2. **Click on the heading Test Drive.**

   The Test drive page (store.yahoo.com/vw/tesdriv.html) appears in your browser window.

3. **If you want to surf around and check out some of the other businesses being hosted by Yahoo! Store, click on the link labeled "See all our users at The Yahoo! Stores;" otherwise, click on the link "Build your own store right now . . ."**

   The Create Your Own Account page appears. This form tells Yahoo! that you want to create a site with them and that you need to have a directory assigned to you on one of the host's Web servers. No matter what kind of Web hosting service you decide to use, the fill-out-a-form page is a pretty much universal one.

4. **Fill out the fields on the Create Your Own Account page (including your name, e-mail address, and online store name) and then click on Create.**

   A page appears that sets the terms of your agreement with Yahoo! to host your temporary site. Yahoo! keeps this temporary account for ten days, at which point you can either call Yahoo! and ask to have your account changed to a permanent one, or you can let the account (and the Web site) be dissolved.

5. **Read the terms and, if you agree to them, click on I Accept.**

   The first in a series of "guided tour" Web pages appears. These pages explain how to create your store.

6. **Click on Continue.**

   The front page (or home page) of your store appears.

7. **Click on the New Section button at the bottom of the screen.**

   A simple Web form appears with the instructions "Enter a name for the section" at the top of the page.

8. **Type a name for a major section of your Web site and then click on Update.**

   Your new section heading appears on your Web-page-in-progress (see Figure 4-1).

Figure 4-1: After you fill out a simple form, Yahoo! Store gives you instant results: a simple home page.

9. **Click on the New Item button.**

   Another Web form appears, this one with Name, Code, Price, and Caption fields where you can enter information about your merchandise. The Code field is only applicable if you assign numbers to your inventory to keep track of them. The caption field contains a description of the merchandise.

10. **Fill out the information and then click on Update.**

    Your updated Web page appears with the description of your item. If you want to add a new item, click on Up to go back to the section you created in Step 8, and then click on the New Item button again.

11. **If you want to add an image, click on the Image button.**

    A new Web page form appears.

12. **If you know the name of the image file you want to add, type the directory structure and filename in the text box next to File; if you don't remember the name and the directory in which the image file is located, click on Browse.**

If you click on Browse, a dialog box appears enabling you to navigate through the directories or folders on your computer. When you locate the file you want to add, single-click on the file to select it and then click on Open. The name of the image file appears in the text box next to File.

13. **Click on Send.**

After a few seconds, the Web page you're working on reappears, with the image included in a predetermined location to left of the item name and description.

The Yahoo! Store wizard has plenty of other options. By clicking on the Special button at the bottom of a page, you can add a phrase such as "50% Off" or "Reduced for Clearance."

14. **When you finish adding sale merchandise, click on the Info button.**

A page appears that lets you add your address, phone number, or other contact information for your online business.

15. **Add your contact information and then click on Update to see the results.**

16. **When you're satisfied with your Web page, click on Publish to transfer your new Web page files to the Yahoo! Store site.**

You can visit your new site by entering your own Web address, which takes the form `http://store.yahoo.com/storename` (where `storename` is the name you entered in Step 4).

Setting up shop with America Online

If you're one of the millions of folks who already have an account with America Online, by all means consider setting up your online store with AOL as your host. Even if you don't have an account with AOL presently, you might consider signing up in order to create and publish a simple Web site. Plenty of entrepreneurs either started an online business with AOL and then moved on to another Web host, or continue to maintain their business Web site on one of AOL's Web servers.

When you sign up for an account with America Online, you're entitled to 2MB of space for your own Web pages. That may not seem like a lot of room, but consider that the average Web page is only 5 to 10K in size. Even if each page contains images that are perhaps 10 to 20K in size, that still means you have room for 70 to 100 Web pages. Besides that, an account with AOL provides for five separate usernames. Each username is entitled to 2MB of Web site space. In theory, at least, you have 10MB of space at your disposal. This is more than enough to accommodate most moderately-sized Web sites.

If AOL is so great, why doesn't everyone publish Web sites with them? Well, AOL has its downsides, too. For one thing, its servers seem (to me, at least) to be noticeably slower than others, perhaps because of the sheer volume of users. AOL has had problems with members being unable to get online during busy times. And unless you pay AOL's flat monthly rate for unlimited access, you're liable to run up some sizable hourly access charges in the course of creating, revising, and maintaining your business site. Finally, there's a subtle but important difference between AOL and a Web host that's on the Internet: AOL isn't really part of the Internet. It's on its own online network. E-mail sent from an AOL user to someone on the Internet has to go through a computer connection called a gateway. If the gateway goes down or if some other aspect of AOL's operation experiences a problem, all AOL users are suddenly inaccessible from the Internet. Your business may be inaccessible to many potential customers for a time. Although AOL does seem to be getting more reliable, the fact that it's separate from the Internet is an important consideration to keep in mind if you're thinking about setting up shop there.

America Online presents several resources for customers who want to publish Web pages for their business or personal use. Some of these re- sources are only accessible through America Online, but because AOL is making an effort to branch out onto the Web itself, other resources are located on the Web, not within AOL.

Collectively, AOL's Web page publishing options are known as My Place, shown in Figure 4-2.

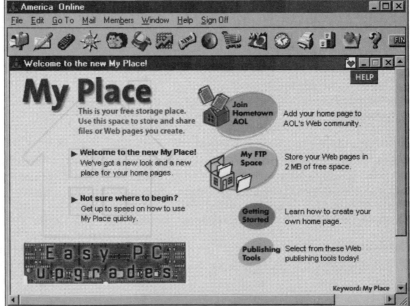

Figure 4-2:
My Place is AOL's collection of resources for members who want to publish their own Web sites.

Within My Place, you can find plenty of resources, including

- ✔ **Personal Publisher for Windows:** This is a service that performs roughly the same function as the Web page generators provided by GeoCities, iCat Online Commerce, or Yahoo! Store. You fill out a form using your AOL browser. The information on the form is presented in the form of a very rudimentary Web page. The information requested is personal, however, and not intended for business use. (Keyword: **Personal Publisher**.)

- ✔ **AOLpress:** This is AOL's own Web page editor. It lets you create and preview your own pages without having to learn HTML. Versions are available for both Windows and Macintosh users.

- ✔ **Other Web page editors:** AOL also provides links to shareware and commercial Web editors you can download and use to create your business site.

- ✔ **My FTP Place:** This is the service that transfers Web pages you have already made to your directory on one of AOL's servers using FTP (File Transfer Protocol). My FTP Place doesn't create your Web pages for you, however. You can use any Web page authoring tool to do that. (Keyword: **My Place**, and then click on My FTP Place.)

- ✔ **Hometown AOL:** After you publish your Web site on AOL using My FTP Place, you can add the site to AOL's online community on the Web. Hometown AOL (`hometown.aol.com`) is a "real" Web site on the Internet: It's not part of AOL's own domain the way My Place is. Hometown AOL is open to America Online members and other Internet users alike. AOL members who go through the extra effort of including their site on Hometown AOL get double exposure. Their site is accessible both within AOL (through My Place) and on the Web itself (through Hometown AOL).

- ✔ **PrimeHost:** This is AOL's Web-based business Web site hosting service. For $99 a month, AOL will host your site on the Web (that's not within AOL's own network, but on the wider Internet), list your site on AOL's business indexes, and help you get a user-friendly domain name like `www.mycompany.com`.

If you're an AOL customer and you want to start a home-based business for virtually nothing by claiming your space on My Place, read on. The following steps describe how to set up your site and install AOL's own Web site creation tool, AOLpress.

1. **Create a new screen name.**

   The first step is to pick a screen name for your site. This doesn't need to be the same as your usual AOL username. AOL lets you use up to five different screen names, and it's generally a good idea to reserve one for your personal use and one for your business site. To create a new screen name, connect to AOL using your master screen name, enter keyword **Names**, and then follow the instructions for creating a new screen name.

Your choice of screen name is important when you use My Place as your Web site host. The screen name appears as part of your Web site URL. For example, if your business is called WidgetWorld, you might choose the screen name *widgets*. When you transfer your files online using My FTP Place, you and your visitors can then access your site using the URL http://members.aol.com/widgets. If you want AOL to give you a shorter domain name, like www.widgets.com, you have to sign up for the PrimeHost service.

2. Install AOLpress.

If you want to use AOL's Web page creation software, AOLpress, to build your site, go to keyword **My Place**, click on Publishing Tools, and then click on the button labeled Go to AOLpress. Follow the steps for downloading the version of AOLpress you need. (The 16-bit version is for Windows 3.*x* users. The other versions are for Macintosh users and Windows 95 or 98 users.) After you download the program, install it by double-clicking on the file and following the AOL Press installer wizard as it guides you through the setup process (approving the license agreement, specifying a location for AOLpress, and so on).

3. Design your Web page.

From the Welcome to AOLpress page that appears when you start up the program, you can read about the program by clicking on the links (such as AOLpress Tutorial, Online Documentation & Templates, and Local Help & Readme) to find out more about using the program. Refer to Chapter 5 for the steps involved in using this and other Web page editors.

4. Publish your site with PrimeHost.

You can use AOLpress to create a secure, commercial Web site hosted by AOL's PrimeHost service (www.primehost.com). Various service packages provide you with your own unique domain (www.mysite.com), access to the AOLserver database functionality, and the ability to use your own scripts.

To publish the pages you create with AOLpress, open the page you want to publish and choose File⇨Save As. In the File Selection window, type **http://members.aol.com/screenname/filename.html** into the Page Location field, replacing "screenname" with the screen name you are signed on with and "filename.html" with the name of the file you want to publish. Click on OK and AOLpress saves the page and all the image files (lines, bullets, photos) associated with it. Saving the file across the network may take from a few seconds to several minutes.

If a page with the filename you typed already exists, a window appears, asking you whether to save the file, not save it, or rename the page. If any of your images already exist in this directory, AOLpress asks you if you want to save the image, not save it, rename it, or cancel.

Investigating electronic storefront software

All the other options this chapter provides for publishing your business site are ones that you access and utilize online. Yet another option for creating a business site and publishing it online is to purchase an application that carries you through the entire process of creating an electronic storefront.

Like hosting services such as Yahoo! Store, GeoCities, and iCat, electronic storefront software is designed to facilitate the process of creating Web pages and to shield you from having to learn HTML. Most storefront software provides you with predesigned Web pages, called *templates,* that you customize for your particular business. Some types of electronic storefront options go a step or two beyond the other options by providing you with shopping cart systems that enable customers to select items and tally the cost at checkout. They may also provide for some sort of electronic payment option, such as credit card purchases.

Usually, you purchase the software on disk or CD-ROM, you install the package like any other application, and you follow a series of steps that detail the primary aspects of a business:

- ✔ **The storefront:** These are the Web pages you create. Some packages, like QuickSite, include predesigned Web pages that you can copy and customize with your own content.

- ✔ **The inventory:** You can stock your virtual storefront's shelves by presenting your wares in the form of an online catalog or product list.

- ✔ **The delivery truck:** Some storefront packages streamline the process of transferring your files from your computer to the server. Rather than using FTP software, you publish information simply by pushing a button in your Web editor or Web browser.

- ✔ **The checkout counter:** Most electronic storefront packages give you the option to accept orders by phone, fax, or credit card.

Besides providing you with all the software you need to create Web pages and get them online, electronic storefronts instruct you on how to market your site and present your goods and services in a positive way. In addition, some programs provide you with a "back room" for your business, where you can record customer information, orders, and fulfillment.

CASE STUDY

Basing an online business on career experience

Kathie Turner is an AOL member who decided to start her own online business, Health Care Provider Services (members.aol.com/medinsbill/index.html) using My Place as her host.

A licensed psychotherapist, Kathie started a business that does research, consulting, and administrative tasks for a wide variety of health care professionals.

Q. Why did you decide to start your business?

A. I already had an America Online account when I made the decision to start the business in May, 1988. I knew I was taking a long shot: I had no real money to invest in startup. But I have time. I am on disability due to various health problems. So I have more time than money.

So, last May, I checked out the "easy" AOL Web publishing resources, which include lots of tutorials. I had my first Web page up by mid-May, and by the end of May, I had five pages linked together.

I'm now taking (free) tutorials online to learn Dynamic HTML and JavaScript. I have learned to make forms and use CGI scripts to process the form data — so not only am I my own Webmaster, but I've even made a site for one client and have inquiries from others. I have added Web design to my list of services.

I am continually updating my pages whenever I see room for improvement. When I get an idea from another Web site that I like, I try to integrate some aspect of the design into my site.

I use Allaire ColdFusion as my Web editing program.

Q. What were your startup costs?

A. My startup costs were approximately $1,000. It's difficult to give an exact figure, because some of those purchases I may have made regardless: Supplies for brochures, business cards, upgrading my computer, a new printer and phone, mailing and long distance expense: That's really about it.

Q. What is the goal of your online business?

A. The initial primary goal was to have a purpose, and the second was to make some extra money.

Q. How much work do you put in on your site?

A. I work probably 10 hours a week on my site, or on other sites experimenting with design.

Q. How do you promote your online business?

A. I have promoted my business in many ways. I got listed on free search engines. I participate in mailing lists, such as those for psychologists; I can join a list discussion and put my URL in my signature. This is how I've gotten some business and inquiries. I subscribe to e-zines about marketing and use some of their tips. I also created a mailing list sponsored by Health Care Provider Services. In addition to the list, I put out a weekly newsletter with a lot of useful info that I've found through search engines, other mailing lists, and so on. I found a way to publish my list on several list services, and within a week, I had 15 new subscribers. I update my e-mail signature often, and have several versions depending on who I am e-mailing. I added a special page for psychologists to my site, and am in the process of creating a page with links of psychotherapists organized by geographic location and clinical orientation.

Q. What advice would you have for anyone thinking of starting an online business?

A. I would advise anyone starting an online business to be conservative with their money and to market locally as well as online. Use a free service initially. I think the marketing and how you present yourself in mailing lists, newsgroups, and face-to-face local marketing are more important that whether or not your Web site is an advertising award winner.

I have gotten my most lucrative connection by doing the work for free initially. I continue to offer free services, and the people I do these things for help to market my business in return.

The problem with many electronic storefront packages is that they're very expensive — some cost $5,000 to $10,000 or more. They're not intended for individuals starting their own small businesses, but rather for large corporations that want to branch out to the Web. However, a few packages (two of which I describe in the following sections) provide a Ford-type alternative to the Rolls-Royce storefronts.

QuickSite

QuickSite, by Primecom Interactive, Inc. (`primecom.net/quicksite/index.html`), is a CD-ROM that guides you through the process of setting up a Web site, from coming up with a strategy and identifying your market to handling secure transactions. Besides the extremely well-written instructions on how to strategize and market a commercial Web site (all right, I admit, I wrote the instructions, so I'm not an impartial observer here!), QuickSite comes with a slew of Web site templates designed for various types of businesses. Check out the online demo at `primecom.net/quicksite/download/index.html`.

Custom programs make easy work of copying templates, adding items you want to sell, and getting your Web pages online. QuickSite uses a separate hosting service called QShost for its customers. Several hosting options are available through QShost (you can find out more about these options at `primecom.net/partners/qshost/index.html`):

- ✔ **Basic:** This low-priced account is for a straightforward Web site. Features include 10MB of storage space, one e-mail account, weekly Web site statistics, and space on a Web server that uses secure data encryption (see Chapter 12).

- ✔ **Standard:** In addition to the Basic features, this package provides 20MB additional storage space and a shopping cart system for your site.

- ✔ **Credit Card:** In addition to the Standard features, this package gives you 20MB more of storage space (50MB total) plus a merchant account with a bank and the capacity to process and verify credit card orders.

You also have the option of creating your site using QuickSite's tutorial and templates and then choosing your own Web host. QuickSite Gold comes with more than 350 templates and costs about $89; the Premier version includes 50 Web site templates and costs $49.

ShopSite Express

ShopSite Express is storefront software that's available for free and is designed for small to medium-sized businesses. It comes from Open Market, a longtime developer of electronic commerce software. ShopSite Express doesn't include a built-in Web page editor and limits the user to 25 products for sale. ShopSite Express works with your existing Web editor to add ordering, payment, and shipping features to a conventional Web site. It's not a product that you download or install on your computer, but rather, you access the program by connecting to the Web server on which it resides, using your existing Web browser and Web page editor.

The Express version of ShopSite is actually the most affordable (after all, it's free) of three varieties of this product: ShopSite Pro costs $1,295 and includes features that large businesses will enjoy, including a built-in search engine and site statistics. ShopSite Manager costs $495 and includes secure ordering capability.

If you already have a Web site that's being hosted online, you can use ShopSite Express to add secure commerce capability to your site for no charge. Otherwise, you can sign up with a Web hosting service called AnaServe (www.anaserve.com), which is set up with ShopSite Express server software. AnaServe charges a $50 setup fee, $70 for a domain name, and $24.95 for a monthly hosting fee. Before you sign up, you can try out an online demo of ShopSite Express at express.shopsite.com/demo.html.

Moving into an online mall

In addition to Web site kits, Internet Service Providers, and businesses that specialize in Web hosting, online shopping malls provide another form of Web hosting. You set up your site, either on your own or using special Web page authoring utilities that some malls provide. You pay a monthly fee, you transfer your files to the mall's Web site, and your store appears online. The basic steps are the same with an online mall as with any of the other hosting businesses mentioned in this chapter.

What's the difference, then, between a shopping mall that does Web hosting, an Internet Service Provider that does hosting, and a Web hosting service? The features they offer differ slightly, and the names they call themselves differ slightly, but the important thing to remember is that they all do essentially the same thing. After you open your virtual business on the Web, your customers can't always tell whether you're part of America Online, a mall, or a Web host like MindSpring.

What *is* an online shopping mall, anyway? It's a collection of online businesses that are listed in a directory or index provided by a single organization. The directory may be a simple list of stores on a single Web page. For larger malls with a thousand stores or more, the online businesses are arranged by category and can be found in a searchable index.

In theory, an online shopping mall helps small businesses by giving them additional exposure. A customer who shops at one of the mall's stores might notice other businesses on the same site and visit them, too. Some malls function as Web hosts that let their customers transfer Web page files and present their stores online, using one of the mall's Web servers. Other malls let people list their business in the mall with a hyperlink, even if the store is actually hosted by another company.

Perhaps the only thing that really distinguishes online malls from other hosting services is presentation:

✔ Some malls, like Downtown Anywhere (`www.awa.com`), use the metaphor of a town square to organize their businesses. Stores are presented as being on particular streets, and the visitor browses the shops as though walking around the streets of a small town.

✔ The Internet Mall (`www.internet-mall.com`) is a more traditional online mall, in the sense that it organizes its businesses into categories and fills its Web pages with plenty of enticing giveaways and promotions, as shown by its home page shown in Figure 4-3.

Figure 4-3:
An Internet mall helps provide promotions and lots of stores to attract visitors.

✔ Another online mall to look into is iCat (`www.icatmall.com`), which hosts a number of small businesses. iCat's online presentation closely resembles that of Yahoo! Store. You can test out the service first, trying the Web page creation system for free. Then you pay a monthly fee to locate your own business with the site permanently. The difference is that iCat presents itself as an online shopping mall where visitors can locate many types of online storefronts, including yours.

Consider joining an online mall if you find one that offers an attractive hosting package, and particularly if it has Web page forms that will help you set up your site or create an online catalog quickly. But remember that, to Web shoppers, it doesn't matter who your host is; what's more important is that you develop compelling content for your site to attract customers and encourage sales.

Turning to your ISP for Web hosting

People sometimes talk about Internet Service Providers (ISPs) and Web hosts as two separate types of Internet businesses, but that's not necessarily the case. Providing users with access to the Internet and hosting Web sites are two different functions, to be sure, but they may well be performed by the same organization.

In fact, it's only natural to turn to your own ISP first to ask about their Web hosting policies for their customers. Like Kathie Turner (see the previous sidebar, "Basing an online business on career experience"), if you already go online with AOL, it makes sense to try out their Web hosting facilities. If you install the software provided by MindSpring Enterprises (`www.mindspring.com`) that's included on this book's CD, and if you sign up for an Internet access account, by all means, consider MindSpring as a Web host for your business site.

MindSpring has different Web hosting options depending on the kind of account you have. Like most Internet Service Providers, however, MindSpring provides Web space to its customers so they can publish Web pages that are primarily personal in nature. Yes, you *can* publish a business Web site, and MindSpring won't complain or cancel your account. But they really suggest business users "spring" for special business service that includes oodles of Web space, support for forms and CGI scripts, and a "vanity" URL of the `www.company.com` variety.

MindSpring's Unlimited package ($26.95 per month) provides individual users with the following Web hosting options:

✔ 10MB of storage space

✔ Three separate e-mail accounts for personal or family members' use

✔ A popular Web page editor called Hot Dog Express

✔ A simple reporting service that shows how many people have visited your site

✔ A Web page URL that takes one of these two forms:
`http://www.mindspring.com/~username` or
`http://username.home.mindspring.com`

What should you look for in an ISP Web hosting account, and what constitutes a "good deal"? For one thing, price: A rate of $19.95 per month for unlimited access and 5 to 10MB of Web site space is currently a pretty good deal. Look for a site that doesn't limit the amount of Web pages you can create. Also find one that gives you at least one e-mail address with your account, and that lets you add extra addresses for a nominal fee. Finally, look for a host that gives you the ability to include Web page forms on your site so visitors can send you feedback.

What to expect from an ISP Web hosting service

The process of setting up a Web site varies from ISP to ISP. Here are some general features you should look for, based on my experience with my own ISP:

✔ **Web page editor:** You don't necessarily need to go with a provider that gives you a free Web editor. You can easily download and install the editor of your choice. I tend to use one of two programs, either Microsoft FrontPage Express or Netscape Composer, to create Web pages. (I describe both these programs later in this chapter.)

✔ **Password and username:** When my Web pages are ready to go online, I get to use the same username and password to access my Web site space that I use when I dial up to connect to the Internet. Although you don't need to enter a password to view a Web site through a browser (well, at least at most sites), you do need a password to protect your site from being accessed with an FTP program. Otherwise, anyone can enter your Web space and tamper with your files.

✔ **FTP software:** When I signed up for an account with Interaccess, I received a disk containing a basic set of software programs, including a Web browser and an FTP program. FTP is the simplest and easiest-to-use software to transfer files from one location to another on the Internet. When I access my Web site space from my Macintosh, I use an FTP program called Fetch; from my PC, I use a program called WS-FTP. CuteFTP (`www.cuteftp.com`) is another program that many Web site owners use. Most FTP programs are either available for free on the Internet or can be purchased for a nominal fee.

> ✔ **URL:** When you set up a Web site using your ISP, you are assigned a directory on a Web server. The convention for naming this directory is ~username. The ~username designation goes at the end of your URL for your Web site's home page. For example, my home page URL is `http:// homepage.interaccess.com/~gholden`.

After you have your software tools together and have a user directory on your ISP's Web server, it's time to put your Web site together. Basically, when I want to create or revise content for my Web site, I open the page in my Web editor, make the changes, save the changes, and then transfer the files to my ISP's directory with my FTP program. Finally, I preview the changes in my browser.

What's the ISP difference?

What's the big difference between using a kit (like Yahoo! Store) to create your site and using your own inexpensive or free software to create a site from scratch and post it on your ISP's server? It's the difference between putting together a model airplane from a kit and designing the airplane yourself. If you use a kit, you save time and trouble; your plane ends up looking pretty much like everyone else's, but you get the job done faster. If you design it yourself, you have absolute control. Your plane can look just the way you want. It takes longer to get to the end product, but you can be sure you get what you wanted.

On the other hand, the difference between an ISP-hosted site and a site that resides with a company that does *only* Web hosting, rather than providing Internet dial-up access and other services, is threefold:

> ✔ A business that does only Web hosting charges you for hosting services, whereas your ISP may not.
>
> ✔ A Web hosting service lets you have your own domain name (`www.company.com`), whereas an ISP may not. (Some ISPs require you to upgrade to a "business" hosting account in order to obtain the vanity address. See the nearby sidebar, "What's in a name," for more about how Web hosting services offer an advantage in the domain-name game.)
>
> ✔ A Web hosting service often provides lots of frills, such as super-fast connections, one-button file transfers using Web editors like Microsoft FrontPage, and tons of site statistics, as well as automatic backups of your Web page files.

To find out more about using a real, full-time Web hosting service, skip to "Going for the works with a Web hosting service" later in this chapter.

Where to find an ISP

What if you don't already have an Internet Service Provider, or you're not happy with the one you have? On today's Internet, you can't swing a dead mouse without hitting an ISP. How do you find the one that's right for you? In general, you want to look for the provider that offers you the least expensive service with the fastest connection and the best options available for your Web site.

Bigger does not necessarily mean cheaper or better; many regional or local ISPs provide good service at lower rates than the giants like Netcom or UUNet. When you're shopping around for an ISP, be sure to ask such questions as:

- ✔ What types of connections do you offer?
- ✔ How many dial-up numbers do you have?
- ✔ What is your access range (do you provide only local coverage, or regional or international coverage as well)?
- ✔ What type of tech support do you offer? Do you accept phone calls or e-mail inquiries around the clock, or only during certain hours? Are real human beings always available on call, or are clients sent to a phone message system?

Some Web sites are well-known for listing Internet Service Providers by state or by the services they offer. Here are a few good starting points in your search for the ideal ISP:

- ✔ **The List (**thelist.internet.com**):** This site lists about 5,000 ISPs. You can search the list by area code or by country code, or you can focus on the United States or Canada.
- ✔ **Providers of Commercial Internet Access (**www2.celestin.com/pocia**):** This site lists more than 1,500 Internet Service Providers around the world. It also has a section for Web hosting companies.
- ✔ **Yahoo's List of Internet Access Providers (**dir.yahoo.com/Business_and_Economy/Companies/Internet_Services/Access_Providers**):** This is a good source for directories of national and international Internet Service Providers.

Going for the works with a Web hosting service

After you've had your site online for a while with a free Web host such as AOL (at least, AOL is free if you already have an account with them) or GeoCities, you may well decide you need more room, more services (such as Web site statistics), and a faster connection that can handle many visitors at once. In that case, you want to locate your online business with a full-time Web hosting service.

What's in a name?

Most hosts assign you a URL that leads to your directory (or folder) on the Web server. For example, my account with my Internet Service Provider includes space on a Web server where I can store my Web pages. The address is as follows:

```
http://homepage.interaccess
    .com/~gholden
```

This is a common form of URL that many Web hosts use. It means that my Web pages reside in a directory called ~gholden on a computer named homepage. The computer, in turn, resides in my provider's domain on the Internet: interaccess.com.

However, for an extra fee, some Web hosts allow you to choose a shorter domain name, provided that the one you want to use isn't already taken by another site. For example, if I'd paid extra for a full-fledged business site, my provider would have let me have a catchier, more memorable address, like this:

```
http://www.gregholden.com
```

As the preceding sections attest, many kinds of businesses now host Web sites. But in this case, I'm defining *Web hosting service* as a company whose primary mission is to provide space on Web servers for individual, non-profit, and commercial Web sites.

What to look for in a Web host

Along with providing lots of space for your HTML, image, and other files (typically, you get 20 to 50MB of space), Web hosting services offer a variety of related services, including some or all of the following:

- ✔ **E-mail addresses:** You're likely to be able to get several e-mail addresses for your own or your family members' personal use. Besides that, many Web hosts give you special e-mail addresses called *autoresponders*. These are e-mail addresses, such as info@yourcompany.com, that you can set up to automatically return a text message or a file to anyone looking for information.

- ✔ **Domain names:** Virtually all of the hosting options mentioned in this chapter give customers the option of obtaining a short domain name, such as www.mycompany.com. But some Web hosts simplify the process by providing domain-name registration in their flat monthly rate.

- ✔ **Web page software:** Some hosting services include Web page authoring/editing software, such as Microsoft FrontPage. Some Web hosting services even offer Web page forms that you can fill out online in order to create your own online shopping catalog. All you have to provide is a scanned image of the item you want to sell, along with a price and a description. You submit the information to the Web host, and it's added to an online catalog that's part of your site. Figure 4-4 shows the online catalog form provided by one Web host, Home Pages, Inc. (www.homepages.com).

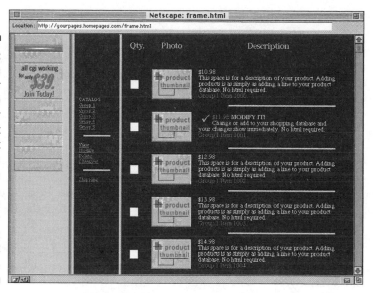

Figure 4-4:
Along with space for your Web site, look for a Web host that provides you with secure commerce, online catalog, or shopping cart features.

✓ **Multimedia/CGI scripts:** One big thing that sets Web hosting services apart from other hosts is the ability to serve complex and memory-intensive content, such as RealAudio sound files or RealVideo video clips. They also let you process Web page forms that you include on your site by executing computer programs called CGI scripts. These programs receive the data that someone sends you (such as a customer service request or an order form) and present the data in readable form, such as a text file, e-mail message, or an entry in a database. See Chapter 6 for more about how to set up and use forms and other interactive Web site features.

✓ **Shopping cart software:** If part of your reason for going online is to sell specific items, look for a Web host that can streamline the process for you. Some organizations provide you with Web page forms that you can fill out to create sale items and offer them in an online shopping cart, for example.

✓ **Automatic data backups:** some hosting services automatically back up your Web site data to protect you against data loss.

✓ **Site statistics:** Most Web hosting services also provide you with site statistics that give you an idea (perhaps not a precisely accurate count, but a good estimate) of how many visitors you have received, where your visitors are from, how they found you, which pages on your site are the most frequently viewed, and so on.

✔ **Shopping and electronic commerce features:** If you plan to give your customers the ability to order and purchase your goods or services online using their credit cards, be sure to look for a Web host that provides you with secure commerce options. A *secure server* is a computer that can encrypt sensitive data (such as credit card numbers) that the customer sends to your site. For a more detailed discussion of secure electronic commerce, see Chapter 12.

Having so many hosting options available is the proverbial blessing and curse. It's good that you have so many possibilities and that the competition is so fierce, because that could keep prices down. On the other hand, deciding which site is best for you can be difficult. In addition to asking about the preceding list of features, here are a few more questions to ask prospective Web hosts about their services to help narrow the field:

✔ **Do you limit file transfers?** Many services charge a monthly rate for a specific amount of electronic data that is transferred to and from your site. Each time a visitor views a page, that user is actually downloading a few kilobytes of data in order to view it. When you transfer your graphics and other files to your site, that adds to the transfer rate. Be sure to find out whether your host puts a limit on the number of megabytes or kilobytes of data you can transfer per month — if you go over the limit, you may face extra charges.

✔ **What kind of connection do you have?** Your site's Web page content appears more quickly in Web browser windows if your server has a super-fast T-1 or T-3 connection, as opposed to sharing an ISDN line with hundreds of other Web sites. (See Chapter 3 for explanations of ISDN, T-1, and other connection options.)

✔ **Will you promote my site?** Some hosting services (particularly online shopping malls) help publicize your site by listing you with Internet search indexes and search services, so visitors are more likely to find you.

Besides these, the other obvious questions (How long have you been in business? Can you suggest customers who will give me a reference?) that you would ask of any contractor apply to Web hosting services, as well.

The fact that I include a screen shot of a particular Web hosting service's site doesn't mean that I'm endorsing or recommending that particular organization. Shop around carefully and find the one that's best for you. Check out the hosts with the best rates and most reliable service. Visit some other sites they host, and e-mail the owners of those sites for their opinion of their hosting service.

Competition is tough among hosting services, which means that prices are going down. But it also means that hosting services may seem to promise the moon in order to get your business. Be sure to read the fine print and talk to the host before you sign a contract, and always get statements about technical support and backups in writing.

What's it gonna cost?

Due to the increasing competition in the industry, prices for Web hosting services vary widely. If you look in the classified sections in the back of magazines that cover the Web or the whole Internet, you'll see adds for hosting services costing from $14.95 to $24.95 per month. Chances are, these prices are for a basic level of service: Web space, e-mail addresses, domain name, and software. This may be all you need.

The second level of service provides CGI script processing, the ability to serve audio and video files on your site, regular backups, and extensive site statistics, as well as consultants who can help you design and configure your site. This more sophisticated range of features typically runs from $34.95 per month up to $150 or more per month. Hosts that let you conduct secure electronic commerce on your site are charging about $99 per month at this writing. By the time you read this, however, more affordable options may be available as the market settles down and prices become more standardized.

Choosing a Web Page Editor

A woodworker has his or her favorite hammer and saw. A cook has an array of utensils and pots and pans. Likewise, a Web site creator has software programs that facilitate the presentation of words, colors, images, and multimedia in Web browsers.

A little HTML is a good thing — but just a little. Knowing HTML comes in handy when you need to add elements that Web page editors don't handle. Some programs, for example, don't provide you with easy buttons or menu options for adding META tags. META tags let you add keywords or descriptions to a site so search engines can find them and describe your site correctly.

If you really want to get into HTML or to find out more about creating Web pages, read *HTML 4 For Dummies,* by Ed Tittel and Steve James, or *Creating Web Pages For Dummies,* 4th Edition by Bud Smith and Arthur Bebak, both published by IDG Books Worldwide, Inc.

It pays to spend time choosing a Web page editor that has the right qualities. What qualities should you look for in a Web page tool, and how do you know which tool is right for you? To help narrow the field, I've divided this class of software into different levels of sophistication. Pick the type of program that best fits your technical skill.

For the novice: Use your existing programs

A growing number of word processing, graphics, and business programs are adding HTML to their list of capabilities. You may already have one of these programs at your disposal. By using a program with which you're already comfortable, you can avoid having to install a Web page editor.

Here are some programs that let you generate one type of content, then give you the option of outputting that content in HTML, which means that your words or figures can appear on a Web page:

- ✔ **Microsoft Word:** The venerable word processing standby has an add-on called Internet Assistant. The Assistant works with older versions of Word such as 6.0 and 7.0. Word 97 has HTML support built in. Once you obtain and install the Assistant, you can save a Word document as HTML. Just choose File➪HTML files.

- ✔ **Adobe PageMaker/Quark Xpress:** The most recent versions of these two popular page layout programs let you save the contents of a document as HTML — only the words and images are transferred to the Web, however; any special typefaces become generic Web standard headings.

- ✔ **Microsoft Office 98:** Word, Excel, and PowerPoint all give users the option of exporting content to Web pages.

- ✔ **Corel Presentations:** You can save each slide of a Corel presentation as an HTML page or a GIF image. The program adds clickable arrows to each slide in your presentation so viewers can skip from one slide to another (if you have chosen to present one slide per Web page).

Although these solutions are convenient, they probably won't completely eliminate the need to use a Web page editor. Odds are, you'll still need to make corrections and do special formatting after you convert your text to HTML.

For intermediate needs: User-friendly Web editors

If you're an experienced Web surfer and eager to try out a simple Web editor, try a program that keeps the HTML transparent and that provides you with plenty of functionality while still being easy to use. Here are some user-friendly programs that are inexpensive (or, better yet, free), yet allow you to create a functional Web site.

Editors that'll flip your whizzy-wig

Web browsers are multilingual; they understand exotic-sounding languages such as FTP, HTTP, and GIF, among others. But one language browsers don't speak is English. Browsers don't understand instructions such as "Put that image there" or "Make that text italic." HyperText Markup Language, or HTML, is a translator, if you will, between human languages and Web languages.

If the thought of HTML strikes fear into your heart, relax. Thanks to modern Web page creation tools, you don't have to learn HTML in order to create Web pages. Although knowing a little HTML does come in handy at times, you can depend on these special user-friendly tools to do almost all your English-to-HTML translations for you.

The secret of these Web page creation tools is their WYSIWYG (pronounced whizzy-wig) display. WYSIWYG stands for "What You See Is What You Get." A WYSIWYG editor lets you see on-screen how your page will look when it's on the Web, rather than forcing you to type (or even see) HTML commands like this:

```
<H1> This is a Level 1 Heading
    </H1>
<IMG = "lucy.gif"> <BR>
<P>This is an image of Lucy.
    </P>
```

A WYSIWYG editor, such as Microsoft FrontPage Express (see below), shows you how the page appears even as you assemble it. Besides that, it lets you format text and add images by means of familiar software shortcuts such as menus and buttons.

Insert Image button

The following programs don't include some of the bells and whistles you need to create complex, interactive forms, format a page using frames, or access a database of information from one of your Web pages. These goodies are served up by Web editors that have a higher level of functionality, which I describe in the upcoming section for advanced commerce sites.

Adobe PageMill

If you work on a Macintosh, PageMill is one of the best choices you can make for a Web page tool. Although PageMill is also available for Windows, it originally came out for the Mac, and is tailored to use the Mac's highly visual interface. You can use Macintosh drag-and-drop to add an image file to a Web page in progress by dragging the image's icon into the PageMill window, for example. PageMill also comes with a ton of images, audio files, animations, Web page templates, and more. Find out more about PageMill at the Adobe Systems Inc. Web site (www.adobe.com/prodindex/pagemill/main.html).

Other good choices of Web editors for the Macintosh are World Wide Web Weaver by Miracle Software Inc. (www.miracleinc.com/Products/W4), FrontPage (www.microsoft.com/frontpage), and Home Page by Filemaker Inc. (www.filemaker.com).

Microsoft FrontPage Express

One of the best things about FrontPage Express, if you're a Web site creator working on a tight budget, is that it comes bundled with Windows 98. If Windows 98 is already installed on your computer, you don't have to do a thing to install FrontPage Express. Just choose Start⇨Programs⇨Internet Explorer⇨FrontPage Express to open FrontPage Express.

Either begin working on the new blank screen (if you're creating a Web page from scratch) or choose File⇨Open from the FrontPage Express menu bar. To open an existing file from the Open dialog box, navigate to the Web page file you want to open, single-click on the filename, and then click on Open. The document appears on-screen.

That's all there is to it. You can begin typing and formatting text using the FrontPage Express menu options. You can add an image by clicking on the Insert Image toolbar button. Or use the Forms toolbar to create the text boxes and radio buttons that make up an interactive Web page form.

FrontPage Express doesn't include the wizards, templates, and other bonuses that come with its big-brother program, FrontPage. But it does have everything you need to create a basic Web page.

Netscape Composer

When I read reviews of Web page software, I don't often see Netscape Composer included in the list. I can't figure out why. To me, it's an ideal program for an entrepreneur on a budget. Why? Let me spell it out for you: F-R-E-E.

Netscape Composer is the Web page editing and authoring tool that comes with Netscape Communicator. All you have to do is download Communicator from the Netscape Web site (www.netscape.com), and Composer is automatically installed on your computer along with Navigator (the Netscape Web browser) and several other Internet programs.

With Composer, you can create sophisticated layout elements, such as tables (see Chapter 5), with an easy-to-use graphical interface. After you edit a page, you can preview it in Navigator with the click of a button. Plus, you can publish all your files by choosing a single menu item. If you already have Communicator installed, check out Composer right now!

For advanced commerce sites: Programs that do it all

If you plan to do a great deal of business online, or even to add the title of Web designer to your list of talents (as some of the entrepreneurs profiled in this book have done), it makes sense to spend some money up front and use a Web page tool that can do everything you want — today and for years to come.

The advanced programs I describe here go beyond the simple designation of "Web page editors." They not only let you edit Web pages, but they can also help you add interactivity to your site, link dynamically updated databases to your site, and keep track of how your site is organized and updated. Some programs (notably, FrontPage) can even transfer your Web documents to your Web host with a single menu option. This way, you get to concentrate on the fun part of running an online business — meeting people, taking orders, processing payments, and the like.

Macromedia Dreamweaver

What's that, you say? You can never hear enough bells and whistles? The cutting edge is where you love to walk? Then Dreamweaver, a Web authoring tool by Macromedia (www.macromedia.com), is for you. Dreamweaver is a feature-rich, professional piece of software.

Dreamweaver's strengths aren't so much in the basic features like making selected text bold, italic, or a different size; rather, Dreamweaver excels in producing Dynamic HTML (which makes Web pages more interactive through scripts) and HTML style sheets. Dreamweaver has ample FTP (File Transfer Protocol) settings, and it gives you the option of seeing the HTML codes you're working with in one window and formatting your Web page in a second, WYSIWYG window. Dreamweaver is available for both Windows and Macintosh computers; find out more at the Macromedia Web site (www.macromedia.com/software/dreamweaver).

Microsoft FrontPage

The full-featured (as opposed to the Express) version of FrontPage (www.microsoft.com/frontpage) is unique among Web authoring tools. It has some features that no other programs have. For one thing, it provides you with a way to organize a Web site visually. The main FrontPage window is divided into two sections. On the left, you see the Web page on which you're currently working. On the right, you see a tree-like map of all the pages on your site, arranged visually to show which pages are connected to each other by hyperlinks.

Another nice thing about FrontPage — something that you're sure to find helpful if you haven't been surfing the Web or working with Web pages for very long — is the addition of wizards and templates. The FrontPage wizards let you create a discussion area on your site where your visitors can post messages to one another. The wizards also help you connect to a database or design a page with frames. (See Chapter 5 for more about creating frames.)

NetObjects Fusion

Fusion, a highly popular Web page tool by NetObjects (www.netobjects .com/products/html/nof.html), is an especially good choice if you want to exert a high level of control over how your Web page looks. It helps you make use of the latest HTML style-sheet commands that precisely control the positioning of text and images on a page.

Fusion (which is available in versions for Windows 95/98/NT and for the Macintosh) is also famous for letting you work with an external database of information. You can publish your database on the Web, and your visitors can then access records to see current inventory and status information.

What's more, Fusion helps with site management, which can save you time if your site grows to be big and complex due to all the success you're having online. Fusion generates a list of all the documents on your site, and helps you update the documents automatically.

Chapter 5

Organizing and Designing
Your Business Site

● ●

In This Chapter

▶ Coming up with a clear organization for your business site

▶ Establishing a graphic identity through color and type

▶ Scanning, cropping, and retouching photos

▶ Creating animations and other graphics

▶ Using Web page frames and tables effectively

● ●

*T*he business bandwagon known as the World Wide Web is getting so crowded it's in danger of tipping over. A new, high-speed version of the Net, called Internet II, is in the works to help relieve slowdowns and traffic jams due to the skyrocketing popularity of "going online."

For an individual like you, who's planning to start a new business by squeezing onto the bandwagon, all this popularity is a great opportunity. But it's also a challenge: As cyberspace fills up with small businesses trying to find their niches, it becomes increasingly difficult to stand out from the crowd and attract attention.

This chapter discusses one of the best ways for a new business to attract attention online: through a well-organized and eye-catching Web site. (Another strategy for attracting visitors — developing promotions and content that encourages interaction — is the subject of Chapter 6.)

Organizing Your Web Site

Although it's tempting to jump right into the creation of a cool Web page, take a moment to plan. Whether you're exploring the Alaskan wilderness or building a playhouse for the kids, you'll progress more smoothly by drawing a map of where you want to go. I mean that literally: Grab a pencil and a sheet of paper and make a list of the elements you want to have on your site.

Look over the items on your list and try to break them into two or three main categories. These main categories will branch off your *home page,* which functions as the welcome mat for your online business site. You can then draw a map of your site that assumes the shape of a triangle, as shown in Figure 5-1.

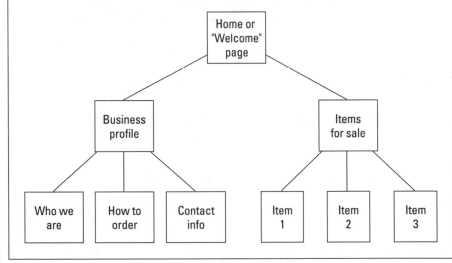

Figure 5-1:
A home page is the point from which your site branches into more specific levels of information.

Think of your home page as a person at the door of your store who greets all the guests attending your grand opening and who hands folks a sheet listing sale items or a map of the departments in the store. Remember to include the following items on your home page:

✔ The name of the store or business

✔ Your logo, if you have one

✔ Links to the main areas of your site or, if your site isn't overly extensive, to every page

✔ Contact information, such as your e-mail address, phone/fax numbers, and (optionally) your address so people know where to find you in the Land Beyond Cyberspace

Making a good first impression

First impressions are critical on the Web, where shoppers jump from site to site with a click of the mouse button. In this atmosphere, a few extra seconds of downtime waiting for complex images or mini-computer programs called *Java applets* to download can make the difference between a purchase and a rejection.

How do you make your welcome page a winner rather than a dud? Here are some suggestions:

✔ **Keep it simple:** Don't overload any one page with too many images. Keep all images 20K or less in size.

✔ **Find a fast host:** Web servers are not created equal. Some have super-fast connections to the Internet, and others use slower lines. Test your site out; if your pages take 10 or 20 seconds or more to appear, ask your host company why and find out whether they can move you to a faster machine.

✔ **Provide sales hooks:** Nothing attracts attention like a contest, a giveaway, or a special sales promotion. If you have anything that you can give away, either through a contest or a deep discount, do it. See Chapter 6 for more ideas.

✔ **Keep it short:** Make sure that your most important information appears at or near the top of your page. Readers on the Web don't like having to scroll through several screens worth of material in order to get to the information they want.

Establishing Your Store's Identity — Visually

Designing Web pages may seem complicated if you haven't tried it before, but it really boils down to a simple principle: effective visual communication that conveys a particular message. The first step in creating graphics is not to open up a painting program and start drawing, but to plan out your page's message. Next, determine the audience you want to reach with that message and think about how your graphics can best communicate what you want to say. Here are some ways to do this:

✔ Gather ideas from Web sites that use graphics well — both award-winning sites and sites created by designers who are using graphics in new or unusual ways.

✔ Use graphics consistently from page to page to create an identity.

✔ Know your audience. Create graphics that meet visitors' needs and expectations. If you're selling skateboards to teenagers, go for neon colors and out-there graphics. If you're selling insurance to senior citizens, choose a distinguished and sophisticated typeface.

How do you "get to know" your audience when you can't actually see them face-to-face in cyberspace? Find newsgroups and mailing lists in which potential visitors to your site are discussing subjects related to what you plan to publish on the Web. Read the posted messages to get a peek into the concerns and vocabulary of your intended audience.

Choosing your Web page wallpaper

The technical term for the wallpaper that sits behind the contents of a Web page is its *background*. Most Web browsers display the background of a page as light gray, unless you specify something different. The default gray, background is so widespread that, if you don't change it, viewers are likely to get the impression that the page is poorly designed or that the author of the page hasn't put a great deal of thought into the project. So it's a good idea to change the background of all your pages, even if you only make them a neutral color like white.

You can change the background of your Web page by tinkering with the HTML source code — but why bother? Most Web page creation programs offer a simple way to specify a color or an image file to serve as the background of a Web page. For example, in AOLpress (a Web page design tool described in Chapter 4), you use the Page Attributes dialog box (see Figure 5-2) to set your Web page wallpaper.

Using color to convey your message

You can use colors to elicit a particular mood or emotion, and also to convey your organization's identity on the Web. The right choice of color can create impressions ranging from elegance to professionalism to the energy of youth.

The conservative colors chosen by package-delivery company United Parcel Service (www.ups.com) assure customers that it is a staid and reliable company, and the U.S. Postal Service (www.usps.gov) sticks to the solid-citizen choice of red, white, and blue. In contrast, the designers of the HotHotHot hot sauce site (www.hothothot.com) combine fiery colors and original art to convey a spicy, mouth-watering atmosphere.

When selecting colors for your own Web pages, consider the tastes of your target audience. Ask yourself what emotions or impressions different colors evoke in you. Try to determine which colors best convey the mission or identity of your business.

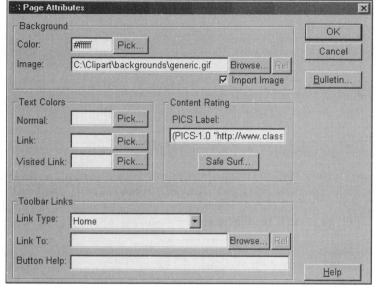

Figure 5-2:
Most Web
page
editors let
you specify
background
image/color
options in a
dialog box
like this.

The best color choices for Web backgrounds are ones that don't shift dramatically from browser to browser or platform to platform. The best palette for use on the Web is a set of 216 colors that is common to all browsers. These are called browser-safe colors, because they appear pretty much the same from browser to browser and on different monitors. The palette itself appears on Bob Cunningham's Web site (www.connect. hawaii.com/hc/webmasters/Netscape.colors.html).

Keep in mind that the colors you use must have contrast so that they don't blend into one another. For example, you don't want to put purple type on a brown or blue background, or yellow type on a white background. Remember to use light type against a dark background, and dark type against a light background. That way, all your page's contents will show up.

As long as your type and graphics are visible, there is no right or wrong color choice. Go with your instincts and then get feedback from your colleagues and a sample of your audience before you make your final decision.

Tiling images in the background

You can use an image, instead of a solid color, to serve as the background of a page. You specify an image in the HTML code of your Web page, and browsers automatically *tile* the image, reproducing it over and over to fill up the current width of the browser window.

For an example, see Kathie Turner's business page (members.aol.com/medinsbill/index.html). Kathie's choice of background image works because it's subtle; it doesn't interfere with the page contents. It literally looks like beige wallpaper. The potential downside to using a background image is that, if not chosen correctly, it can make the page unreadable. Be careful to choose an image that doesn't have any obvious lines that will create a distracting pattern when tiled.

Using special Web typefaces

If you create a Web page and don't specify that the text be displayed in a particular font, the browser that displays the page will use its default font — which is usually Times or Helvetica (although individual users can customize their browsers by picking a different default font).

However, as a Web page designer, you can exercise a degree of control over the appearance of your Web page by specifying that the body type and headings be displayed in a particular nonstandard font, such as Arial, Garamond, Century Schoolbook, and so on. But you don't have ultimate control over whether a given browser will display the specified typeface. That's because you don't know for sure whether the individual user's system has access to your preferred typefaces. If the particular font you specified is not available, the browser will fall back on its default font (which, again, is probably Helvetica or Times).

That's why, generally speaking, when you design Web pages, you want to pick a generic typeface that is built into virtually every computer's operating system. This convention ensures that your Web pages look more or less the same no matter what Web browser or what type of computer displays them.

To add some variety to the way Web page text looks, Microsoft is taking steps to help users download the fonts that Web page designers are likely to specify. Microsoft Typography offers an assortment of TrueType typefaces, designed to be used with Windows 95, that you can download for free from its Web site (www.microsoft.com/typography/default.asp). These typefaces do not come with Windows 95, so you're not likely to have them already available on your system. After you download the special font, you install it into your system and then add it to your Web page.

Where, exactly, do you specify type fonts, colors, and sizes for the text on a Web page? Again, special HTML tags tell Web browsers what fonts to display, but you don't need to mess with these tags yourself if you're using a Web page creation tool. The specific steps you take depend on what Web design tool you're using. In AOLpress (the Web design tool available from America Online, as described in Chapter 4), you use the Font Preferences dialog box (see Figure 5-3) to specify typeface. Check the Help files with your own program to find out exactly how to format text and what typeface options you have.

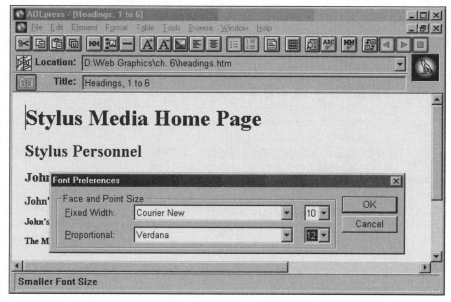

Figure 5-3:
Most Web
page design
tools let you
specify a
preferred
font for your
Web page
in a dialog
box like this.

Copying and using clip art

Clip art is a quick and economical way to add graphic interest to Web pages, particularly if you don't have the time or resources to scan photos or create your own original graphics. Many Web page designers add clip-art bullets, diamonds, or other small images next to list items or major Web page headings to which they want to call special attention. You can also use clip art to provide a background pattern for a Web page or to highlight sales headings such as *Free! New!* or *Special!*

Clip art gets its name from the catalogs of illustrations that publishers can buy to clip out art and paste it down. In keeping with the spirit of exchange that has been a part of the Internet since its inception, some talented and generous artists have created icons, buttons, and other illustrations in electronic form and offered them free for downloading.

Here are some suggestions for sources of clip art on the Web:

- ✔ Barry's Clip Art Server (`www.barrysclipart.com`)
- ✔ ArtToday (`www.arttoday.com`)
- ✔ The Yahoo! page full of links to clip art resources (`dir.yahoo.com/Business_and_Economy/Companies/Computers/Software/Graphics/Clip_Art`)

Be sure to read the "fine print" before you copy graphics. Sometimes, the authors require you to pay a small fee, or they may restrict use of their work to nonprofit organizations.

Adding scanned images

Unless your customers are looking for something very specific, like a particular variety of silverware or a carburetor for a 1956 Edsel, you need to add images to help entice them into your site and encourage them to move from one item or catalog page to another.

Even if you only use some basic clip art, like placing spheres or arrows next to sale items, your page will likely be the better for it. A much better approach, though, is to scan your sale items and provide compact, clear images of them on your site.

Step 1: Choose images to scan

After you purchase a scanner (see the suggestions in Chapter 3), the next step is to select images that have the following qualities:

- **Moderate brightness:** Whenever possible, select images that are well illuminated. Subtle images may come out dark and unrecognizable on a computer screen.

- **Good contrast:** Select images that display a clear difference between light and dark areas.

- **Small in size:** Snapshots work well on Web pages. If you scan an entire 8½" x 11" sheet of paper, you end up with an image that's far too big to display on the average 7" x 10" computer screen. Inline images on Web pages are generally less than 7 inches wide. Often, photos are only 1 to 4 inches wide, and perhaps 1 to 5 inches tall.

The overall quality of the image is just as important as how you scan or retouch it. Images that appear murky or fuzzy in print will be even worse when viewed on a computer screen.

Step 2: Create a preview scan

Virtually all scanning programs let you make a quick *preview* scan of an image so that you can get an idea of what it looks like before you do the actual scan. When you press the Preview button, you hear a whirring sound as the optical device in the scanner captures the image. A preview image appears on-screen, surrounded by a *marquee box* (a rectangle made up of dashes), as shown in Figure 5-4.

Figure 5-4:
The marquee box lets you crop a preview image to make it smaller and reduce the file size, too.

Step 3: Crop the image

Cropping an image is highly recommended because it highlights the most important contents and reduces the file size, as well. In the case of scanning software, *cropping* means that you resize the box around the image in order to select the portion of the image that you want to keep and leave out the parts of the image that aren't essential.

Almost all scanning and graphics programs present separate options for cropping an image and reducing the image size. By cropping the image, you eliminate parts of the image you don't want, and this *does* reduce the image size. But it doesn't reduce the size of the objects within the image. Resizing the overall image size is a separate step; it enables you to change the dimensions of the entire image without eliminating any contents.

Step 4: Select an input mode

After you crop your image, the next step is to tell the scanner how you want it to capture the visual data. Select one of the following options in your scanning software's Mode menu:

- ✔ **Color:** When scanning a color photo, choose this option.
- ✔ **Line art:** Use this setting to scan black-and-white drawings, signatures, cartoons, or other art.
- ✔ **Grayscale:** This option is for scanning a black-and-white photo.

No one's going to turn you in to the Web design police if you scan a black-and-white drawing in color mode. You'll just end up with an image file that's far larger than it needs to be. It'll use up more space on your hard disk, and take longer to appear on-screen.

Step 5: Set the resolution

In Chapter 3, I note that scanned images are made up of little bits (dots) of computerized information called *pixels*. The more pixels per inch, the higher the level of detail. When you scan an image, you can tell the scanner to make the dots smaller (creating a smoother image), or larger (resulting in a more jagged image). This adjustment is called *setting the resolution* of the image.

How many dots per inch (dpi) do you want your image to be? When you're scanning for the Web, you expect your images to appear primarily on computer screens. Because many computer monitors can only display resolutions up to 72 dpi, this is an adequate resolution for a Web image. 72 dpi is a relatively rough resolution. By contrast, many laser printers print at a resolution of 300 dots per inch. But using this coarse resolution has the advantage of keeping the image's file size small. Remember, the smaller the file size, the more quickly an image appears when your customers load your page in their Web browsers.

Step 6: Adjust contrast and brightness

You're probably aching to make your scan by this point, but wait! You have one final step. The more preparatory work you do up front, the better your image will appear when it gets online.

Take a look at your preview scan: Does the image seem dark or muddy? Virtually all scanning programs provide brightness and contrast controls that you can adjust with your mouse to improve the image. If you're happy with the image as is, leave the brightness and contrast set where they are. (You can also leave the image as is and adjust brightness and contrast later in a separate graphics program, such as Paint Shop Pro.)

Step 7: Reduce the image size

You can do even one *more* thing to improve your scan. Just keep repeating this mantra to yourself: "Make my image small . . . make my image small." If your preview scan is much larger than you want the image to be when it appears on the Web, you can tell your scanner to reduce the size as it scans the image.

Do some quick math and estimate how much the image has to be reduced. For example, if an image is 8" x 10", and you're sure that it needs to be about 4" x 5" when it appears on your Web page, scan it at 50 percent of the original size. This step reduces the file size right away and makes the file easier to transport, in case you have to put it on a floppy disk to move it from one computer to another.

Accommodating your viewers

Lack of bandwidth is one of the major roadblocks to presenting such content as live video, teleconferencing, and complex graphics files on the Web. But some Web surfers with very slow Internet connections (or very low tolerances for waiting) may not have the bandwidth to display even ordinary images quickly enough. After many minutes or even just seconds of waiting, the surfer is likely to hit the browser's Stop button, with the result that no graphics appear at all.

How do you prevent customers from slamming the door on your graphics like this? Some alternatives include:

✔ Creating low-resolution alternatives to high-resolution graphics, such as thumbnails (postage-stamp sized versions of larger images).

✔ Cropping images to keep them small.

✔ Using line art whenever possible, instead of high-resolution photos.

By using the same image more than once on a Web page, you can give the impression of greater activity and while speeding up the appearance of the entire page. Why? If you repeat the same image three times, your customer's browser only has to download the image file once. It stores the image in a storage area, called *disk cache,* on the user's hard disk. To display the other instances of the image, the browser retrieves the file from the disk cache, so the second and third images appear much more quickly than the first one did.

Users can also disable image display altogether, so they don't see graphics on any of the sites they visit. The solution: Always provide a simple textual alternative to your images so that, if the user has disabled the display of a particular image, a word or two describing that image appears in its place.

Step 8: Scan away!

Finally, you get to flex your mouse-clicker finger and choose your scanning program's Scan button. Listen to your scanner whir away as it turns those colors into pixels. Because you're only scanning at 72 dpi, your image shouldn't take too long to scan. When the machine finishes, the image appears again in your scanning program's window.

Step 9: Save the file

Now you can save your image to disk. Most programs let you do this by choosing File⇨Save. In the dialog box that appears, enter a name for your file and select a file format. (Because you are scanning images to be published on the Web, remember to save either in GIF or JPEG format.)

When you give your image a name, be sure to add the correct filename extension. Web browsers recognize only image files with extensions like .gif, .jpg, or .jpeg. If you name your image product and save it in GIF format, call it product.gif. If you save it in JPEG format, and you're using a PC, call it product.jpg. On a Macintosh, call it product.jpeg.

Creating a logo

An effective logo establishes your online business's graphic identity in no uncertain terms. A logo can be as simple as a rendering of the company name that imparts an official typeface or color. Whatever text it includes, a logo is a small, self-contained graphic object that conveys the group's identity and purpose. Figure 5-5 shows an example of a logo.

A logo doesn't have to be a fabulously complex drawing with drop-shadows and gradations of color. A simple type-only logo often works just fine. See the logo for the Collectible Exchange in Chapter 2, for example. Pick a typeface you want, choose your graphic's outline version, and fill the letters with color.

Using Advanced Web Page Layouts

If you're just starting out and creating your first Web site, I advise you to stay away from more complicated ways of designing Web pages, such as frames and tables. On the other hand, you're the adventurous type; that's why you want to start an online business in the first place, right? So this section includes some quick explanations of what tables and frames are so that you know where to start if the time comes when you do want to use them.

GIF versus JPEG

Web site technology and HTML may have changed dramatically over the past several years, but, for the most part, Web pages still only display two types of images: GIF and JPEG. Both formats use compression methods that compress computer image files so the visual information contained within them can be transmitted easily over computer networks. (PNG, a third format designed as a successor to GIF, is not yet widely used.)

GIF (pronounced either "jiff" or "giff") stands for Graphics Interchange Format. GIF is best suited to text, line art, or images with well-defined edges. Special types of GIF allow images with transparent backgrounds to be interlaced and animated.

JPEG (pronounced "jay-peg") stands for Joint Photographic Experts Group, the name of the group that originated the format. JPEG is better suited for large photos and continuous tones of grayscale or color that need greater compression.

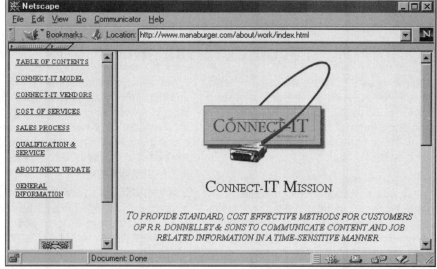

Figure 5-5:
A good logo
effectively
combines
color, type,
and
graphics to
convey an
organization's
identity or
mission.

Setting the tables for your customers

Tables give designers another means to present information in a graphically interesting way on a Web page. Tables were originally intended to present "tabular" data in columns and rows, much like a spreadsheet. But by using advanced HTML techniques, you can make tables a much more integrated and subtle part of your Web page.

Because you can easily create a basic table by using Web page editors such as HotDog, Netscape Composer, and FrontPage, it makes sense to start with one of these tools. However, some HTML tinkering is probably unavoidable, especially if you want to use tables to create blank columns on a Web page (as I explain later in this section). Here is a quick rundown of the main HTML tags used for tables:

- ✔ `<TABLE> </TABLE>` encloses the entire table. The BORDER attribute sets the width of the line around the cells.

- ✔ `<TR> </TR>` encloses a table row, a horizontal set of cells.

- ✔ `<TD> </TD>` defines the contents of an individual cell. The `HEIGHT` and `WIDTH` attributes control the size of each cell. For example, the following code tells a browser that the table cell is 120 pixels wide:

```
<TD WIDTH=120> Contents of cell </TD>
```

Don't forget that the cells in a table can contain images as well as text. Also, individual cells can have different colors from the cells around them. You can add a background color to a table cell by adding the `BGCOLOR` attribute to the `TD` table cell tag.

A quick HTML primer

Although, thanks to Web page creation tools, you don't have to learn HyperText Markup Language in order to create your own Web pages, some knowledge of HTML is helpful when it comes to editing pages and understanding how they are put together.

As the name says, HTML is a markup language, not a computer programming language. You use it in much the same way that old-fashioned editors marked up copy before they gave it to typesetters. A markup language allows you to identify major sections of a document, such as body text, headings, title, and so on. A software program (in the case of HTML, a Web browser) is programmed to recognize the markup language and display the formatting elements you have marked.

Markup tags are the basic building blocks of HTML. They enable you to structure the appearance of your document so that, when it is transferred from one computer to another, it will look the way you described it. HTML tags appear within carrot-shaped brackets. Most HTML commands require a *start tag* at the beginning of the section and an *end tag* (which usually begins with a backslash) at the end.

For example, if you place the HTML tags ⟨B⟩ and ⟨B⟩ around the phrase "This text will be bold," the words appear in bold type on any browser that displays them, no matter if it's running on a Windows-based PC, a UNIX workstation, a Macintosh, an Amiga, or any other computer.

Many HTML commands are accompanied by *attributes,* which provide a browser with more specific instructions on what action the tag is to perform. In the following lines of HTML, SRC is an attribute that works with the IMG tag to identify a file to display:

```
<IMG SRC="house.jpg">
```

Each attribute is separated from an HTML command by a single blank space. The equal sign (=) is an operator that introduces the value on which the attribute and command will function. Usually, the value is a filename or a directory path leading to a specific file that is to be displayed on a Web page. The straight (as opposed to curly) quotation marks around the value are essential for the HTML command to work.

The clever designer can use tables in a hidden way to arrange an entire page, or a large portion of a page, by doing two things:

- Set the table border to 0. Doing so makes the table outline invisible, so the viewer sees only the contents of each cell, not the lines bordering the cell.

- Fill some table cells with blank space so they act as empty columns that add more white space to a page.

An example of the first approach, that of making the table borders invisible, appears in Figure 5-6: David Nishimura's Web Vintage Pens Web site (www.vintagepens.com) where he sells vintage writing instruments.

Figure 5-6:
This page is divided into table cells, which give the designer a high level of control over the layout.

Framing your subject

Frames are subdivisions of a Web page, each consisting of its own separate Web document. Depending on how the designer sets up the Web page, visitors may be able to scroll through one frame independently of the other frames on the same page. A mouse click on a hypertext link contained in one frame may cause a new document to appear in an adjacent frame.

Simple two-frame layouts like the one used by one of my personal favorite Web sites, Maine Solar House (see Figure 5-7), can be very effective. A page can be broken into as many frames as the designer wants, but you typically want to stick with only two to four frames, because they make the page considerably more complex and slower to appear in its entirety.

Frames fit within the BODY section of an HTML document. In fact, the <FRAMESET> </FRAMESET> tags actually take the place of the <BODY> </BODY> tags, and are used to enclose the rest of the frame-specific elements. Each of the frames on the page is then described by <FRAME> </FRAME> tags.

Only the more advanced Web page creation programs provide you with menu options and toolbar buttons that let you create frames, without having to enter the HTML manually. Luckily, two of the programs on this book's CD do this: Macromedia Dreamweaver and HotDog Professional 5 Webmaster Suite. See each program's Help topics for specific instructions on how to implement framing tools.

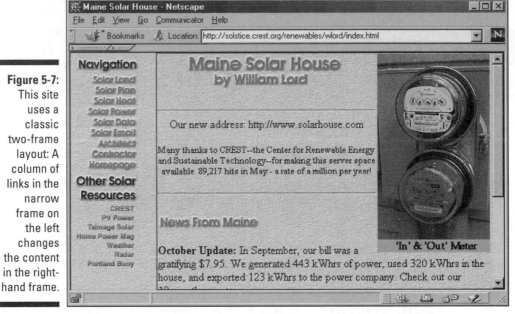

Figure 5-7:
This site
uses a
classic
two-frame
layout: A
column of
links in the
narrow
frame on
the left
changes
the content
in the right-
hand frame.

Frames add interactivity and graphic interest to a page, but many users dislike the extra time they require. As a Web page designer, be sure to provide a "no frames" alternative to a "frames" layout.

Turning to a Professional Web Designer

Most of the entrepreneurs I interviewed in the course of writing this book do their own Web page design work. They learned how to create Web sites by reading books or taking classes on the subject. But in many cases, the initial cost of hiring someone to help you design your online business can pay off in the long run. For example:

- ✔ If you need business cards, stationery, brochures, or other printed material, in addition to a Web site, it's worth hiring someone to come up with a consistent look for everything at the beginning.

- ✔ You can pay a designer to get you started with a logo, color selections, and page layouts. Then you can save money by adding text yourself.

- ✔ If, like me, you are artistically impaired, consider the benefits of having your logo or other artwork drawn by a real artist.

Most professional designers charge $40 to $60 per hour for their work. You can expect a designer to spend five or six hours to create a logo or template, but your company may use that initial design for years to come.

Chapter 6

Adding Content and Interactivity to Your Site

· ·

In This Chapter

▶ Creating compelling content through links and hooks

▶ Promoting your business through objective, useful information

▶ Making less do more through concise, well organized content

▶ Writing friendly, objective prose that sells your products and services

▶ Inviting customer interaction through forms, e-mail, and more

· ·

*P*eople often say that Content Is King when it comes to the Web, and although I believe that to be true, I would add that not just any content makes an online business work. You need the *right* content, presented in the *right* way, to make prospective clients and customers want to explore your site the first time and then come back for more later on.

So what's the *right* content? you ask. Well, that's the subject of this chapter. However, because one of my primary points in this chapter is that you need to express your main message on your business site up front, I'll do the same by explaining what I consider to be the right content for an online business. The material you include on your site should do the following:

✔ Take into account the way people absorb information online

✔ Make it easy for visitors to find out who you are and what you have to offer

✔ Be friendly and informal in tone, concise in length, and clear in its organization

✔ Help develop the all-important one-to-one-relationship with customers and clients by inviting dialogue and interaction, both with you and with others who share the same interests

There you have the main topics of this chapter in a nutshell. Another one of my main points in this chapter is that you need to be straightforward about who you are and where you're coming from on your business site. Accordingly, my "mission statement" for this chapter is to get you to think, not so much about writing for the Web, but about being a provider of useful, exciting, well organized, and easily digestible information. Now, on to the specifics of how you can put these goals into action.

Give 'Em What They Want!

Long ago, when mail-order merchandising was revolutionizing retail commerce (much the way the Internet is today), Marshall Field uttered his famous quote, "Give the lady what she wants." Today, on the Internet, the message is the same, albeit in a gender-free, '90s sort of way: "Give your Web surfers what they want." Half the battle with developing content for a business Web site is knowing what shoppers online want and determining strategies for providing it to them.

Studies of how people absorb the information on a Web page indicate that people don't really read the contents from top to bottom (or left to right, or frame to frame) in a linear way. In fact, most Web surfers don't *read* in the traditional sense at all. Instead, they browse. They "flip through pages" by clicking on link after link.

People who are looking for things on the Web are often in a state of hurried distraction. Think about the office worker at 4 p.m. on a Friday, waiting for the week to end. Imagine this person surfing with one hand on a mouse, the other on a cookie or a cup of coffee. Imagine the noise of the office in the background: phones ring, voices mumble. This person isn't in the mood to read ten pages of beautifully written prose describing your life story, why you started your business, and what you love about your field of expertise. Here's what this shopper is probably thinking:

> "Look, I don't have time to read all this. I'm on my coffee break. My boss gets out of that meeting in ten minutes. I'm not supposed to be surfing the Web anyway."

> "What's this? Why does this page take so long to load? And I have a direct connection here at the office. I swear, sometimes I wish the Web didn't have any graphics. Here, I'll click on this. No, wait! I'll click on that. . . ."

The following sections describe some ways to attract the attention of the distracted and point their tired, jittery eyes where you want them to go.

Get it all out in the open

Don't make anyone wait to find out who you are and what you do. Keep in mind that people who come to a Web site give that site less than a minute (in fact, I've heard only 20 seconds) to answer their primary questions:

- Who are you, anyway?

- All right, so, what is your main message or mission?

- Well, then, what do you have here for me?

- Why should I believe you, pay attention to you, investigate your site . . . ?

This is a pretty hard-nosed perspective, I admit. But I really believe that this is what most Web surfers are thinking as they scan sites for information.

When it comes to Web pages, it pays to put the most important elements up front first: who you are, what you do, how you differ from any competing sites, and how you can be contacted.

You probably can't fit every article or catalog item you have to offer right on the first page of your site. Even if you could, you wouldn't want to: As in a newspaper, it's better to prioritize the contents of your site so that the "top stories" or the best contents appear at the top, and the remainder of the contents are arranged in order of importance.

Encourage visitors to click, click, click!

Having a row of links at the top of your home page, each of which points the visitor to an important area of your site, is always a good idea. Such links give visitors an idea of what your site contains in a single glance and imme- diately encourage viewers to click on a primary subsection of your site and explore further. By placing an interactive table of contents right up front, you let often impatient surfers get right to the material they want.

The links can go at or near the top of the page on either the left- or right- hand side. Nancy Roebke takes a bit of a risk by filling the top of her Profnet, Inc. home page with a sizeable, though eye-catching, drawing. She makes up for the lost space by placing links along *both* the left and right sides (see Figure 6-1).

Netscape: Profnet, Inc. – Business Leads, Marketing, Networking

Location: http://www.profnet.org/

Helping Business Professionals Find More Business

PROFNET

Propaganda

Chapter Info

Membership Info

F.A.Q.

Business Development

Lead Generation

I N C.

Figure 6-1:
It's a good idea to get at least five or six links near the top of your home page.

The following steps show how to create links to local files on your Web site using FrontPage Express, the Web page creation tool that is bundled with the version of Microsoft Internet Explorer that's on this book's CD-ROM. The steps assume that you have started up the program and that the Web page you want to edit is already open:

1. **Select the text or image on your Web page that you want to serve as the jumping-off point for the link.**

   If you select a word or phrase, the text is highlighted in black. If you select an image, a black box appears around the image.

2. **Choose Insert⇨Hyperlink (or click on the Create or Edit Hyperlink toolbar button).**

   The Edit Hyperlink dialog box appears, as shown in Figure 6-2.

3. **Click on the Hyperlink Type drop-down menu list and select (other).**

4. **In the box next to URL, enter the name of the file you wish to link to the selected text or image.**

   If the page you want to link to is in the same directory as the page that contains the jumping-off point, you only need to enter the name of the Web page. If the page is in another directory, you need to enter a path relative to the Web page that contains the link.

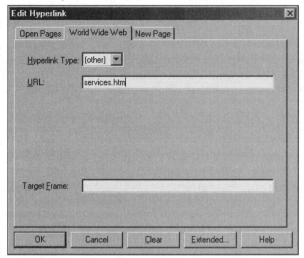

Figure 6-2:
If you keep
all your
related
Web pages
in the same
directory,
you only
have to
enter a
simple
filename as
the link
destination.

5. Click on OK.

The Edit Hyperlink dialog box closes, and you return to the FrontPage
Express window. If you made a textual link, the selected text is underlined and in a different color. If you made an image link, when you pass
your mouse arrow over the image, the link destination appears in the
status bar at the bottom of the FrontPage Express window.

Presenting the reader with links up front indicates that your site is content-
rich and worthy of exploration.

Tell us a little about yourself

One thing you need to get out in the open as soon as possible on your Web
site is who you are and what you do. Profnet does this by condensing its
mission statement into a single phrase:

Helping Business Professionals Find More Business

Can you identify your primary goal in a single sentence? If so, great. If not,
two or three sentences will do just fine. Whatever you do, make your
mission statement more specific and customer-oriented than simply saying,
"Out to make lots of money!" Tell prospects what you can do for them; the
part about making money goes without saying.

Keep your pages short and sweet

If you're worried about having to hire someone like me to write reams of golden prose in order to fill your pages with Pulitzer Prize content, I have news for you: Making a Web site compelling is simple. You're not writing an essay, a term paper, or a book here. Rather, you need to observe a couple of simple rules:

- ✔ Provide lots of links and hooks that readers can scan.
- ✔ Keep everything concise!

The shorter you can keep everything, the better. Keep sentences short. Limit paragraphs to one or two sentences in length. You may also want to limit each Web page to no more than one or two screens in length so that viewers don't have to scroll down too far to find what they want.

Make your content scannable

When you're writing something out on paper, your contents have to be readable. On the Web, things are a little different: Content has to be *scannable*. This rule has to do with the way people absorb information online. Eyes that are staring at a computer screen for many minutes or many hours tend to jump around a Web page, looking for an interesting bit of information on which to rest. This section suggests ways to attract those nervous eyes and guide them toward the products you have to sell or the services you want to provide.

I'm borrowing the term *scannable* from John Morkes and Jakob Nielsen of Sun Microsystems, who use it in their article "Concise, Scannable, and Objective: How to Write for the Web" (`www.useit.com/papers/webwriting/writing.html`). I include this article in the Internet Directory portion of this book and accompanying CD-ROM, along with other tips on enriching the content of your Web pages. See the section of the Directory called "Developing Compelling Content" for more.

Point the way with headings

One prominent Web page element that's sure to grab the attention of your readers' eyes is a heading. Every Web page needs to contain headings that direct the reader's attention to the most important contents. This book provides a good example. The chapter title (hopefully) grabs your attention first. Then the section headings and subheadings direct you to the topics you want to read about.

As a general rule, I usually suggest following the convention of newspaper headlines when it comes to writing headings: Put the biggest headings at the top of the page. Most Web page editing tools designate top-level headings with the style Heading 1. Beneath this, you place one or more Heading 2 headings. Beneath each of those, you may have Heading 3 and, beneath those, Heading 4. (Headings 5 and 6 are too small to be useful, in my opinion.) The arrangement may look like this (I've indented the following headings for clarity; you don't have to indent them on your page):

Stan and Bud's Surfer Dude Paradise (Heading 1)

HangTen Surfboards (Heading 2)

The Surfer Dude Story (Heading 2)

Catch a Wave Surfin' School (Heading 2)

Registration (Heading 3)

Course Schedule (Heading 3)

New Bodysurfing Course Just Added! (Heading 4)

 You can energize virtually any heading by telling your audience something specific about your business. Instead of "Fred's Shopping Mall," for example, say something like "Fred's Shopping Mall: Your One-Stop Shopping Spot for New and Used Hand Tools." Instead of simply writing a heading like "Mary Murano, Certified Public Accountant," say something specific, like "Mary Murano: The Oldest Accounting Firm in San Diego."

Become an expert list maker

Lists are simple and effective ways to break up text and make your Web content easier to digest. They're simple to create, and they give your customers' eyes more places on which they can rest. For example, suppose that you roast your own coffee and you want to offer certain varieties at a discount. Rather than bury the items you're offering within an easily over-looked paragraph, why not list them prominently so visitors can't help but see them.

The following example shows how easy lists are to implement if you use a Web page editor like Microsoft FrontPage Express. You have your Web page document open in FrontPage Express, and you're at that point in the page where you want to insert a list. Just do the following:

1. **Type a heading for your list and then select the entire heading.**

   For example, you might type and then select the words **Today's Specials**.

Your Web page title: The ultimate heading

When you're dreaming up clever headings for your Web pages, don't overlook the "heading" that appears in the narrow black bar at the very top of your visitor's Web browser window: the *title* of your Web page.

The two HTML tags `<TITLE>` and `<TITLE>` contain the text that appears within the browser title bar. But you don't have to mess with these nasty HTML codes: All Web page creation programs give you an easy way to enter or edit a title for a Web page. In FrontPage Express, you follow these steps:

1. **With the Web page you're editing open in the FrontPage Express window, choose File⇨Page Properties.**

   The Page Properties dialog box appears.

2. **In the Title text box, enter a title for your page.**

3. **Click on OK.**

   The Page Properties dialog box closes and you return to the FrontPage Express window. The title doesn't automatically appear in the title area at the top of the window. However, when you view the page in a Web browser, the title is visible.

Make the title as catchy and specific as possible, but be sure to keep the title 64 characters or less. An effective title refers to your goods or services while grabbing the viewer's attention. If your business is called Lydia's Cheesecakes, for example, you might make your title "Smile and Say Cheese! With Lydia's Cakes" (40 characters).

2. **Click on the triangle next to the Change Style drop-down menu.**

   A list of paragraph styles appears.

3. **Click on a heading style, such as Heading 3, to select it from the list of styles.**

   The name of the style you chose appears in the Change Style menu, and your text is now formatted as a heading.

4. **Click anywhere in the FrontPage Express window to deselect the heading you just formatted.**

5. **Press Enter to move to a new line.**

6. **Type the first item of your list, press Enter, and then type the second item on the next line. Repeat until you have entered all the items of your list.**

7. **Select all the items of your list (but not the heading).**

8. **Click on the Bulleted List toolbar button at the far right of the FrontPage Express Formatting menu.**

   A bullet appears next to each list item, and the items appear closer together on-screen so they look more like a list. That's all there is to it! Figure 6-3 shows the result.

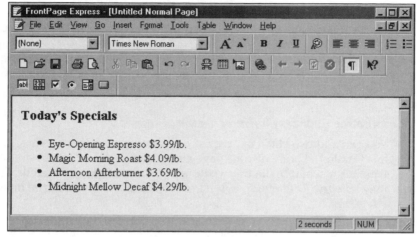

Figure 6-3:
A bulleted
list is an
easy way
to direct
customers'
attention
to special
promotions
or sale
items.

Most Web editors let you vary the appearance of the bullet that appears next to a bulleted list item. For example, you can make it a hollow circle rather than a solid black dot, or you can choose a rectangle rather than a circle.

Lead your readers on with links

I mean for you to interpret the heading above literally, not figuratively. In other words, I'm not suggesting that you make promises on which you can't deliver. Rather, I mean that you should do anything you can to lead your visitors to your site and entice them to enter and explore individual pages. You can accomplish this goal with a single hyperlinked word that leads to another page on your site:

More . . .

I see this word all the time on Web pages that present a lot of content. At the bottom of a list of their products and services, businesses place that word in bold type: **More. . . .** I'm always interested in finding out what more they could possibly have to offer me.

Television newscasts use the same approach. Before the newscast actually goes on the air, someone appears during a commercial break to give you a "tease" about the kinds of stories that are coming up next. You can do the same kind of thing on your Web pages. For example, which of the following links is more likely to get a response?

<u>Next</u>

<u>Next: Paragon's Success Stories</u>

Whenever possible, tell your visitors what they can expect to encounter as a benefit when they click on a link. Give them a promise — then, live up to that promise.

Enhance your text with well placed images

You can add two kinds of images to a Web page: an *inline image,* which appears in the body of your page along with your text, or an *external image,* which is a separate file that visitors access by clicking on a link. The link may take the form of highlighted text or a small version of the image called a *thumbnail.*

The basic HTML tag that inserts an image in your document takes the following form:

```
<IMG SRC="URL">
```

This tag tells your browser to display an image (<IMG>) here. "URL" gives the location of the image file that serves as the source (SRC) for this image. Whenever possible, you should also include WIDTH and HEIGHT attributes (as follows), because they help speed up graphics display for many browsers:

```
<IMG HEIGHT=51 WIDTH=48 SRC="target.gif">
```

Most Web page editors add the WIDTH and HEIGHT attributes automatically when you insert an image. Typically, you click on the location in the Web page where you want the image to appear. Then you click on an Image toolbar button or choose Insert⇨Image to display an image selection dialog box. You then enter the name of the image you want to add, click on OK, and the image is added to your Web page. (For more information, see Chapter 5.)

A well-placed image points the way to text that you want people to read immediately. Think about where your own eyes go when you first connect to a Web page. Most likely, they go to any images on the page; then they go to the headings; finally, they settle on text to read. If you can place an image next to a heading, you virtually ensure that viewers will read the heading.

Give something away for free

Raise your right hand and repeat after me. "I, [your name]" — no, don't say "your name," say your name. Oh, never mind. Just promise me that you'll use one of the following words in the headings on your online business site's home page:

- ✔ Free
- ✔ New
- ✔ Act (as in Act Now!)
- ✔ Sale
- ✔ Discount
- ✔ Win

Contests and sweepstakes

The word *free* and the phrase *Enter Our Contest* can give you a big bang for your buck when it comes to a business Web page. In fact, few things are as likely to get viewers to click into a site as the promise of getting something for nothing.

Giveaways have a number of hidden benefits, too: Everyone who enters sends you personal information that you can use to compile a mailing list or prepare marketing statistics. Giveaways get people involved with your site, and they invite return visits — especially if you hold contests for several weeks at a time.

Of course, in order to hold a giveaway, you need to have something to *give away*. If you make crafts or sell shoes, you can designate one of your sale items as the prize. If you can't afford to give something away, offer a deep (perhaps 50 percent) discount.

You can organize either a sweepstakes or a contest. A *sweepstakes* chooses its winner by random selection; a *contest* requires participants to compete in some way. The most effective contests on the Internet tend to be simple. If you hold one, consider including a "Rules" Web page that explains who is eligible, who selects the winner, and any rules of participation.

Be aware of the federal and state laws and regulations that cover sweepstakes and contests. Such laws often restrict illegal lotteries as well as the promotion of alcoholic beverages. Telemarketing is sometimes prohibited in connection with a contest. Here are some other things to consider:

✔ Unless you are sure that it's legal to include Web surfers from other countries to participate, you're safest limiting your contest to U.S. residents only.

✔ On the contest rules page, be sure to clearly state the starting and ending dates for receiving entries. Some states have laws requiring you to disclose this information.

✔ Don't change the ending date of your contest, even if you receive far fewer entries than you had hoped for.

Before your contest goes online, make sure that you've observed all the legal guidelines by visiting the Arent Fox Contests and Sweepstakes Internet site (www.arentfox.com/features/sweepstakes).

If you do hold a contest, be sure to announce it at the top of your Web page, and hint at the prizes people can win. Use bold and big type to attract visitors' attention.

Expert tips and insider information

Giveaways aren't just for businesspeople in retail or wholesale sales who have merchandise they can offer as prizes in a contest. If your work involves professional services, you can give away something just as valuable: your knowledge. Publish a simple newsletter that you e-mail to subscribers on a periodic basis (see Chapter 7 for instructions on how to do this). Or, answer questions by e-mail. Plenty of Web page designers work for free initially, until they build a client base and can charge for their services.

Make your site searchable

People just love those searchable text boxes that let them specify a word or phrase that they are most interested in finding within your Web site. If you can provide your visitors with a way to access the entire contents of your Web site at once, you provide them with another user-friendly way to interact with you.

Actually creating a Search This Site utility for your Web site is no small matter, however. To do this from scratch, you would have to index your site's contents and create a computer script that searches for the keywords that people enter in the Search text box. Or you can download and install an existing script. Ask your Web host whether you can run scripts on your Web site, and how to make a script work.

The artist Joseph Wu's beautifully designed Origami Page, which is shown in Figure 6-4, includes a searchable text box so prospective customers and other interested visitors can find out more about his work and about the art of origami in general.

Figure 6-4:
A "Search this site" text box lets visitors instantly match their interests with what you have to offer.

You say you're up to making your site searchable, and you aren't afraid of dealing with computer scripts? Then head over to Extropia.com (www.extropia.com) and check out the application SiteSearch. You can also add a search box to your Web page that lets visitors search the entire Internet by making a link to the search service Excite. Find out more at www.excite.com/Info/linking3.html.

Writing for an Online Business Site

Business writing on the Web differs from the dry, linear report writing one is often called upon to compose (or, worse yet, read) in the corporate world. So loosen up your tie, kick off your pumps, and relax: You're online, where sites that are funny, authors who have a personality, and content that's quirky are most likely to succeed.

Striking the right tone

When your friend meets you at the train station, how does he pick you out from all the other passengers who have arrived on the 8:40? Maybe it's your signature haircut or that hat you'll probably take to the grave. Your business also has a personality, and the more striking you make its description on your Web page, the better. Use the tone of your text to define what makes your business unique and what distinguishes it from your competition.

Letting others speak for you

Don't go overboard with promotional prose that beats readers over the head. Web readers are looking for objective information they can evaluate for themselves. An independent review of your site or your products carries far more weight than your own ravings about how great your site is. Sure, *you* know your products and services are great, but you'll be more convincing if your offerings can sell themselves, or you can identify third parties to endorse them.

What's that you say? *Wired* magazine hasn't called to do an in-depth interview profiling your entrepreneurial skills? Yahoo! hasn't graced you with the coveted "glasses" icon (indicating, in the estimation of Yahoo!'s Web site reviewers, a cool site worthy of special attention) on one of its long index pages? Take a hint from what my colleagues and I do when we're writing computer books like the one you're reading now: We fire up our e-mail and dash off messages to anyone who may want to endorse our books: our mentors, our friends, and people we admire in the industry.

People should endorse your business because they like it, not simply because you asked for an endorsement. If they have problems with your business setup, they can be a great source of objective advice on how to improve it. Then, after you make the improvements, they're more likely than ever to endorse it.

Satisfied customers are another source of endorsements. Approach your customers and ask if they're willing to provide a quote about how you helped them. If you don't yet have satisfied customers, ask someone to try out your products or services for free and then, if they're happy with your wares, ask permission to use their comments on your site. Your goal is to get a pithy, positive quote that you can put on your home page or on a page specifically devoted to quotes from your clients.

Don't be afraid to knock on the doors of big-wigs, too. Send e-mail to an online reporter or someone prominent in your field, and ask for an endorsement. People love to give their opinions and see their names in print. You just may be pleasantly surprised at how ready they are to help you.

Sharing your expertise

Few things build credibility and ensure return visits like a Web site that presents "inside" tips and goodies you can't get anywhere else. The more you can make your visitors feel that they're going to find something on your site that they can't get anywhere else, the more success you'll have.

Tell what you know. Give people information about your field that they may not have. Point them to all sorts of different places with links.

LinkExchange (`www.linkexchange.com`) provides many services that Web site owners can access and use online for free. One utility, SiteInspector, checks your site to make sure that your links work, your pages load quickly, your HTML commands are correct, and your page will be accepted by another useful service, Submit-It!, which sends your business URL to a variety of search engines and indexes. After you have designed your pages, added your content, and gone online, enter your URL and submit your site to SiteInspector to make sure that everything works efficiently.

Getting Your Customers to Talk Back

Quick, inexpensive, and *personal:* These are among the advantages that the Web has over traditional printed catalogs. The first two are obvious pluses. You don't have to wait for the ink to dry on an online catalog. On the Web, your contents are published and available to your customers right away. And, as the little birdie said, it's *cheap, cheap, cheap.* Putting a catalog on the Web eliminates (or, if publishing a catalog on the Web allows you to reduce your print run, dramatically reduces) the cost of printing, which can result in big savings.

But the fact that online catalogs can be more personal than the printed variety is perhaps the biggest advantage of all. The personal touch comes from the Web's potential for *interactivity.* Getting your customers to click on links makes them actively involved with your catalog.

Inviting e-mail feedback

Don't leave your customers looking for bread crumbs to find their way to you. What's the single most important piece of content on a Web site? It could be the way you provide for your customers to interact with you so that they can reach you quickly.

Add a simple *mailto* link like this:

Questions? Comments? Send e-mail to: info@mycompany.com

A mailto link gets its name from the HTML command that programmers use to create it. When visitors click on the e-mail address, their e-mail program opens a new e-mail message window with your e-mail address already entered. That way, they only have to enter a subject line, type the message, and click Send to send you their thoughts.

Most Web page creation programs make it easy to create a mailto link. For example, if you use Microsoft FrontPage Express, follow these steps:

1. **Launch FrontPage Express and open the Web page to which you want to add your e-mail link.**

2. **Position your mouse arrow and click at the spot on the page where you want the address to the appear.**

   The convention is to put your e-mail address at or near the bottom of a Web page. A vertical blinking cursor appears at the location where you want to insert the address.

3. **Click on the Create or Edit Hyperlink button in the FrontPage Express toolbar.**

   The Create Hyperlink dialog box appears.

4. **Click on the triangle next to the <u>H</u>yperlink Type drop-down menu.**

   A list of menu options drops down.

5. **Select mailto: from the drop-down list.**

   The list disappears, and `mailto:` now appears in the box next to Hyperlink Type as well as in the URL text box.

6. **Click your mouse inside the URL text box and, after the word mailto:, type your e-mail address.**

   For example, this is how my e-mail address would appear: **mailto:gholden@interaccess.com** (note that you don't want to include a space after mailto: when you enter your address).

7. **Click on OK.**

   The Create Hyperlink dialog box closes, and you return to the FrontPage Express window, where your e-mail address appears in blue and is underlined to signify that it is a clickable link.

Other editors work similarly. For example, in World Wide Web Weaver, a shareware program for the Macintosh, you choose Tags⇨Mail. A dialog box called Mail Editor appears. Enter your e-mail address and the text you want to appear as the highlighted link and then click on OK to add the mailto link to your page.

Using Web page forms

You don't have to do much Web surfing before you become intimately acquainted with how Web page forms work, at least from the standpoint of someone who has to fill them out in order to sign up for Web hosting or to download software.

When it comes to creating your own Web site, however, you become conscious of how useful forms are as a means of gathering essential marketing information about your customers. They give your visitors a place to sound off, ask questions, and generally get involved with your online business.

Be clear and use common sense when creating your order form. Here are some general guidelines on how to organize your form and what you need to include:

- ✔ **Make it easy on the customer.** Whenever possible, add pull-down menus with pre-entered options to your *form fields* (text boxes that visitors use to enter information). That way, users don't have to wonder about things like whether you want them to spell out a state or use the abbreviation.

- ✔ **Validate the information.** You can use a programming language called JavaScript to ensure that users enter information correctly, that all fields are completely filled out, and so on. You may have to hire someone to add the appropriate code to the order form, but it's worth it to save you from having to call customers to verify or correct information that they missed or submitted incorrectly.

- ✔ **Provide a help number.** Give people a number to call if they have questions or want to check on an order.

- ✔ **Return an acknowledgment.** Let customers know that you have received their order and will be shipping the merchandise immediately, or contacting them if more information is needed.

As usual, the growing crop of Web page authoring and editing programs makes it a snap to create the text boxes, check boxes, buttons, and other parts of a form that the user fills out. The other part of a form, the computer script that receives the data and processes it so you can read and use the information, is not so simple. See Chapter 9 for details.

Providing a guestbook

A *guestbook* on a Web page performs roughly the same function as a guestbook in a hotel or at a museum: It gives your customers a place to sign in and provide some brief comments about your business. When you add a guestbook to one of your business's Web pages, your clients and other visitors can check out who else has been there and what others think about the site.

If you set out to create your own Web page guestbook from scratch, you'd have to create a form, write a script (fairly complicated code that tells a computer what to do), test the code, and so on. Lucky for you, there's an easier way to add a guestbook — you register with a special Web business that provides free guestbooks to users. Two organizations that offer guestbook services are LinkExchange (www.linkexchange.com) and GuestWorld (saturn.guestworld.tripod.lycos.com).

If you register with GuestWorld's service, you can have your own guestbook right away with no fuss. (Actually, GuestWorld created the guestbook program, which resides on one of its Web servers; You just add the text-entry portion to your own page.) Here's how to do it:

1. **Connect to the Internet, start up your Web browser, and go to the following URL:** `saturn.guestworld.tripod.lycos.com`.

   This step takes you to the World Famous Guestbook Server page (see Figure 6-5).

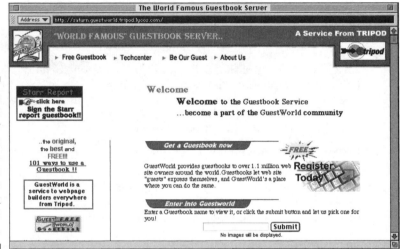

Figure 6-5:
If you register with GuestWorld, you can add a free guestbook to your own Web page.

2. **Click on the link called <u>Get a Guestbook now</u>, which is near the top of the World Famous Guestbook Server page.**

   You go to the GuestWorld Guestbook Registration page (`callisto.guestworld.tripod.lycos.com/registration.cfm`).

3. **Fill out the Guestbook Registration form.**

   The program asks you to choose a name and password for your guestbook, and to enter the URL of the Web page on which you want the guestbook to appear.

4. **When you finish filling out the form and reading the Terms of Service Agreement near the bottom of the registration page, click on the Register button.**

   After a few seconds, a page called You Are Registered! appears. This page lets you know that your registration was successfully submitted. It also contains the HTML code that will add the guestbook *text-entry fields* (the text boxes and other items that visitors use to submit information to you) to your Web page.

5. **Scroll down the page to the green box labeled Code.**

   This box contains the code you need to copy and add to the HTML for your Web page.

6. **Position your mouse arrow at the beginning of the code (just before the first line, which looks like this:** `<!—start of code—>`**), press and hold down your mouse button, and scroll across the code to the last line, which reads:** `<!—end of code—>`**.**

   The code is highlighted to show that it has been selected.

7. **Choose Edit⇨Copy to copy the selected code to your computer's clipboard.**

8. **Launch your Web editor, if it isn't running already, and open the Web page you want to edit in your Web editor window.**

   If you're working in a program (like HotDog Pro), that shows the HTML for a Web page while you edit it, you can move on to Step 9. If, on the other hand, your editor hides the HTML from you, you have to use your editor's menu options to view the HTML source for your page. The exact menu command varies from program to program. Usually, though, the option is contained in the View menu. In FrontPage Express, for example, the command is View⇨HTML. With this command, a new window opens that contains the HTML for the Web page you want to edit.

9. **Scroll down and click on the spot on the page where you want to paste the HTML code for the guestbook.**

   How do you know where this spot is? Well, you have to add the code in the BODY section of a Web page. This is the part of the page that is contained between two HTML commands, `<BODY>` and `</BODY>`. You can't go wrong with pasting the code just before the `</BODY>` tag — or just before your return e-mail address or any other material you want to keep at the bottom of the page. The following example indicates the proper placement for the guestbook code:

   ```
   <HTML>
   <HEAD>
   <TITLE>Sign My Guestbook</TITLE>
   </HEAD>
   <BODY>
   The body of your Web page goes here;
        this is the part that appears on the Web.
   Paste your guestbook code here!
   </BODY>
   </HTML>
   ```

10. **Choose Edit⇨Paste.**

    The guestbook code is added to your page.

11. **Click the close box (X) in the upper-right corner of the HTML window, if you are working in a Windows environment. (If you're working on a Mac, close the window by clicking on the close box in the upper-left corner of the window that displays the HTML.)**

    The HTML code disappears, and you return to your Web editor's main window.

12. **Choose File⇨Save to save your changes.**

13. **Preview your work in your Web browser window.**

    Exactly how you do this varies from editor to editor. Some editors have a Preview toolbar button on which you can click to view your page in a Web browser. Otherwise, double-click on the icon to launch your Web browser, if you haven't launched it already. Then

    • If you use Netscape Navigator, choose File⇨Open Page, single-click on the name of the file you just saved in the Open Page dialog box, and then click on Open to open the page.

    • If you use Internet Explorer, choose File⇨Open, single-click on the name of the file you just saved in the Open dialog box, and click on Open to open the page.

    The page opens in your Web browser, with a new Guestbook button added to it (see Figure 6-6).

Figure 6-6:
Add a
guestbook
link to your
Web site.

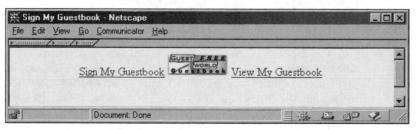

Now, when visitors to your Web page click on the highlighted Sign My Guestbook link, they go to a page that has a form they can fill out (see Figure 6-7). Clicking on the View My Guestbook link enables visitors to view the messages that other visitors have entered into your guestbook.

The problem with adding a link to a service that resides on another Web site is that it makes your Web pages load more slowly. First, your visitor's browser loads the text on your page. Then, it loads the images from top to bottom. Besides this, it has to make a link to the GuestWorld site in order to load the guestbook. If you decide to add a guestbook, images, or other elements that reside on another Web site, be sure to test out your page and make sure that you're satisfied with how long the contents take to appear.

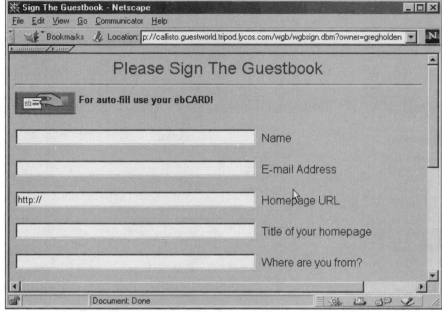

Gathering 'round the water cooler

You put your business online, you created some great content, and you're excited by the response you're receiving. You're getting plenty of e-mail inquiries, and, once in a while, someone gives you a big thrill by placing an order for your products or services.

Congratulations are certainly in order. But because I'm here to see that your online business is a real success, it's my duty to tell you not to stop there. After visitors start coming to your site, the next step is to retain those visitors. A good way to do this is by building a sense of community by posting a bulletin-board-type discussion area.

A discussion area takes the form of back-and-forth messages on topics of mutual interest. Each person can read previously posted messages and either respond or start a new topic of discussion. For an example of a discussion area that's tied to an online business, visit the Australian Fishing Shop (www.ausfish.com) discussion areas, one of which is shown in Figure 6-8.

The talk doesn't have to be about your own business per se. In fact, the discussion will be more lively if your visitors can discuss general concerns about your area of business, whether it's computers, psychotherapy, automotive repair, antiques, or whatever.

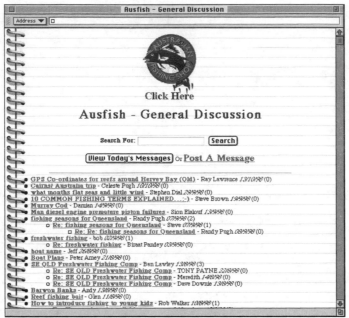

Figure 6-8:
A
discussion
area
stimulates
interest and
interaction
among like-
minded
customers.

How, exactly, do you start a discussion area? Generally speaking, you need to install a special computer script on the computer that hosts your Web site (again, it's essential to discuss this prospect with your Web hosting service beforehand). When visitors come to your site, their Web browsers access the script, enabling them to enter comments and read other messages.

Here are some specific ways to make your site discussion-ready:

✔ Install Microsoft FrontPage, which includes the scripts you need to start a discussion group. You have to purchase FrontPage, because no demo or beta version of the software is available as this time. It comes in versions for Macintosh and Windows platforms.

✔ Copy a bulletin board or discussion-group script from Extropia.com (`www.extropia.com`) or Matt's Script Archive (`www.worldwidemart.com/scripts/readme/wwwboard.shtml`).

✔ Start your own forum on a service like HyperNews, by Daniel LaLiberte, or install the HyperNews program yourself (`www.hypernews.org/HyperNews/get/hypernews.html`).

Because chat rooms and discussion groups are for a more advanced business Web site, rather than one that's just starting out, I don't discuss them in detail in this book. I do, however, explore the topic in my book *Small Business Internet For Dummies,* published by IDG Books Worldwide, Inc.

Chapter 7

Marketing to a Worldwide Audience

*E*very businessperson wants to attract a wide range of customers. Even the vendors who seem to have the smallest reach, such as the barber who has a shop on the corner or moppets selling lemonade from a table in front of their house, wouldn't turn away a customer who comes from across town or even from a neighboring community.

As an online businessperson, you aren't limited to finding customers on the street where you live. In fact, you have a tremendous advantage when it comes to how far your business reaches. Although the *Inter-* in the word *Internet* doesn't stand for *international,* the effect is the same. Your customer base stretches across the globe. Networks, computers, and Web browsers eliminate the restrictions of language barriers, political borders, and time zones to create a truly worldwide marketplace.

In fact, one of the most exciting moments for many online merchants occurs when they receive their first order from overseas. That's when a host of new concerns pops up, too: How do I ship this order to Australia, Norway, Mexico, or Japan? How do I accept payment? After that, questions arise about how to attract more business from overseas. This chapter provides pointers to help you attract and fulfill business orders, not just from around the neighborhood, but also from around the world.

Speaking Their Language

What is it that attracts shoppers to your business and encourages them to place orders from thousands of miles away? It's what you have to sell and how you present it. But how can customers understand what you're selling if they speak a different language? It's up to you to make your site accessible to *all* your potential customers.

Minding your Ps and Qs (puns and quips)

Put yourself in your customer's place. Suppose that you're from Spain. You speak a little English, but Spanish is your native tongue, and other Romance languages like French and Italian are definitely easier for you to understand than English. You're surfing around an Internet shopping mall, and you come across sentences such as these:

> Hey, rachet-jaws. Shoot me some e-mail with your handle, and steer clear of Smokeys with ears.

> Whatever. All you home boys will be down with my superfly jive.

> Like, this cable modem is totally awesome to the max.

Get the picture? Your use of slang and local dialect may have customers from your own hometown or region in stitches, but it can leave many more people scratching their heads and clicking on to the next site. The first rule in making your site accessible to a worldwide audience is to keep your language simple so people from all walks of life can understand you.

Using the right salutations

First impressions mean a lot. The way you address someone can mean the difference between getting off on the right foot or stumbling over your shoelaces. The following useful tidbits are from the International Addresses and Salutations Web page (www.bspage.com/address.html) which, in turn, borrowed them from *Merriam Webster's Guide to International Business Communication:*

- ✔ In Austria, address a man as *Herr* and a woman as *Frau;* don't use *Fräulein* for business correspondence.

- ✔ In southern Belgium, use *Monsieur* or *Madame* to address someone, but the language spoken in northern Belgium is Flemish, so be sure to use *De heer* (Mr.) when addressing a man, or *Mevrouw,* abbreviated to *Mevr.* (Mrs.), when addressing a woman.

- ✔ In India, use *Shri* (Mr.) or *Shrimati* (Mrs.). Don't use a given name unless you are a relative or close friend.

✔ In Japan, given names aren't used in business. Use the family name followed by the job title. Or, add *-san* to the family name (for example, Fujita-san), or the even more respectful *-sama* (Fujita-sama).

Adding multilingual content to your Web site is a nice touch, particularly if you deal on a regular basis with customers or clients from a particular area. Regional differences abound, so it's prudent to find a person familiar with the area you are trying to target to read your text before you put it up on the Web. Let a friend, not the absence of orders, tell you that you've committed a cultural *faux paus*.

Making your site multilingual

One of the best ways to expand your business to other countries is to provide alternate translations of your content. You can either hire someone to prepare the text in one or more selected languages, or use a computer program to do the work for you. Then provide links to the Web pages that contain the translated text right on your site's home page, like this:

```
Read this page in:
French
Spanish
German
```

One translation utility that's particularly easy to use — and, by the way, free — is available from the search service AltaVista. Just follow these steps to get your own instant translation:

1. **Connect to the Internet, launch your Web browser, and go to the following URL:** `babelfish.altavista.digital.com`.

   The AltaVista: Translations Web page appears.

2. **If you have a specific bit of text that you want to translate, click in the text box on this page and either type in the text or paste it from a word processing program. If you want the service to translate an entire Web page, enter the URL in the text box. Be sure to include the first part of the URL (for example, `http://www.mysite.com` rather than just `mysite.com`).**

   Obviously, the shorter and simpler the text, the better your results.

3. **Choose the translation path (that is, *from* what language you want to translate) by clicking on the Translate From drop-down menu.**

   At this writing, the service offers only English, French, Spanish, German, Italian, and Portuguese.

4. **Click on the Translate button.**

   Almost as fast as you can say, "Welcome to the new Tower of Babel," a new Web page appears on-screen with the foreign language version of your text, as shown in Figure 7-1. (If you selected a Web page to translate, the Web page appears in the new language. The title of the page, however, remains in the original language.)

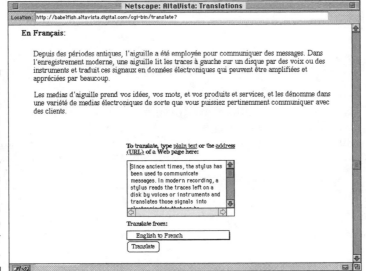

Figure 7-1:
AltaVista's online translation service instantly translates selected text or an entire Web page for free.

Instead of creating a foreign-language version of your Web page, you can provide a link to AltaVista's translation page on your own page. That way, your visitors can translate your text for themselves.

You can download the software behind AltaVista's translation service, Systran Personal, from the Systran Software, Inc. Web site (www.systransoft.com). The program is available for Windows 95 or NT only, and requires at least 16MB of RAM and 15MB of hard disk space. The cost is $29 for unidirectional translation, and $49 for a bidirectional package. If you need translation to or from Japanese, Chinese, or Russian, look into Systran Professional, which costs $995. This program has the same software requirements as the Personal package, as well as an Asian font display driver for Asian language translation.

The limitations of a computer translation

The problem with having a computer perform a translation is that you don't have the benefit of a real human being's judgment in choosing the right words and phrases. And in most cases, you have no idea just how good a job the program is doing in conveying your message. Suppose that you want to say your business deals in "vintage and collectible" watches, and the program says your watches are "juicy and delectable"?

To test out AltaVista's online translation service, I took two paragraphs from my own business Web site and turned them into French. Then, I had my friend Caroline Dauteuille evaluate the translation. Caroline is a native French speaker and professional translator.

Here is the original text:

> Since ancient times, the stylus has been used to communicate messages. In modern recording, a stylus reads the traces left on a disk by voices or musical instruments into electronic data that can be amplified and enjoyed by many. Stylus Media takes your ideas, your words, and your products and services, and styles them into a variety of electronic media so that you can effectively communicate with customers.

If you have really good eyes, you can read AltaVista's translation in Figure 7-1.

When Caroline first read AltaVista's translation, she rated it a six on a scale of one to ten, because she got the basic idea of what the text was trying to say. But, when she took a second look, she noticed two big mistakes:

✔ The program took my company's name, Stylus Media, and translated it as a regular phrase: "The media of the stylus," with no capital letters.

✔ The word "left" in the phrase "traces left" was translated as the direction "left" (*á gauche*) rather than a word meaning "something remaining behind."

So Caroline downgraded her rating of the translation to a three on a scale of one to ten. Although the computer program got most of the literal meanings right, the misunderstanding that could have resulted from the few big mistakes would have made a really bad impression.

Okay, I realize that this isn't a scientific test, and the results aren't surprising. Systran Systems, Inc., which provided the software used in AltaVista's translation service, has a disclaimer on its Web site stating that a computer is no match for a human translator. But if you only have a short, *very* simple bit of content that you need to translate, this is a cost-effective and quick alternative for a small business on a tight budget.

You don't have to translate your entire Web site. In fact, just providing an alternate version of your home page may be sufficient. The important thing is to give visitors an overview of your business and a brief description of your products and services in a language they can understand easily. Most importantly, include a mailto link (see Chapter 6) so people can send mail to you. However, if you aren't prepared to receive a response in Kanji or Swahili, request that your guests send their message in a language that you can read.

Although you probably don't have sufficient resources to pay for a slew of translation services, it may be worthwhile to have someone translate your home page so you can provide an alternate version, especially if you sell products that are likely to be desirable to a particular market. Plenty of translation services are available online. Clarity (`www.netjuice.es`) will translate your home page for a fee if you supply them with your URL. Yahoo! has an index of translation services at `dir.yahoo.com/ Business_and_Economy/Companies/ Communications_and_Media_Services/Translation_Services`.

Using the right terms

Sometimes, communicating effectively with someone from another country is a matter of knowing the terms they use to describe important items. The names of the documents you use to draw up an agreement or pay a bill are often very different in other countries than they are in your own. For example, if you are an American merchant and someone from Europe asks you to provide a *proforma invoice,* you may not know what the person wants. You're used to hearing the document in question called a *quote*.

When you and your European buyer have come to terms, a Commercial Invoice is an official form you may need to use for billing purposes. Many of these forms have to do with large-scale export/import trade, and you may never have to use them. But if you do undertake trade with someone overseas, be aware that they may require you to use their own forms, not yours, in order to seal the deal. To avoid confusion later on, ask your overseas clients about any special requirements that pertain to business documents before you proceed too far with the transaction.

Joining the International Trade Brigade

International trade may seem like something that only multinational corporations practice. But the so-called little guys, like you and me, can be international traders, too. In fact, the term simply refers to a transaction between two or more individuals or companies in different countries. If you are a designer living in the U.S. and you create some stationery artwork and Web pages for someone in Germany, you have been involved in international trade.

Keeping up with international trade issues

If you really want to be effective in marketing yourself overseas and become an international player in world trade, you need to follow the tried-and-true business strategies: networking, education, and research. Join groups that promote international trade, become familiar with trade laws and restrictions, and generally get a feel for the best marketing practices around the world.

Here are some suggestions for places you can start:

- ✓ **NASBITE, the National Association of Small Business International Trade Educators** (`www.nasbite.dcccd.edu/nasbite.htm`): This group is particularly good because it's aimed at educating small businesses about international trade issues. The group gives you a way to interact with an international network of trade educators, consultants, and policy makers. Find out about upcoming international trade legislation, attend workshops, and get answers to your international marketing questions. Membership costs $75 per year.

- ✓ **The EPDWeb International Trade, Small Business, and Intellectual Property Web site** (`www.irlgov.ie/entemp/intern.htm`): This site is part of the Irish government's Department of Enterprise, Trade, and Employment.

- ✓ **International Business Resources On The WWW** (`ciber.bus.msu.edu/busres.htm`): This site (shown in Figure 7-2) is published by Michigan State University and includes hundreds of international trade links.

Figure 7-2:
If you want to do business with overseas customers, this is a must-visit site.

The Newsletter Access Web site (`www.newsletteraccess.com/subject/intertrade.html`) has information on how to subscribe to hundreds of different newsletters that discuss international trade issues.

Researching specific trade laws

Rather than waiting for overseas business to come to you, you can be proactive. A good first step is to do some research into the appropriate trade laws that apply to countries with which you might do business. The Internet has an amazing amount of information pertaining to trade practices for individual countries.

You can seek out international business by using one or more message boards designed specifically for small business owners who want to participate in international trade. These message boards let users post *trade leads*, which are messages that announce international business opportunities.

For example, at the Global Marketplace – World Business Network bulletin board (`worldbusiness.net/marketplace/trade.phtml`), you may find a message from a Dutch brewery offering beer for export, an international investment firm in Rhode Island that needs managers, or a Mexican company that's offering Mayan hammocks for sale. Advertisements on this site typically include the URL for the business's Web site. The site charges a fee to post your own notices. (See Figure 7-3.)

Figure 7-3: Follow trade leads or advertise your own goods and services for sale by posting on an international trade message board.

Be aware of export restrictions

If you're in the business of creating computer software or hardware, you need to be aware of restrictions that the U.S. government imposes on the export of some computer-related products.

For example, you can run into complications if you try to export commercial products that use 56-bit DES and equivalent encryption keys. (However, products with asymmetric encryption key sizes of up to 1,024 bits are permitted.)

You also cannot export to certain people and places. In fact, you may incur a fine of more than $100,000 from the U.S. Treasury Department and the U.S. State Department for exporting to a Denied Person, Specially Designated National, or Restricted Country. The list of these people and countries changes frequently. Look for links to the current ones at www.bxa.doc.gov/thesite.htm.

DigiLead (www.digilead.com) lets you post your own trade leads or search for other leads by keyword. The International Trade Leads page of the incredibly extensive International Business Resources On The WWW site (ciber.bus.msu.edu/busres/tradlead.htm) includes links to sites that post trade leads in countries such as Egypt, India, and Taiwan.

Exploring free trade zones

A *free trade zone* (FTZ) is an officially designated business or industrial area within a country where foreign and domestic goods are considered to be outside of the territory covered by customs. You don't have to pay customs duty, taxes, or tariffs on merchandise brought into, handled, or stored in an FTZ. You can find FTZs in many countries as well as in many U.S. states.

The purpose of FTZs is to reduce customs costs and make it easier for businesses to send goods into a country. You can store your items there for a while, exhibit them, and, if necessary, change them to comply with the import requirements of the country in question, until the time comes when you want to import them into the country.

A list of links to free trade zones in countries around the world is available at www.ceemail.com/zone_franche.html.

Shipping Overseas Goods

It never hurts to state the obvious, so here goes: Don't depend on ground mail (appropriately nicknamed *snail mail*) to communicate with overseas customers. Use e-mail and fax to get your message across and, if you have to ship information or goods, use airmail express delivery. Surface mail can take weeks or even months to reach some regions of some countries — if it gets there at all.

Your customer may ask you to provide an estimate of your export costs, called *incoterms*. Incoterms (short for international commercial trade terms) are a set of standardized acronyms that were originally established in 1936 by the International Chamber of Commerce. They establish an international language for describing business transactions to prevent misunderstandings between buyers and sellers from different countries. Incoterms thus provide a universal vocabulary that is recognized by all international financial institutions.

Incoterms are most likely to apply to you if you're shipping a large number of items to an overseas factory, rather than, for example, a single painting to an individual's home. But just in case you hit the big time, it helps to be aware of common incoterms such as:

- **EXW (Ex Works):** This term means that the seller fulfills his or her obligation by making the goods available to the buyer at the seller's own premises (or *works*). The seller doesn't have to load the goods onto the buyer's vehicle, unless otherwise agreed.

- **FOB (Free on Board):** This term refers to the cost of shipping overseas by ship — not something you're likely to do in this high-tech day and age. But if you sell a vintage automobile to a collector in France, who knows?

- **CFR (Cost and Freight):** This term refers to the costs and freight charges necessary to transport items to a specific overseas port. CFR only describes costs related to items that are shipped by sea and inland waterways and that go to an actual port. Another incoterm, CPT (Carriage Paid To) can refer to any type of transport, not just shipping, and refers to the cost for the transport (or *carriage*) of the goods to their destination.

You'll find a detailed examination of incoterms at the Scheneker International Web site (www.schenkerusa.com/incoterms.html). The Trade Law Project has another list at itl.irv.uit.no/trade_law/documents/sales/incoterms/nav/inc_mode.html.

If the item you're planning to ship overseas by mail is valued at more than $500 (or, for items that are to be shipped by other means, more than $2,500), the U.S. requires you to fill out and submit a Shipper's Export Declaration (SED) and submit it to a U.S. customs agent. The SED requires you to provide your name, address, and either your social security number or your Internal Revenue Service Employer Identification Number (EIN). You also have to describe what's being sent, where it is being sent from, and the ultimate destination. You can obtain an SED from your local U.S. customs office or purchase one from the Government Printing office, 202-783-3238. Detailed instructions on how to fill out the SED are available on the U.S. Census Bureau's Web site (www.census.gov/foreign-trade/www/correct.way.html).

Some nations require a certificate of origin or a signed statement that attests to the origin of the exported item. You can usually obtain such certificates through a local chamber of commerce.

Some purchasers or countries may also ask for a certificate of inspection stating the specifications met by the goods shipped. Inspections are performed by independent testing organizations.

Wherever you ship your items, be sure to insure them for the full amount they are worth. Tell your customers about any additional insurance charges up front. Finally, choose an insurance company that is able to respond quickly to claims made from your own country and from your customers' country, as well.

Getting Paid in International Trade

Having an effective billing policy in place is especially important when your customers live thousands of miles away. The safest strategy is to request payment in U.S. dollars and to ask for cash in advance. This approach prevents any collection problems and gets you your money right away.

What happens if you want to receive payment in U.S. dollars from someone overseas but the purchaser is reluctant to send cash? You can ask the purchaser to send you a personal check — or, better yet, a cashier's check — but it's up to the buyer to convert the local currency to U.S. dollars. You can also suggest that they obtain an International Money Order from a U.S. bank that has a branch in their area, and specify that the money order be payable in U.S. dollars. Suggest that your customers use an online currency conversion utility like the Bloomberg Currency Calculator (www.bloomberg.com/markets/currency/currcalc.cgi) to do the calculation.

You can also use an online escrow service such as TradeSafe Online Corporation (www.tradesafe.com) or I-Escrow (www.iescrow.com), which holds funds in escrow until you and your customer strike a deal. The escrow service holds the customer's funds in a trust account so that the seller can ship an item knowing that he or she will be paid. Then the escrow service transfers the funds from seller to buyer after the buyer has inspected the goods and approved them.

Escrow services usually accept credit card payments from overseas purchasers; this is one way to accept credit card payments even if you don't have a merchant account yourself. The credit card company handles conversion from the local currency into U.S. dollars.

If you're going to do a lot of business overseas, consider getting export insurance to protect yourself against loss due to damage or delay in transit. Policies are available from the Export-Import Bank of the United States (www.exim.gov) or from other private firms that offer export insurance.

Marketing through global networking

Someone who has done a lot of research on international marketing and who knows the importance of reaching out to a worldwide audience is Nancy Roebke. Roebke is executive director of Profnet, Inc., a company that helps businesses network, follow leads and referrals, and generally increase their level of success.

Q. Has your online business been profitable financially?

A. The company started making money in its first year when it was only three months old, and it continues to be profitable financially.

Q. How do you promote your site?

A. I use all the following strategies. Articles and autoresponders pull the absolute best, and I use both every single day for marketing:

✔ **Classified ads:** My Web site (www. profnet.org/classifieds.htm) includes a whole list of places online that publish classified ads for free. It helps to offer something FREE in your ad, like a catalog, report, or newsletter, to get your prospect's attention.

✔ **E-mail marketing:** My absolute favorite marketing tool is sharing lists and doing a dual promotion with a firm that has the same client base but doesn't compete. I always include a signature file; the shorter the tag, the better it pulls.

✔ **Press releases:** I place these offline in newspapers and magazines, and online in Web magazines, newsgroups, and archives.

✔ **Web site URL/e-mail address:** We include these on all pieces of information that leave our office — ads, envelopes, e-mail, letterheads, flyers, and shipping labels.

✔ **Leading or moderating forum discussions:** Conducting an online conference is a great way to boost your credibility and visibility with a receptive audience.

✔ **Autoresponders:** These are e-mail addresses that are configured to respond automatically to a request for information. Put autoresponders in your online classified ads, Web site, and so on. Most Web hosts provide a digest of all e-mail addresses that contacted your autoresponder. Save this list for follow-up marketing.

✔ **Sub-dealer relationships:** Sub-dealing involves allowing other Web sites to sell your products when a sale occurs, you fulfill the order and pay the Web site owner a referral commission.

Q. What special considerations do small businesses have to keep in mind in dealing with a worldwide audience?

A. I hire translators for any country I want to market in. I always choose a *local* person to translate articles, Web site content, or messages I want to write for a foreign audience.

Chapter 8

Conducting E-Commerce on Your Site

Starting up a new business and getting it online is exciting, but believe me, the real excitement occurs when you get paid for what you do. Nothing boosts your confidence and tells you that your hard work is paying off like receiving the proverbial check in the mail or having funds transferred to your business account.

The immediacy and interactivity of selling and promoting yourself online applies to receiving payment, too. You *can* get paid with just a few mouse clicks and some important data entered on your customer's keyboard. But completing an electronic commerce (or, for short, *e-commerce*) transaction isn't the same as getting paid in a traditional retail store. The customer can't personally hand you some cash or a check. Or, if a credit card is involved, you can't verify the user's identity through a signature or photo ID.

In order to get paid promptly and reliably online, you have to go through some extra steps to make the customer feel secure and to protect yourself, as well. Successful e-commerce is about setting up the right atmosphere for making purchases, providing options for payment, and keeping sensitive information private. It's also about making sure that the goods get to the customer safely and on time. This chapter describes ways in which you can implement these essential online business strategies.

What Online Customers Want

Time and again, this book points out how important it is to understand online shoppers' needs and habits and to do your best to address them. Well, I'm still stuck on that broken record groove. When It comes to e-commerce, the more effectively you can address what your customers want, the more tangible results you find in your bank account.

Tell me how much it costs, now!

Don't make your customers search for a price list to find out how much an item costs. Be sure to put the cost right next to the item you are presenting. Remember that speed and convenience are what Web shoppers want most. They don't have the patience to click through several pages. Chances are they're comparison shopping, and they're in a hurry.

FrontPage Express, which is bundled with the copy of Internet Explorer that's on this book's CD-ROM, includes some clip art images that help highlight price information. Figure 8-1 shows an example.

Figure 8-1:
Use
graphics
to call
attention
to the
information
your
customer
wants most:
the price.

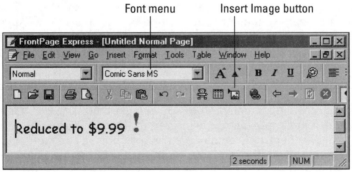

Show me that I can trust you!

All business is based on trust. But for an online business, trust-building is especially important. Electronic commerce is in its early days, and many customers still have fears like these:

✔ How do I know that someone won't intercept my name, phone number, or credit card information and use the data to make unauthorized purchases?

> ✔ How can I be sure that your online business will actually ship me what I order and not "take the money and run"?
>
> ✔ Can I count on you not to sell my personal information to some other businesses that will flood me with unwanted e-mail?

To get an in-depth look at how customers shop online and what constitutes "good" and "bad" shopping for many people, consult the book *Buying Online For Dummies,* by Joseph Lowery, published by IDG Books Worldwide, Inc.

How do you build trust on your Web site? State your policies clearly and often. Tell people that you value their business and will do everything you can to protect their personal information. Assure them you will not give out any customer's data without that person's consent. If you plan to accept credit card orders, be sure to get an account with a Web host that provides a *secure server:* software that encrypts data exchanged with a browser.

If you are a member in good standing of the Better Business Bureau (www.bbb.org), you may be eligible to join the BBBOnLine program (www.bbbonline.org) to build credibility and confidence among your clients. BBBOnLine participating businesses show their commitment to their customers by displaying a BBBOnLine seal on their Web site. Consumers are able to click on the BBBOnLine seal and view a Better Business Bureau company profile on the participating business.

Give me all the information I need!

Remember that one of the big advantages of operating a business online is space. You have plenty of room in which to provide full descriptions of your sale items. You also have no reason to skimp on the details you provide about your business, your products, and your services. Here are some suggestions:

> ✔ If you sell clothing, include a page with size and measurement charts.
>
> ✔ If you sell food, provide weights, ingredients, and nutritional information.
>
> ✔ If you sell programming, Web design, or traditional graphic design, provide samples of your work, links to Web pages you've created, and testimonials from satisfied clients.
>
> ✔ If you're a musician, publish a link to a short sound file of your work.

Don't be reluctant to tell people ways that your products and services are better than others. Visit the Lands' End online catalog (www.landsend.com) for good examples of how this well-established marketer describes the quality of its wares.

Enabling Credit Card Purchases

Having the ability to accept and process credit card transactions makes it especially easy for your customers to follow the impulse to buy something from you. You stand to generate a lot more sales than you would otherwise.

But although credit cards are easy for shoppers to use, they make *your* life as an online merchant more complicated. I don't want to discourage you from becoming credit-card-ready by any means, but you need to be aware of the steps (and the expenses) involved, many of which may not occur to you when you're just starting out. For example, you may not be aware of one or more of the following:

- You have to apply and be approved for a special bank account called a *merchant account* in order for a bank to process credit card orders you receive.

- Fees can be high, but they vary widely, and it pays to shop around. Some banks charge a merchant application fee ($300 to $800). All banks charge a usage fee, deceptively called a *discount rate.* Typically, this fee ranges from 1 to 4 percent of each transaction. Plus, you may have to pay a monthly premium charge of perhaps $30 to $70 to the bank.

- If you want to accept payments from American Express and Discover cardholders, you must make arrangements through the companies themselves. You can apply online to be an American Express card merchant by going to the American Express Small Business Exchange site (www6.americanexpress.com/smallbusiness) and clicking on the Apply to Accept the Card link. The Discover Card site (www.novusnet.com/discover/data/main.htm) does not include applications for credit card merchants, but you can call 1-800-347-2683 for more information.

- You need software or hardware to process the transactions and transmit the data to the banking system. If you plan only to accept credit card numbers online and don't need a device to handle actual "card swipes" from in-person customers, you can use your computer modem to transmit the data. The hardware involved is a terminal or phone line, which you can lease for $25 to $50 per month.

You also need to watch out for credit card fraud, in which criminals use stolen numbers to make purchases. You, the merchant, end up being liable for most of the fictitious transactions. Cardholders are only responsible for $50 of fraudulent purchases. To combat this crime, before completing any transaction, verify that the shipping address supplied by the purchaser is the same (or at least in the same vicinity) as the billing address. You can either do this check yourself or pay a service to do the checking.

Setting up a merchant account

The good news is that getting merchant status is becoming easier, as more banks accept the notion that businesses don't have to have an actual, physical storefront in order to be successful. The bad news is that it still takes a long time to get a merchant account approved, and some hefty fees are involved, as well. Banks look more favorably on companies that have been in business for several years and have a proven track record. What's an entrepreneur just starting out to do?

You can find a long list of institutions that provide merchant accounts for online businesses at one of Yahoo!'s index pages (dir.yahoo.com/ Business_and_Economy/Companies/Financial_Services/Transaction_ Clearing/Credit_Card_Merchant_Services). The list is so long that it's difficult to know which company to choose. I recommend visiting Wells Fargo Bank (www.wellsfargo.com), which has been operating online for several years and is well established. The Wells Fargo Web site provides you with a good overview of what's required to obtain a merchant account.

One advantage of using one of the payment options set up by CyberCash, the widely-used electronic payment company described in "Online Payment Systems," later in this chapter, is that the system is so well-known that a fairly lengthy list of financial institutions support it. If you use CyberCash, you can apply for a merchant account with one of the banks listed at www.cybercash.com/cybercash/financial/partners.html.

In general, your chances of obtaining merchant status are enhanced if you apply to a bank that welcomes Internet businesses and if you can provide good business records proving that you are a viable, money-making concern.

Be sure to ask about the discount rate that the bank charges for Internet-based transactions before you apply. Compare the rate for online transactions to the rate for conventional "card-swipe" purchases. Some banks charge 1 to 2 extra percentage points for online sales.

Finding a secure server

A *secure server* is one that uses some form of encryption (such as Secure Sockets Layer, described in Chapter 12) to protect data that you receive over the Internet. Customers know that they've entered a secure area when the security key or lock icon at the bottom of the browser window is locked shut and a blue security band appears at the top of the browser window.

If you plan to receive credit card payments, you definitely want to find a Web hosting service that will protect the area of your online business that serves as the online store. In literal terms, you need secure-server software protecting the directory on your site that is to receive customer-sent forms. Some hosts charge a higher monthly fee for using a secure server; with others, the secure server is part of a basic business Web site account. Ask your host (or hosts you are considering) whether any extra charges apply.

Verifying credit card data

Unfortunately, the world is full of bad people who try to use credit card numbers that don't belong to them. The very convenience and immediacy of the Web can facilitate fraudulent orders, just as it can benefit legitimate orders.

Protecting yourself against credit card fraud is essential. Always check the billing address against the shipping address. If the two addresses are thousands of miles apart, e-mail the owner to verify that the transaction is legit. Even if it is, the owner will appreciate your taking the time to verify the transaction.

You can use software to help check addresses. Two programs that perform this service are Authorizer (described in the upcoming section, "Processing the orders") and NetVERIFY, which you can purchase from ICVerify (www.icverify.com). Call 1-800-666-5777 for current pricing.

Processing the orders

When someone submits credit card information to you, you need to transfer the information to the banking system. Whether you make this transfer yourself or hire another company to do it for you is up to you.

Do-it-yourself processing

To submit credit card information to your bank, you need POS (point-of-sale) hardware or software. The hardware, which you either purchase or lease from your bank, is a *terminal* — a gray box of the sort you see at many local retailers. The software is a program that contacts the bank through a modem.

The terminal or software is programmed to authorize the sale and transmit the data to the bank. The bank then credits your business or personal checking account, usually within two or three business days. The bank also deducts the discount rate from your account, either weekly, monthly, or with each transaction.

One payment processing program is called Authorizer (see Figure 8-2). You can download a demo version from the Atomic Software Web site (www.atomic-software.com). A single-user version of Authorizer for Windows is available for $349. A multi-user version costs $549.

Automatic processing

You can hire a company to automatically process credit card orders for you. These companies compare the shipping and billing addresses to help make sure that the purchaser is the person who actually owns the card, and not someone trying to use a stolen credit card number. If everything checks out, they transmit the data directly to the bank.

Look into the different options provided by VeriFone, Inc. (www.verifone.com), CheckFree Corporation (www.checkfree.com), or the Octagon Technology Group (www.otginc.com) for such services.

Automatic credit card processing works so fast that your customer's credit card can be charged immediately, whether or not you have an item in stock. If a client receives a bill and is still waiting for an item that is on back order, the person can get very unhappy. For this reason, some business owners, such as Dave Hagan (profiled in the sidebar, "Keeping back-office functions personal"), choose not to use them.

Figure 8-2:
Software that verifies identity and processes payments is important for conducting credit card transactions.

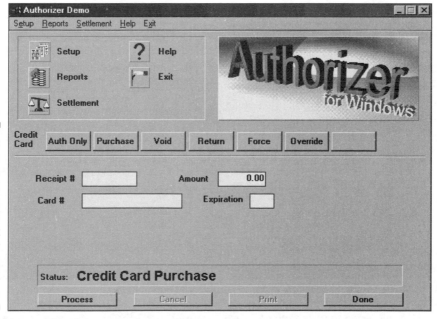

Keeping back-office functions personal

Dave Hagan, Jr. knows the importance of credit card verification and order processing. Yet he tries to make these functions as personal as possible in keeping with the spirit of online business.

Dave is president of both York Internet Services, a Web site design company, and General Tool & Repair, Inc., a tool supplier based in York, Pennsylvania. General Tool has been in business for twelve years, but three years ago, Dave created a simple Web page on America Online to help promote the company. Within two weeks, he received an order from a customer in Florida.

Since then, he has expanded his e-commerce Web site using Microsoft Commerce Server, and he set up shop at www.gtr.com.

Dave estimates that General Tool's Web site receives between 5 and 15 orders each day, and average online sales amount to $25,000 to $30,000 per month. He believes the site takes the place of 50 salespeople. "This is all business we never had until two years ago, so it's basically all gravy for us," he notes happily.

Q. How do you process credit card orders?

A. Our customers send us the credit card information through our Web site, and our secure server encrypts the data. But we don't process orders online. We first check to see if we have the item in stock, and, if we do, we process the order the next business day. That way, we don't "slam" the customer's credit card without having the item ready to ship out.

Q. How do you verify the identity of customers who submit credit card numbers to you?

A. We use a program called Authorizer by Atomic Software. The program lets you check the shipping address against the address of the credit card owner. If the two addresses are in the same state, you're pretty sure that

you can ship the item. Otherwise, you know that you'd better e-mail the card owner and tell the person there's a problem.

There's another advantage to using Authorizer. The program submits data to the bank in such a way that the bank can't tell whether this was a "card-swipe" purchase or one that came over the Internet. The bank then charges you its regular discount rate (in my case, 1.7 percent) rather than the 3 to 3.5 percent it charges for Internet purchases.

Q. Do you get many fraudulent credit card orders?

A. We get bogus orders all the time. Normally, you can tell because they don't have the correct "ship to" address.

Q. Whom do you use for shipping?

A. We get orders from countries like Japan and Finland, and all over the United States, too. If the customer is affiliated with the military, you are required to use the U.S. Postal Service for shipping. If we're shipping to a business address, such as an office in New York City, we use United Parcel Service because they give the option of requiring someone to sign for an item before they deliver it. We add an extra $1 to the shipping charge for this, but we feel that it's worth it because we don't want any items to get lost because they were left without a signature.

Q. How do you tell your customers about shipping options?

A. We contact them by e-mail after they place their order and explain the options to them. That way, they can choose. We don't add on flat-rate shipping or handling charges that might be excessive. There are only five of us here, and I can't justify charging someone $25 shipping and handling for a $3 set of nuts or bolts.

Online Payment Systems

A number of organizations have devised ways to make e-commerce secure and convenient for shoppers and merchants alike. These alternatives fall into one of two general categories:

- ✔ Organizations that help you complete credit card purchases (for example, CyberCash)
- ✔ Organizations that provide alternatives to transmitting sensitive information from one computer to another by using "virtual money" rather than real money (for example, Millicent)

In order to use one of these systems, you or your Web host has to set up special software on the computer that actually stores your Web site files. This computer is where the transactions take place. The following sections provide general instructions on how to get started with setting up each of the most popular electronic payment systems.

For electronic payment systems to work smoothly, you have to set up programming languages such as Perl, C/C++, or Visual Basic on your site. You also have to work with techy documents called *configuration files*. This is definitely an area where paying a consultant to get your business set up saves time and headaches and gets your new transaction feature online more efficiently than if you tackle it yourself. CyberCash provides a list of consultants who are experienced in setting up systems for its merchants.

CyberCash

CyberCash (`www.cybercash.com`) is one of the best-known companies providing payment options for online businesses. The fact that CyberCash is well-known should help you if you decide to use one of its different systems, including CashRegister, PayNow, or CyberCoin. CashRegister helps process credit card transactions, PayNow enables customers to pay bills online, and CyberCoin handles small sums called micropayments.

There's no cost to download and install the CyberCash Merchant Connection Kit, which lets you make use of the CashRegister software on the CyberCash site. However, you do have to pay fees if you need to hire consultants to help you get started, or if you need to get a merchant account with a bank that handles CyberCash transactions. (See "Enabling Credit Card Purchases," earlier in this chapter, for more information about merchant accounts.)

Reach for your wallet!

One of the terms commonly thrown around in the jargon of e-commerce is *wallet*. A wallet is software that, like a real wallet that you keep in your purse or pocket, stores available cash and other records. You reach into the cyberwallet and withdraw virtual cash such as the ecash, scrip, or CyberCoins.

A cybershopper who uses wallet software, such as Microsoft Wallet (www.microsoft.com/wallet/default.asp) or CyberCoin Wallet, is able to pay for items online in a matter of seconds, without having to transfer credit card data. What's more, some wallets can even "remember" previous purchases you have made and suggest further purchases.

Follow these steps to get set up with CyberCash:

1. **Connect to the Internet and go to the CyberCash Merchant page** (www.cybercash.com/cybercash/merchants/servtech.html).

2. **After reading the general information for merchants, click on the I want to get started link, at the bottom of the Web page.**

   The Getting Started as a CyberCash Merchant page appears. This page explains several options for integrating CyberCash payment systems into your online business site:

   • Hiring a Merchant Development Partner to help you

   • Hosting your site with an existing secure server that already uses CyberCash

   • Setting up CyberCash's connection software on your own computer (not recommended for beginners)

3. **Pick one of the first two options.**

   If you decide to work with a Merchant Development Partner, someone will guide you through the process of becoming a CyberCash merchant. This partner may be a Web developer who can help build your site or an ISP that can act as your site's Web host. In either case, you still need to obtain a merchant account with a financial institution, as explained earlier in this chapter, under "Enabling Credit Card Purchases."

In case you're wondering what's so involved about installing CyberCash yourself, here's an overview. CyberCash requires a Unix or Windows NT computer (a Windows 98/95 version is not available at this writing). You also need a merchant account with a financial institution that supports CyberCash transactions, plus special software or hardware to process credit card transactions. You also need a server that uses Secure Sockets Layer security and a valid certificate (see Chapter 12). You also have to make sure that one of the following scripting environments is operating on your system so you can run the scripts that come with the Merchant Connection Kit: Perl version 5.003 or later, an ANSI compatible C compiler, or VisualBasic. If all this sounds overwhelming, stick with one of the first two options for integrating CyberCash payment systems into your online business site.

MilliCent

MilliCent (`www.millicent.com`) issues a kind of virtual currency known as micropayments. (Other companies, including CyberCash with its CyberCoin system, offer similar services.)

Micropayments are very small units of currency that are exchanged by merchants and customers. The amounts involved may range from one-tenth of one cent (that's $.001) to a few dollars. Such small payments enable sites to provide content for sale on a per-click basis. In order to read articles, listen to music files, or view video clips online, some sites require micropayments in a special form of electronic cash that MilliCent calls *scrip*.

As a vendor, you authorize a broker to sell scrip on your behalf to your customers. If a customer goes to your site and wants to purchase articles or other content, the customer initiates the process by purchasing, usually with a credit card, a certain amount of scrip (say, $10 or $20) at face value from the broker. The broker then pays you, the MilliCent merchant, the $10 or $20 purchase of scrip that the customer made, minus a service fee. The customer is then free to make purchases from your site by clicking on items that have been assigned a certain value (say, one or two cents). The MilliCent software causes the few cents of scrip to be automatically subtracted from the user's supply of scrip. No credit card numbers are exchanged in these micropayment transactions.

The micropayment system is particularly useful if you're a software developer who wants to accept moderate shareware fees for your products, or if you have any kind of content that you want to charge small amounts to give people access to, such as online courses or articles.

Fulfilling Your Online Orders

Being on the Internet can help when it comes to the final step in the e-commerce dance: order fulfillment. *Fulfillment* refers to what happens after a sale is made. Typical fulfillment tasks include:

✔ Packing up the merchandise
✔ Shipping the merchandise

✔ Solving delivery problems or answering questions about orders that haven't reached their destinations

✔ Sending out bills

✔ Following up to see if the customer was satisfied

Order fulfillment may seem like the least exciting part of running a business, online or otherwise. But from your customer's point of view, it's the most important business activity of all. The following sections suggest how you can use your presence online to help reduce any suspense or anxiety your customers feel about receiving what they ordered.

The back-end (or, to use the Microsoft term, BackOffice) part of your online business is where order fulfillment comes in. If you have a database where you record customer orders, link it to your Web site so your customers can track orders. Allaire Cold Fusion and Macromedia Dreamweaver can help with this. (A trial version of the latter program is included on this book's CD-ROM.)

Provide links to shipping services

One advantage of being online is that you can help customers track packages after shipment. Federal Express's online order-tracking feature (Figure 8-3) gets thousands of requests each day and is widely known as one of the most successful marketing tools on the Web. If you use FedEx, provide a link to their tracking form.

The other big shipping services have followed FedEx's lead and created their own online tracking systems. You can link to these sites, too:

Where are the smart cards?

If you've traveled in Europe recently, you may have noticed lots of people using *smart cards.* These are cards that have an embedded computer chip that stores lots of information, from personal passwords to bank account balances. Cash resides directly on the card, rather than being stored in the banking system.

Smart cards haven't yet caught on in the U.S. Some recent promotions held by two big banks in New York just fizzled for lack of interest. The reason? ATM networks are widespread and familiar here, and the various ATM networks are compatible as well. And smart card readers are expensive. So shoppers are sticking with their credit and debit cards for now.

That doesn't mean that smart cards are dead, however. Microsoft has announced that it will develop a new operating system, due to go on sale in 1999, especially for smart cards. So if you get any inquiries from foreign customers asking whether you accept smart cards, you should probably respond with "Not yet" rather than "Huh?"

✔ United Parcel Service (www.ups.com)

✔ The U.S. Postal Service's Express Mail (www.usps.gov)

✔ Airborne Express (www.airborne.com)

Figure 8-3:
Provide
links to
online
tracking
services
so your
customers
can check
on delivery
status.

Present shipping options clearly

In order fulfillment, as in receiving payment, it pays to present your clients with as many options as possible and to explain the options in detail. Because you are online, you can provide your customers with as much shipping information as they can stand. Web surfers are knowledge hounds — they can never get enough data, whether it's related to shipping or other parts of your business.

When it comes to shipping, be sure to describe the options, the cost of each, and how long each takes. (See the sidebar called "Keeping back-office functions personal," earlier in this chapter, for some good tips on when to require signatures and how to present shipping information by e-mail rather than on the Web.) Here are some more specific suggestions:

✔ **Compare shipping costs.** Make use of an online service such as InterShipper, which allows you to submit via a Web page form the origin, destination, weight, and dimensions of a package that you want to ship, and then returns the cheapest shipping alternatives.

✔ **Make sure that you can track.** Pick a service that lets you track your package's shipping status.

✔ **Be able to confirm receipt.** If you use the U.S. Postal Service, ship the package "return receipt requested," because tracking is not available — unless you use Express Mail.

Many online stores present shipping alternatives in the form of a table. (*Tables* are Web page design elements that let you arrange content in rows and columns, making them easier to read; refer to Chapter 5 for more on adding tables to your site.) You don't have to look very far to find an example; just visit the IDG Books Worldwide Web site and order a book from their online store. When you're ready to pay for your items and provide a shipping address, you see the table shown in Figure 8-4.

Figure 8-4:
Tables help
shoppers
calculate
costs, keep
track of
purchases,
and decide
on shipping
options.

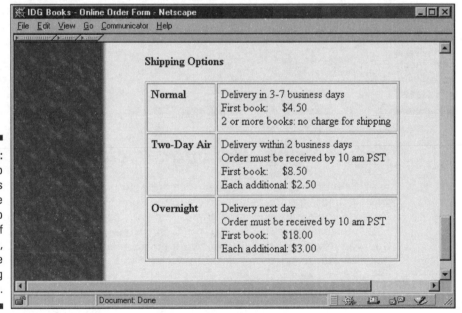

Shipping Options

Normal	Delivery in 3-7 business days First book: $4.50 2 or more books: no charge for shipping
Two-Day Air	Delivery within 2 business days Order must be received by 10 am PST First book: $8.50 Each additional: $2.50
Overnight	Delivery next day Order must be received by 10 am PST First book: $18.00 Each additional: $3.00

Part III
Promoting Your Online Business

The 5th Wave — By Rich Tennant

"So far our Web presence has been pretty good. We've gotten some orders, a few inquiries, and nine guys who want to date our logo."

In this part . . .

*L*ike fish in the ocean, your potential customers are out there — more of them, in fact, than you can begin to count. Part III tells you everything you need to know to reel them in — hook, line, and sinker.

When you run an online business, you need to develop special strategies for getting attention and standing out from the millions of other sites that are your competitors. This means researching your market, delivering on your promises, making sure that your customers are satisfied with your goods and services, exploring all the options for advertising and publicity that are available to you, and choosing an effective marketing strategy that best meets your needs.

Nothing's more frustrating, after all, than feeling a nibble on your line and then having to content yourself with telling your friends about the one that got away.

Chapter 9

Service with a Virtual Smile

●●●

●●●

Customer service is one activity where small, entrepreneurial businesses can outshine larger competitors. On top of that, an online business can provide help and support more quickly and completely than companies that only use conventional help lines or customer service desks. Tools such as e-mail and interactive forms, coupled with the fact that an online commerce site can provide information on a 24-hour-a-day, 7-day-a-week basis, give you a powerful advantage when it comes to retaining customers and building loyalty.

What constitutes good online customer service, particularly for a new business that has only one or two employees? It comes down to the personal touch. For the most part, you're dealing with customers one at a time, and you're connecting to them one to one. Think about the bad customer service experiences you've had: talking to recordings instead of to human beings, encountering bored employees who won't listen to you, having to wait overnight or through a weekend to speak to someone.

Being responsive and available is half the battle. This chapter presents ways to succeed with the other half: providing information, communicating effectively, and enabling your clientele to talk back to you online.

Customer Service = Information

The more information you can provide up front, the fewer phone queries or complaints you'll receive later on. Sure, you can go the traditional route and print pamphlets and brochures describing your products and services at length. But the cheaper and more effective route is to publish as much information as possible online.

Suppose your hire a writer like me to compose a 1,000-word description of your new company and your products and/or services. If I were to take those words and format them to fit on a 4-x-9-inch fold-out brochure, the contents would cover several panels and take at least a few hundred dollars to print.

On the other hand, if I divide my golden prose into a few Web pages and put them online, they'd probably take up no more than 5K to 10K of disk space. The same applies if you distribute your content to a number of subscribers in the form of an e-mail newsletter. In either case, you pay nothing to publish the information.

Sticking to the FAQs

A set of *frequently asked questions* (FAQs) is a familiar feature on many online business sites — so familiar, in fact, that longtime Web surfers like myself practically expect to find a FAQ page on every business site, and we have a pretty good idea of the kind of information we'll find there.

The format of FAQ pages is pretty similar from site to site, and this predictability is itself an asset. FAQ pages are generally presented in Q-and-A format, with topics appearing in the form of questions that have either literally been asked by other customers or that have been made up to resemble real questions. Each question has a brief answer that provides essential information about the business.

Because FAQ pages tend to be pretty long, it's an effective strategy to list the questions all at once at the top of the page. By clicking on a hyperlinked item in the list, the reader jumps to the spot down the page where you present the question and its answer in detail.

Not all FAQs are created equal. The best ones are easy to use and comprehensive. Take a look at one of the most famous of the genre, the venerable World Wide Web FAQ by Thomas Boutell (www.boutell.com/faq/oldfaq/index.html) to get some ideas for your own FAQ page. Or search through the many FAQs listed at FAQ.org (www.faq.org).

Because you know your own business so well, thinking up questions about it from the perspective of an outsider can be difficult. Yet you often have to create both the questions and the answers yourself when you first go online, rather than waiting for visitors to ask real questions. Enlist the help of friends and family to come up with questions about your own business. Some topics to consider include the following:

✔ **Contact information:** If I need to reach you in a hurry either by mail, fax, or phone, how do I do that? Are you available only at certain hours?

✔ **Instructions:** What if I need more detailed instructions on how to use your products or services? Where can I find them?

✔ **Service:** What do I do if the merchandise doesn't work for some reason, or breaks? Do you have a return policy?

✔ **Sales tax:** Is sales tax added to the cost I see on-screen?

✔ **Shipping:** What are my shipping options?

Starting an online newsletter

Sharing information with customers and potential customers through an e-mail newsletter is a great way to build credibility for yourself and your business.

For added customer service (not to mention a touch of self-promotion), consider producing a regular publication that you send out to a mailing list. You can compile your mailing list from customers and prospects who visit your Web site and indicate that they want to subscribe.

An e-mail newsletter does require some effort to create and distribute, but it can provide your business with great long-term benefits, including:

✔ **Customer tracking:** You can add subscribers' e-mail addresses to a mailing list that you can use for other marketing purposes.

✔ **Low-bandwidth:** An e-mail newsletter doesn't require much memory.

✔ **Timeliness:** You can get breaking news into your electronic newsletter much faster than you can put it in print.

Assuming that you already have a name for your newsletter and have assembled content that you want to include, follow these steps to create your publication:

1. **Create your newsletter by typing the contents in plain-text (ASCII) format.**

   Optionally, you can also provide an HTML-formatted version. You can then include headings and graphics that will show up in e-mail programs that support HTML e-mail messages.

   If you use a plain-text newsletter, format it using capital letters; rules that consist of a row of equal signs, hyphens, or asterisks; or blank spaces to align elements.

2. **Save your file with the proper filename extension: .txt for the text version, and .htm or .html if you send an HTML version.**

3. **Attach the file to an e-mail message by using your e-mail program's method of sending attachments.**

4. **Address your file to the recipients.**

   If you have lots of subscribers (many newsletters have hundreds or thousands), save their addresses in a mailing list. Use your e-mail program's address book function to do this.

5. **Send out your newsletter.**

If you have a large number of subscribers, I recommend sending your publication late at night or in several stages, rather than sending out all the e-mail messages at once. That way, your words will reach their destination much more quickly and reliably.

Managing a mailing list can be time-consuming because you have to keep up with all the messages from people who want to subscribe or unsubscribe and who ask for more information. You can save time and trouble by hiring a company like SkyList (www.skyweyr.com/skylist/hosting) to do the day-to-day list management for you.

Helping Customers Talk Back to You

The simplest and most essential element of customer service you can provide is your contact information. When you're online, this information can take several forms. Be sure to include:

- Your mailing address
- Your e-mail address(es)
- Your phone and fax numbers, and a toll-free number (if you have one)

Because most Web hosting services (such as the types of hosts I describe in Chapter 4) give you more than one e-mail inbox as part of your account, consider setting up more than one e-mail address. One address can be for people to communicate with you personally, and the other can be where people go for general information. You can also set up e-mail addresses that respond to messages by automatically sending a text file in response (see "Setting up autoresponders," later in this chapter).

Keep your site as personal and friendly as possible. A contact page is a good place to provide some brief biographical information about the people visitors can contact: you and any employees or partners in your company, that is.

You don't have to put your contact information on a separate Web page. Doing so only makes your patrons have to wait a few seconds to access it. If your contact data is simple and your Web site consists only of a few pages, by all means put it right on your home page.

Using advanced e-mail techniques

E-mail communication is a must for every online business. The more you learn about the finer technical points of e-mail, the better you are able to meet the needs of your clients. The following sections suggest ways to go beyond simply sending and receiving e-mail messages, to becoming a power business e-mail user.

Setting up autoresponders

An *autoresponder,* which also goes by the name *mailbot,* is software that you can set up to send automatic replies to requests for information about a product or service, or to respond to people subscribing to an e-mail publication or service.

You can provide automatic responses either through your own e-mail program or through your Web host's e-mail service. If you use a Web host to provide automatic responses, you can usually purchase an extra e-mail address that can be configured to return a text file (such as a form letter) to the sender.

Look for a Web host that provides you with one or more autoresponders along with your account. Typically, your host assigns you an e-mail address that takes the form: info@mycompany.com. In this case, someone at your hosting service configures the account so that when a visitor to your site sends a message to info@yourcompany.com, a file of your choice, such as a simple text document that contains background information about you and your services, automatically goes out to the sender as a reply.

Noting by quoting

Responding to a series of questions is easy when you use *quoting* — a feature that lets you copy quotes from a message to which you are replying. Quoting, which is available in almost all e-mail programs, is particularly useful for responding to a mailing list or newsgroup message, because it indicates the specific topic being discussed.

How do you tell the difference between the quoted material and the body of the new e-mail message? The common convention is to put a carrot (>) character in the left margin, next to each line of the quoted material.

When you tell your e-mail software to quote the original message before you type your reply, it generally quotes the entire message. To save space, you can *snip* (delete) out the part that isn't relevant. However, if you do so, it's polite to type the word **<snip>** to show that you've cut something out. A quoted message looks something like this:

```
Mary Agnes McDougal wrote:
>I wonder if I could get some info on <snip>
>those sterling silver widgets you have for sale...
Hi Mary Agnes,
Thank you for your interest in our premium collector's line
           of widgets. You can place an order online or call
           our toll-free number, 1-800-WIDGETS.
```

Attaching files

A quick and convenient way to transmit information from place to place is to attach a file to an e-mail message. In fact, attaching files is one of the most useful things you can do with e-mail. Attaching, which means that you send a document or file along with an e-mail message, allows you to include material from any file on your hard disk. Attached files appear as separate documents that recipients can download to their computers.

Many e-mail clients allow users to attach files with a simple button or other command. Compressing a lengthy series of attachments using software such as StuffIt or WinZip conserves bandwidth. Using compression is also a necessity if you ever want to send more than one attached file to someone whose e-mail account (such as an AOL account) doesn't accept multiple attachments.

Protocols such as MIME (Multipurpose Internet Mail Extensions) are sets of standards that allow you to attach graphic and other multimedia files to an e-mail message. Recipients must have an e-mail program that supports MIME (which includes almost all of the newer e-mail programs) in order to download and read MIME files in the body of an e-mail message. In case your recipient has an e-mail client that doesn't support MIME attachments, or if you aren't sure whether or not it does, you must encode your attachment in a format such as BinHex (if you are sending files to a Macintosh) or UUCP (if you are sending files to a newsgroup).

Creating a signature file that sells

One of the easiest and most useful tools for marketing on the Internet is called a *signature file,* or a *sig file.* A *signature file* is a text blurb that your system automatically appends to the bottom of your e-mail messages and newsgroup postings. You want your signature file to tell the readers of your message something about you and your business; you can include information such as your company name and how to contact you.

Creating a signature file takes only a little more time than putting your John Hancock on the dotted line. First, you create the signature file itself, as described in these steps:

1. **Open up a text editing program.**

   This example uses Notepad, which comes built in with Windows. If you are a Macintosh user, you can use SimpleText. With either program, a new blank document opens on-screen.

2. **Press and hold down on the hyphen (–) or equal sign (=) key to create a dividing line that will separate your signature from the body of your message.**

   Depending on which symbol you use, a series of hyphens or equal signs forms a broken line. Don't make this line too long, or it will run onto another line, which doesn't look good; 30 to 40 characters is a safe measure.

3. **Type the information about yourself that you want to appear in the signature, pressing Enter after each line.**

   Include such information as your name, job title, company name, e-mail address, and Web site URL, if you have one. A three- or four-line signature is the typical length.

   If you're feeling ambitious at this point, you can press the spacebar to arrange your text in two columns. My agent (who's an online entrepreneur himself) does this with his own signature file, as shown in Figure 9-1.

Figure 9-1: A signature file often uses divider lines and can be arranged in columns to occupy less space on-screen.

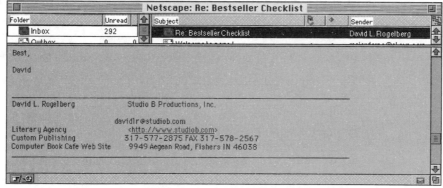

Netscape: Re: Bestseller Checklist

Folder	Unread		Subject			Sender	
Inbox	292		Re: Bestseller Checklist			David L. Rogelberg	
Outbox	0						

Best,

David

_____

David L. Rogelberg   Studio B Productions, Inc.

                      davidlr@studiob.com
Literary Agency   <http://www.studiob.com>
Custom Publishing   317-577-2875 FAX 317-578-2567
Computer Book Cafe Web Site   9949 Aegean Road, Fishers IN 46038

Always include the URL to your business Web site in your signature file, and be sure to include it on its own line. Why? Most e-mail programs will recognize the URL as a Web page by its prefix (http://). When your reader opens your message, the e-mail program displays the URL as a clickable hyperlink that, when clicked, opens your Web page in a Web browser window.

4. **Choose File⇨Save.**

   A dialog box appears, enabling you to name the file and save it in a folder on your hard disk.

5. **Enter a name for your file that ends in the filename extension .txt.**

   This extension identifies your file as a plain text document.

6. **Click on the Save button.**

   Your text file is saved on your computer's hard disk.

Now that you've created a plain-text version of your electronic signature, the next step is to identify that file to the computer programs that you use to send and receive e-mail and newsgroup messages. Doing so enables the programs to make the signature file automatically appear at the bottom of your messages. The procedure for attaching a signature file varies from program to program; the following steps show how to do this using Netscape Messenger for Windows:

1. **Access Messenger's preferences options by choosing Edit⇨ Preferences from the Messenger or Netscape Navigator menu bar.**

   The Preferences dialog box opens. The list of preference topics appears under Category. The specific options change depending on which category you select.

2. **Click on the plus sign (+) next to Mail & Groups.**

   The set of e-mail and newsgroup preference topics expands beneath Mail & Groups.

3. **Single-click on Identity.**

   The word Identity is highlighted, and the Identity preferences appear in the right half of the Preferences dialog box.

4. **Click on the Choose button, next to the Signature File text box.**

   The Signature File dialog box appears. This is a standard Windows navigation dialog box that lets you select folders and files on your computer.

5. **Locate the signature file you created in the previous set of steps by selecting a drive or folder from the Look in drop-down list. When you locate the file, single-click on the filename and then click on the Open button.**

   The Signature File dialog box closes, and you return to the Preference dialog box. The selected file is named in the Signature File text box.

6. Click on OK.

The Preferences dialog box closes, and you return to the Netscape Messenger or Navigator window you were in originally. Your signature file will now be automatically added to your messages.

To test out your new signature file, choose File⇨New⇨Message from the Messenger or Navigator menu bar. A new message composition window opens. Your signature file should appear in the body of the message composition window. You can compose a message by clicking before the signature and starting to type.

Creating simple Web page forms

Forms are a convenient and effective way to conduct customer service. They give customers a means to provide you with feedback as well as essential marketing information. Using forms, you can find out where customers live, how old they are, and so on. Customers can also use forms to sound off and ask questions. The speed of the Internet enables your customers to dash off information right away, and you to immediately send a response that's tailored to the individual's needs and interests.

The two components of Web page forms

Forms consist of two parts, only one of which is visible on a Web page:

- ✔ The visible part includes the text-entry fields, buttons, and check boxes that an author creates with HTML commands.

- ✔ The part you don't see is a computer script that resides on the server that receives the page. This script, which is typically written in a language such as Perl, AppleScript, or C++, processes the form data that a reader submits to a server and presents that data in a format that the owner or operator of the Web site can read and use.

How the data gets to you

What exactly happens when customers connect to a page on your site that contains a form? First, they fill out the text-entry fields, radio buttons, and other areas you have set up. When they finish, they click a button, often marked Submit, in order to transmit, or *post,* the data from the remote computer to your Web site.

A computer script called a Common Gateway Interface (CGI) program receives the data submitted to your site and processes it so that you can read it. The CGI may cause the data to be e-mailed to you, or it may present the data in a text file in an easy-to-read format.

Optionally, you can also create a CGI program that prompts your server to send the user a Web page that acknowledges that you have received the information and thanks them for their feedback.

Writing the scripts that process form data is definitely in the province of Webmasters or computer programmers, and is far beyond the scope of this book. But you don't have to hire someone to write the scripts: You can use a Web page program (such as Microsoft FrontPage or FrontPage Express, or Macromedia Dreamweaver) that not only helps you create a form but also provides you with scripts that process the data for you.

Using FrontPage Express to create a form

You can use the Form Page Wizard that comes with FrontPage Express to create both parts of forms: the data-entry parts (such as text boxes and check boxes) as well as the behind-the-scenes scripts, called *WebBots,* that process form data.

FrontPage Express is bundled with Microsoft Internet Explorer, which is included on the CD-ROM that accompanies this book. You don't have to install FrontPage Express separately. After you install Internet Explorer, you can access FrontPage Express from your Start menu. FrontPage Express is only for Windows users. If you're on a Mac, look into the Macintosh version of Microsoft FrontPage or a very good shareware program called World Wide Web Weaver by Miracle Software, Inc. (www.miracleinc.com).

The first step in setting up a Web page form is determining what information you want to receive from someone who fills out the form. Your Web page creation tool then gives you options for ways to ask for the information you want. You create your form using the following buttons on the Forms toolbar:

`abl`	Single-Line Text Box
	Scrolling Text Box
☑	Check Box
◉	Radio Button
	Drop-Down Menu
	Push Button

All six of these button commands are also available on the FrontPage menu bar under Insert. A seventh command, Image field, is also available under the Insert menu. This option enables you to add an image to the form you're creating. Figure 9-2 shows the most common form fields and the toolbar buttons that you click on in order to insert them in your Web page.

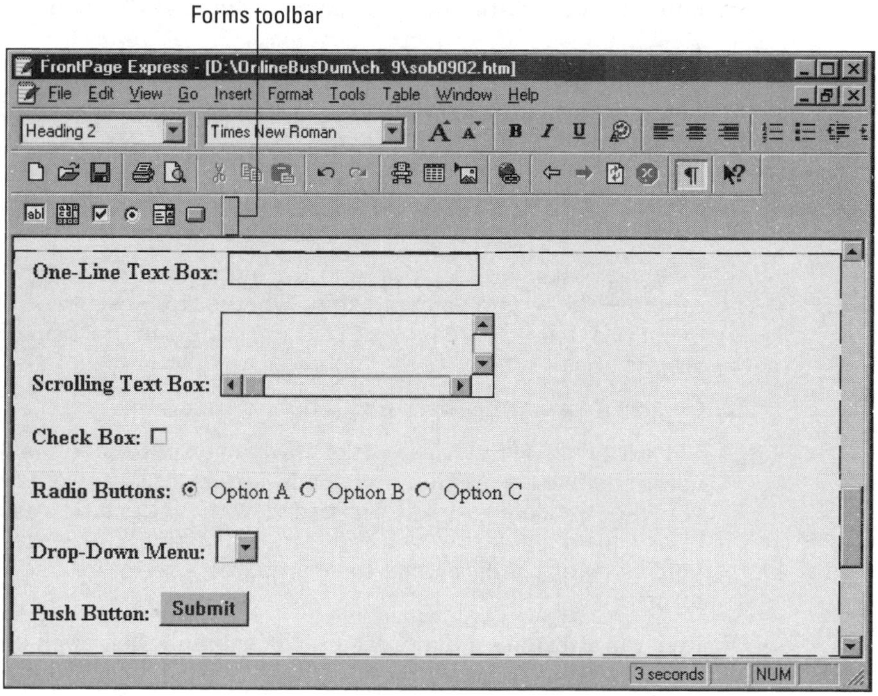

Forms toolbar

Figure 9-2:
FrontPage
Express
provides
you with
menu
options and
toolbar
options for
creating
form
elements.

When you click on any of the buttons in the Forms toolbar, FrontPage Express inserts a dashed, marquee-style box in your document to signify that you are working on Web page form fields rather than normal Web page text.

The Form Page Wizard is a great way to set up a simple form that asks for information from visitors to your Web site. It lets you concentrate on the type of data you want to collect, rather than the buttons and boxes needed to gather it. To create such a form, follow these steps:

1. **Choose Start⇨Programs⇨Internet Explorer⇨FrontPage Express.**

   FrontPage Express starts up and a blank window appears.

2. **Choose File⇨New.**

   The New Page dialog box appears.

3. **Select the Form Page Wizard option and click on OK.**

   The Form Page Wizard dialog box appears.

4. **Click on Next.**

   A new set of options appears in the next Form Page Wizard dialog box. (You can click on Finish at any time to see your form and begin editing it.)

5. **Enter a URL and title for your page in the next dialog box.**

   The URL for the page, in this case, is simply the filename of the document that contains the form. You don't need to type the http:// prefix. Just type form.htm, or whatever you want to name the document.

   The title is what appears at the top of the browser window. Choose something simple, like Registration Form or Contact Form.

6. **Click on Next to move to the next page of the wizard.**

   This page asks you how you want the information to be formatted. For example, the wizard wants to know whether to present the list of questions that you plan to ask your customers in the form of paragraphs or as a bulleted or numbered list.

7. **Choose a formatting option and then click on Next.**

   The next page of the wizard asks how you want to save the data that users submit to you. This decision is important because it controls how you view the data yourself. You can view the information as a Web page or as a plain text file, or you can use a CGI script to process the data for you, if you or a programmer have prepared a script for use with this form.

8. **Pick the alternative that's easiest for you and then click on Next.**

   A page appears telling you that the form creation process is complete.

9. **Click on Finish.**

   The wizard window closes and your form appears in the FrontPage Express window.

When you finish, be sure to add your own description of the form and any special instructions at the top of the Web page. Also add your copyright and contact information at the bottom of the page. Follow the pattern you've set on other pages on your site.

Be sure to change the background of the form page from the default gray that the wizard provides. See Chapter 5 for more specific instructions on changing the background of Web pages you create.

Turning Customers into Members

Think about what it means to be a customer at a typical retail store: You go to the store, make a purchase, and then leave. You don't go back until you need to buy something else or make a return. Now think about what it means to be a member of a club or other organization: You meet with the group on a regular basis, hold discussions, and attend special events. You're part of a community.

Good customer service can make your customers feel like members of a community — the community of satisfied individuals who regularly use your goods and services. The following sections describe some ways to make your customers feel like members, returning to your site on a regular basis and interacting with a community of individuals with similar interests.

A small business can turn its individual customers into a cohesive group by starting its own discussion group on the Internet. Discussion groups work particularly well if you're promoting a particular type of product or if you and your customers are involved in a provocative or even controversial area of interest.

You can create three kinds of discussion groups:

- **A local group:** Some universities create their own discussion areas for their students. Other large companies set aside groups for their employees. Outsiders don't gain access because the groups are not on the Internet, but rather on a local server within the organization.

- **A Usenet newsgroup:** Individuals are allowed to create an Internet-wide discussion group in the alt or biz categories of Usenet without having to go through the time-consuming application and approval process needed to create other newsgroups.

- **A Web-based discussion group:** Microsoft FrontPage includes easy-to-use wizards that enable you to create a discussion area on your business Web site. users can access the area from their Web browsers without having to use special discussion-group software.

Of these three alternatives, the first isn't practical for your business purposes, so the following sections focus on the second two.

In addition to newsgroups, many large corporations also hold interactive chats on subjects related to their area of business. These chats are often moderated by experts in their fields. Small businesses can hold chats, too. The most practical way is to set up a chat room on a site that hosts chat-based discussions. Chapter 17 briefly describes this process. For more information about setting up a free chat room with GeoCities, see my book *Small Business Internet For Dummies*, published by IDG Books Worldwide, Inc., or visit GeoCities at `www.geocities.com`.

Starting an alt discussion group

Usenet is a system of communication on the Internet that enables individual computer users to participate in group discussions about topics of mutual interest. Internet newsgroups have what's referred to as a *hierarchical structure.* Most groups belong to one of seven main categories: comp, misc, news, rec, sci, soc, and talk. The name of the category appears at the beginning of the group's name, such as `rec.food.drink.coffee`. This section discusses a category that's just about as popular as the seven I just mentioned: the `alt` category, which enables individuals like you to establish their own newsgroups.

In my opinion, the `biz` discussion groups aren't taken seriously because they are widely populated by people promoting get-rich-quick schemes and simply blowing their own horns. The `alt` groups, though they can certainly address some wild and crazy topics, are at least as well-known and often address serious topics. Plus, the process of setting up an `alt` group is well documented.

The prefix `alt` didn't originally stand for *alternative,* although it has come to mean that. The term originally stood for Anarchists, Lunatics, and Terrorists. These days, `alt` is a catch-all category where anyone can start a group, if others show interest in the creator's proposal.

The first step to creating your own alt discussion group is to launch your newsgroup software and access the group called `news.announce. newgroups`. This area contains general instructions on starting your own Usenet newsgroup. Also look in `news.answers` for the message "How to Start a New Usenet Newsgroup."

For instructions specific to starting a group in the `alt` category, scroll through the long lists of postings in `alt.answers` and locate the message entitled "So You Want to Create an Alt Newsgroup." (You can also find this message at `www.cis.ohio-state.edu/~barr/alt-creation-guide. html`.) Follow the instructions contained in this message to set up your own discussion group. Basically, the process involves the following steps:

1. You write up a brief proposal describing the purpose of the group you want to create and including an e-mail message where people can respond with comments. The proposal also contains the name of your group in the correct form (`alt.groupname.moreinfo.moreinfo`). Try to keep the group name short and official-looking if it is for business purposes.

2. You submit the proposal to the newsgroup `alt.config`.

3. You gather feedback to your proposal by e-mail.

4. You send a special message called a *control message* to the news server that gives you access to Usenet. The exact form of the message varies from server to server, so you need to consult with your ISP on how to compose the message correctly.

5. Wait a while (a few days or weeks) as news administrators (the people who operate news servers at ISPs around the world) decide whether or not to adopt your request and add your group to their list of newsgroups.

Before you try to start your own group, look through the Big 7 categories (comp, misc, news, rec, sci, soc, and talk) to make sure that a group devoted to your topic doesn't already exist.

Creating a Web discussion area with FrontPage

There's a reason why Microsoft FrontPage is a popular tool for creating Web sites. It lets you create Web page content that you would otherwise need complicated scripts to tackle. One example is the program's Discussion Group Wizard, which lets you create Web pages on which your members (as opposed to customers, remember?) can exchange messages and carry on a series of back-and-forth responses (called *threads*) on different topics. Newcomers to the group can also view articles arranged by a table of contents and accessible by a searchable index.

Don't confuse the program discussed in this section (Microsoft FrontPage) with the free version of the program called FrontPage Express. You have to purchase Microsoft FrontPage, because no demo or beta version of the software is available at the time of this writing. I've seen the program advertised for $137 with a $40 mail-in rebate. At that price, FrontPage is a bargain, considering all that it lets you do. The program comes in versions for Macintosh and Windows platforms.

Creating the discussion area

Follow these steps to set up your own discussion group with Microsoft FrontPage:

1. **After you install the program, start up FrontPage by choosing Start➪Programs➪Microsoft FrontPage.**

   FrontPage is actually a suite of different programs. The program that appears when you first start is called FrontPage Explorer. This application lets you create or edit entire Web sites.

   The Getting Started with Microsoft FrontPage dialog box appears first. This dialog box lets you open a new *web* (that is, a group of interlinked documents that together comprise a Web site) of Web pages or use one of the built-in templates and wizards that come with FrontPage. These templates are predesigned, customizable Web sites that save you the trouble of designing pages from scratch.

2. **To use FrontPage's Discussion Group Wizard, click on the From a Wizard or Template button, next to the section Create a New FrontPage Web. Then click on OK.**

The New FrontPage Wizard dialog box appears. This dialog box presents you, in the big field labeled Template or Wizard, with a list of preconfigured Web sites.

3. **Select Discussion Web Wizard from the Template or Wizard list, and then click on OK.**

The first of a series of Discussion Web Wizard dialog boxes appears. The first dialog box lets you specify the location of your discussion web. By default, the server you specified when you set up Microsoft FrontPage is listed in the box under Web Server.

If you don't have authoring access on a Web server, type in the full name and path of a folder on your local disk. If you enter a path to a folder that does not yet exist, FrontPage creates the folder for you. You can then set up your Web pages on your computer and test them out before you publish them on your remote Internet hosting service's Web server.

4. **In the Name of New FrontPage Web field, enter a name for your discussion group.**

The next Discussion Web Wizard dialog box appears. Go through this and the subsequent dialog boxes, answering the questions they present you with in order to determine what kind of discussion group you're going to have.

At any time, as you go through the series of Discussion Web Wizard pages, you can click on Finish to complete the process.

5. **When you're done, the pre-set pages for your discussion web appear in the FrontPage Explorer main window (see Figure 9-3).**

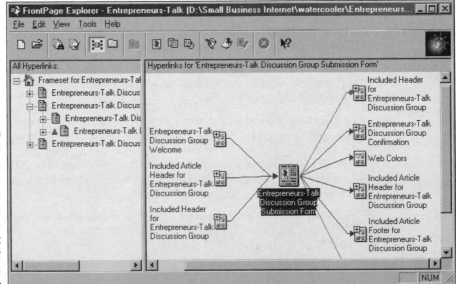

Figure 9-3:
FrontPage's
Discussion
Group
Wizard
helps you
create a set
of pages for
your group.

The left side of the FrontPage Explorer window in Figure 9-3 shows the arrangement of the discussion documents. The right side of the window is a visual map that shows how the discussion group is arranged and how the pages are linked to each other.

When you set up a discussion area with FrontPage, you have the option of designing your pages as a *frameset,* or a set of Web pages that has been subdivided into separate frames. To find out more about frames, see Chapter 5.

Editing the discussion pages

After you use the Discussion Group Wizard to create your pages, the next step is to edit the pages so that they have the content you want. You do this using another FrontPage component application, FrontPage Editor.

With your newly created pages open in FrontPage Explorer, you can access the editor by double-clicking on the icon for the Welcome page in your discussion web. Whatever page you double-click on opens in a new FrontPage Editor window.

The toolbar buttons and menu items in FrontPage Editor let you alter the appearance of your Web pages. For example, it's a good idea to change the default gray background of your pages to make them look more professional. To do so, follow these steps:

1. **Choose Format⇨Background.**

   The Page Properties dialog box appears.

2. **Click on the Specify Background and Colors button.**

   This step activates the other formatting options in the dialog box, including the Background image check box or the Hyperlink, Visited Hyperlink, Active Hyperlink, Background, and Text drop-down menus that enable you to assign colors to specific elements of the page.

3. **Click on the triangle next to Background and then select a color from the drop-down menu.**

4. **Click on OK.**

   The Page Properties dialog box closes and you return to FrontPage Editor, where your page appears with a new background color.

In addition to changing the background color, you should also add a few sentences to the beginning of the Welcome page that you have just created in order to tell participants more about the purpose and scope of the discussion group. You can add text by clicking anywhere on the page and typing.

To edit more pages in your discussion group, choose File➪Open. The Open File dialog box appears with a list of all the documents that make up your discussion group. You can double-click on a file's name in order to edit it. When you finish editing files, choose File➪Save to save your work.

To see how your discussion pages look, use the FrontPage Editor's Preview feature. Choose File➪Preview in Browser, and the page you've been editing appears in your browser window (see Figure 9-4).

Posting your discussion area

The final step is to transfer your discussion web of pages from your own computer to your Web host's site on the Internet. Many Web hosting services support one-step file transfers with Microsoft FrontPage. If you plan to use FrontPage often, it's a good idea to locate a host that offers this support.

With one-step file transfers, you simply connect to the Internet, choose File➪Publish FrontPage Web from the Explorer menu bar, and enter the URL of your directory on your host's Web server where your Web pages are published. Click on OK, and your files are immediately transferred.

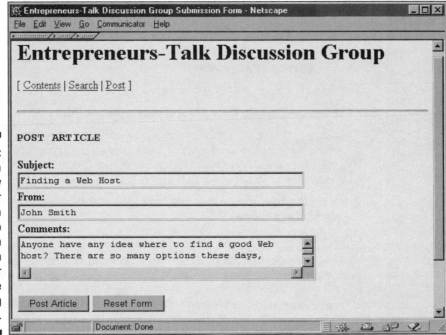

Figure 9-4:
You can preview your discussion group pages on your own computer before putting them online.

Chapter 10

Market, Technical, and Business Research

● ●

In This Chapter

▶ Finding the information you need online

▶ Getting to know your target market

▶ Gathering business statistics

▶ Obtaining technical support

● ●

*I*nformation is the coin of the realm when it comes to starting a business. Merchants who know the competition, make the right contacts, and are well acquainted with the ideal market have a far better chance of success than those who fly by the seats of their proverbial pants, go on gut instinct, or any number of other clichés.

In addition, bankers, investors, and partners may require you to provide measurable data related to your online endeavor. Because e-commerce is still so new, you may be asked to prepare a report that explains not only what you want to do, but also why you chose to start an online business in the first place and how many online businesses achieve success.

This chapter shows you how to support your new Internet presence by becoming an online researcher. Read on to discover search techniques that come in handy whether you are in the planning stages or are already an experienced businessperson. You can also find out how to use the *entire* Internet, not just the Web, to find just about anything you need.

"Online" Means More Than "On the Web"

The Web is the fancy newcomer to the Internet, but it is by no means the only resource when it comes to finding information online. Vast amounts of data are stored on parts of the Net that use little or no graphics, such as FTP and Gopher sites.

Still other online resources are independent of the Internet itself. These include the proprietary services (such as Dialog, LEXIS-NEXIS, and Dow Jones Interactive) that you subscribe to and access by dialing directly to their computers. The following sections describe how you can use Internet-based and proprietary services to research your market and general Internet business topics.

Gopher: No frills information on the Internet

Before the debut of Web-based graphics and multimedia effects, one of the most popular ways of organizing information online was an area of the Internet called *Gopherspace*. Gopher is still around, and it provides a simple, menu-based way of storing and retrieving information online.

Compared to a Web site, a Gopher site is almost Zen-like in its simplicity. Information is presented in little file folders with plain-type descriptions on a plain background. If you want to have a look, you can access a Gopher site with a Web browser. An obvious starting point is `gopher://gopher.tc. umn.edu`. This site, shown in Figure 10-1, belongs to the University of Minnesota, the birthplace of Gopher (which was named for the university's mascot).

For a "pure" Gopher experience, you can download a Gopher client program. This allows you to access Gopher-based information without a Web browser. From the main University of Minnesota Gopher page, shown in Figure 10-1, click on the <u>Information About Gopher</u> link, and then click on the <u>Commercial Gopher Software</u> link. A page appears with links to WinGopher, GUIDE for Macintosh, and other Gopher programs.

Figure 10-1:
You "burrow" into a Gopher site by opening folders and reading text files.

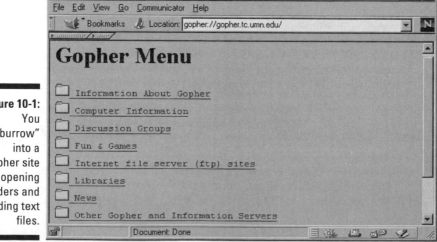

You burrow into a Gopher site with your Web browser like this: First, you open a folder by clicking on the adjacent highlighted hypertext link (or by clicking on the folder itself). When a new page appears, containing another set of folders, you open one by clicking on the link next to it. Repeat the process until you reach a page that contains individual documents (as indicated by icons that look like text documents). Click on the link next to a text document, and the text appears.

What, exactly, can you find using these old-style information tools? For one thing, Gopher servers still contain the contents of many libraries and library catalogs, many of which are not accessible from Web pages. You can also access a good number of electronic books and journals through Gopher. To access all these resources from the main University of Minnesota page, click on the Libraries link.

Mining for FTP treasures

If you're in need of some low-cost, easy-to-use software for your business, and you can't find what you want on this book's CD, you only need to start digging through an FTP site.

FTP sites use File Transfer Protocol (FTP) to provide software programs and other information. FTP is a quick and easy way of transferring data from one computer to another over a network. Some FTP sites only permit access to individuals with an approved username and password. However, many *anonymous FTP sites* let anyone log in and copy files.

You access FTP sites either by using the Swiss Army Knife of Internet programs — your handy-dandy Web browser — or by using an FTP program specially designed for this purpose. One such program, Fetch, is shown in Figure 10-2.

Figure 10-2: FTP programs like Fetch aren't pretty, but they help you quickly transfer programs from an FTP site to your own computer.

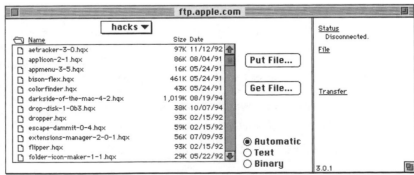

One of the most popular FTP programs is CuteFTP for Windows, by GlobalScape, Inc., which you can download for a free 30-day trial period from www.cuteftp.com and then register for a $34.95 shareware fee. On the Macintosh side, the preeminent program is called Fetch, which was developed at Dartmouth University. You can download Fetch from any Mac shareware site, or by entering the following address in your Web browser's Go To box: ftp://ftp.dartmouth.edu/pub/mac.

You have two alternatives for locating business software or other goodies on FTP sites:

✔ **A Web front door:** Software archives like Shareware.com and Jumbo let you search their contents using FTP from the familiar surroundings of your Web browser window. Typically, you enter the name of the program you're looking for, select your computer operating system from a drop-down menu, and either press Enter or click on a Submit button. In a few seconds, a list of programs that match your search terms appears.

✔ **An Archie search:** In this case, Archie is not a comic book character, but a server that compiles the contents of anonymous FTP sites around the world into a database that you can search quickly if you are looking for a particular program or file.

If you're in a hurry and want to stick with your Web browser, go to one of the shareware sites that provide an easy Web interface for visitors. Try Stroud's consummate Winsock Apps List, which is a great source for Windows shareware programs. This site is so popular that it has several *mirrors* (alternate locations) on the Net. Two of the URLs for the Winsock Apps List are cws.internet.com and cws.icorp.net. If one location is busy, try another.

As Figure 10-3 shows, mining through the wealth of resources on Stroud's site is easy: Just send your Web browser to the home page. You can search through indexes that contain many categories of software by clicking on the buttons labeled *Windows 95/98/NT Apps,* or *Windows 3.x Apps.* Or you can enter the name of the program you want in the Search box at the bottom of the screen.

Virtually all the big shareware sites contain software that's especially designed for businesses, including accounting programs, spreadsheets, billing/customer tracking packages, and more. The following addresses take you directly to business software for Windows users:

✔ Shareware.com (www.shareware.com)

✔ The Jumbo! Download Network (www.jumbo.com)

✔ Tucows, the Ultimate Collection of Winsock Software (www.tucows.com)

Figure 10-3:
If you
search a
software
archive
from the
Web, you
don't
have to
download
or launch
special FTP
software.

Macintosh users can try out a cool program called Anarchie Pro, which speeds up the process of locating software on FTP sites. Anarchie Pro was created by Peter Lewis, and is available as shareware for $35 from www.stairways.com.

Using Telnet to search library card catalogs

Telnet is a program that takes you back to the early days of the Internet — the days when you logged on to the Net by using a terminal. (Telnet, in fact, is a terminal emulation program that lets you connect to another computer the way a modem does.) So why use Telnet at all, if it's such bare-bones computing? Because libraries around the world store their databases on IBM mainframe computers, and Telnet is one of the only ways to connect to those libraries from the Internet.

If you ever need to look up a book in a library practically anywhere in the world, first check your computer to see if you have a version of Telnet already. (Many ISPs hand out Telnet along with other Internet software when you first sign up for access.) If you don't have Telnet, you can download a copy from one of the shareware FTP archives listed in the previous section.

Then, from the comfort of your user-friendly Web browser, go to Galaxy's great index of library catalogs around the world (galaxy.einet.net/hytelnet/SITES1.html). Follow the links to the specific library you want to research. When you find a library, click on a link that lets you access the catalog by Telnet. (For example, if you want to read the Cleveland Public Library's catalog, click on the Telnet LIBRARY.CPL.ORG link.) Your Telnet program launches, and you access the catalog. At that point, you can follow the directions on-screen to find what you're looking for.

Proprietary online database services

Professional database services, such as LEXIS-NEXIS, Dialog, and Dow Jones Interactive, are heavy-duty search services that offer a vast gold mine of information for the online entrepreneur, if you're willing to pay the price of admission.

Although you can access these databases from the Internet and search parts of these services using your Web browser, the contents are independent of the Internet. In most cases, you have to subscribe to a service and pay a monthly fee for access.

If you want to subscribe, you dial up their computers directly:

- **LEXIS-NEXIS (**www.lexis-nexis.com**):** This favorite of law students and lawyers alike is a two-part service. LEXIS offers legal information, and NEXIS offers a vast collection of publications. Together, they boast 1.8 billion documents in their databases. LEXIS-NEXIS Express is designed for smaller business and individuals; call 1-800-843-6476 to find out more.

- **Dialog (**www.dialog.com**):** Run by The Dialog Corporation, this service offers extensive databases on business and the law, current events, science, technology, the environment, arts and letters, and general reference. It claims to be 50 times the size of the Web itself. Check www.dialog.com/pricing for current rates.

- **Dow Jones Interactive (**www.djnr.com**):** This service provides you with *The Wall Street Journal,* plus company and market research reports and a clipping service.

The advantages of using one of these services is that their search engines are often more powerful than those on the Web, the information tends to be more accurate and reliable, and you can cover a vast number of information sources with a single keyword request.

Becoming an Online Power Searcher

The Internet is a constantly changing universe. A search can yield exactly the information you need, or countless useless returns. And the results of your search can differ from one day to the next. Your time is valuable. This section focuses on time-saving tips for using search services more effectively to get the information you want.

Web search engines

Search engines are not all interchangeable. Each specializes in a different method of organizing and accessing information. Yet they all seem to be easy to use. Just enter a few keywords and *voilà!* You have what you want, right? Not necessarily. Using search engines effectively takes a little skill.

Web-based search engines use complex programs called *robots* or *spiders* to retrieve information from the Net. Each one indexes that information differently. The three general types of search engines are

- ✔ **Internet-wide:** Most of the big search services like WebCrawler and AltaVista let you search not only the Web but also Usenet newsgroups and more. Some let you submit keywords that look through specialized information such as weather reports or classified ads.

- ✔ **Multiple-search:** A few sites on the Web are set up to let you search more than one search service's database at a time. See the upcoming section called "Multiple search sites."

- ✔ **Specialized:** Some utilities focus on a particular part of the online world, such as newsgroups, individual Web pages, companies, and much more. See the upcoming section called "Specialized search services."

Some of the Internet search giants (including Lycos, Excite, and Infoseek; see the Internet Directory section of this book for a more detailed list) index Web page contents by concentrating on the major headings. Others record the first 50 or so words on the pages. Still others record a combination of both. What's common to all searchers is that they have you enter keywords in order to specify what you're looking for. And because they all operate a little differently, it can be especially helpful to use more than one search service at a given time.

Multiple search sites

Multiple search sites are Web sites that search more than one search service at a time. You enter a keyword or words in a single form, and the site submits your search terms to a variety of services.

What makes a good keyword?

A *keyword* is a word or series of words that you submit to a search engine by means of an online form. The choice of keyword is important; the more specific the information you provide to the search service, the better your results. Here are some tips on how to pick good keywords:

✔ Combine a string of specific nouns that are related to the topic rather than a word or two. If you're looking for loans, for example, type **small business loans finance grants** rather than just **business loans**.

✔ Use connector words such as *and* and *or* that help refine a search. The connector *and* makes the search less inclusive, whereas *or* widens the search considerably. For example, a search for **business and trademarks** turns up only pages that contain both words used together, whereas a search for **business *or* trademarks** turns up many more pages — those that contain the word *business* plus those that contain the word *trademarks*.

✔ I often find it helpful to enclose search terms in quotation marks. Some services (like AltaVista) return pages that contain the exact terms contained within the quotation marks. If you're looking for the Web site for the Better Business Bureau, a search for **"The Better Business Bureau"** will probably give you the results more quickly than **better business bureau**.

Some of these tips apply to one service, and some to another. Check each searcher's Help pages to get more specific information on how that server uses keywords.

The good news about multiple search sites is that they save you time and effort, but the bad news is that they use only those features that are common to all the search engines they cover. So you can't take advantage of the unique features of the various search engines. Multiple search sites also only return a limited number of results from each search engine.

The following are a few of the well-known multiple search engines:

✔ **Internet Sleuth:** This site (`www.isleuth.com`) lets you pick up to six of the main search engines, or you have the option of running your query through hundreds of specialized databases, guides, and references in particular subject areas (see Figure 10-4). In order to find the cream of the crop, you can run your search through up to six of the Web sites that review new Web sites, such as "The Best of the Web."

✔ **Galaxy:** This site (`galaxy.tradewave.com`) allows you to burrow down from general categories to the exact topic you want. Information includes articles and references to other sites and archives. You can extend your search beyond the Web to Gopher and Telnet sites.

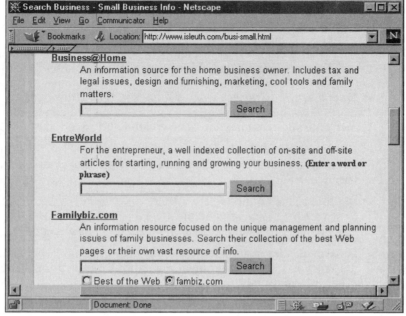

Figure 10-4:
The Internet Sleuth's Small Business Info page lets you search many databases of interest to entrepreneurs.

✔ **Savvy Search:** This site (`guaraldi.cs.colostate.edu:2000/form`) is an experimental project based at Colorado State University. Its main claim to fame is that it offers numerous ways to tune your search, and it presents you with a "Search Plan" which predicts which of the search engines it uses is likely to produce the best results.

✔ **Ask Jeeves:** This site (`www.askjeeves.com`) lets you ask actual questions in plain English. You enter your question, and Jeeves lists your question along with six or seven questions that "he" can answer that most closely resemble your question. (If you're lucky, Jeeves can answer your exact question.) Then Jeeves shows you the search engines he has researched on your behalf and the number of hits from each, which you can then peruse at your leisure.

✔ **ProFusion:** This site (`www.profusion.com`) has an interesting updating service which notes what you're interested in and notifies you of any new information it finds on a weekly basis. You register a query and provide ProFusion with your name, a password, your e-mail address, and the frequency with which to rerun your query. The service sends you periodic updates by e-mail.

✔ **Dogpile:** This colorfully named site (`www.dogpile.com`) can run your query through up to 25 search engines, including general search engines, specialized search engines, and FTP file-locating programs. This site works best for very simple searches.

Specialized search services

Some search services cover a particular area of interest rather than the entire Internet. Specialized search services are available for career hunters, medical researchers, software developers, and businesses too numerous to list here. Here are several useful services for the online businessperson:

- **MapQuest:** This service (www.mapquest.com) allows you to browse a world atlas and zoom in on an exact address. You can link from your own Web site to a map you have created and saved at MapQuest.

- **Yahoo! People Search:** This online "white pages" (people.yahoo.com) allows you to search for the e-mail addresses and phone numbers of individuals.

- **BigBook:** This online "yellow pages" (www.bigbook.com) enables you to search for businesses online, by name or by category, in a particular city or state. You can also search by zip code or area code.

- **FedWorld:** This search service (www.fedworld.gov) is dedicated to helping you locate government regulations, publications, statistics, and other information.

- **SciCentral:** This site (www.scicentral.com) provides a gateway to more than 50,000 online resources in the sciences, including engineering, chemistry, and physics.

You can even find a specialized search site that catalogs the ever expanding number of search engines. Beaucoup (beaucoup.com) has a mind-boggling collection of more than 1,200 listings of search engines, directories, and indexes from across the world, in categories such as business, malls, classifieds, science/technology, and employment.

Internet subject catalogs

Like a teenager's bedroom, the Web will probably never be a neat and perfectly organized place. Nevertheless, some Mary Poppins-like organizations have attempted to tidy things up, arranging Web sites and other resources into a their own categorized indexes, called *subject catalogs*.

Subject catalogs are good when you know what type of information you want, but you don't know the names of any sites that may have it. You can burrow into a particular subject that's covered by the index, clicking on page after page of links. Eventually, you come to a list of sites that address the subject you want to research.

Subject catalogs also differ from search engines in that they don't claim to be comprehensive; rather, they only include what they consider to be most important. Real human beings make those decisions, instead of the computerized, mathematical, or linguistic formulas that drive search engines.

Here are some subject catalogs to start with if you don't exactly know what you're looking for, or if you're looking for general background on a topic:

- **Yahoo!:** In addition to being a prominent Internet search engine, this site (www.yahoo.com) is also the most well-known subject catalog and one of the single most frequently visited sites on the Internet.

- **Galaxy:** This site (galaxy.tradewave.com) calls itself "The professional's guide to a world of information." Like Yahoo!, Galaxy is a subject catalog as well as a multiple Internet search site.

- **Argus Clearninghouse:** This site (clearinghouse.net) is a subject catalog of subject catalogs with a scholarly bent. No fluff here.

- **The Mining Company:** This site (www.theminingcompany.com) is an unusually personal guide to the Internet. The company hires experts (called *guides*) not only to choose the sites for the various subjects, but also to interact with you in the form of newsletters, e-mail, bulletin boards, and chats. Instead of wading though the vast sea of information on the Web, you can go right to an expert and get the lowdown on whatever it is you want to know.

Virtual reference resources

Sometimes, you just need to get your hands on a fact — the kind you can find at the library buried in a standard reference book like a dictionary, almanac, encyclopedia, or atlas. Happily, many reference resources are available online for when you need just such a fact or statistic:

- **The Internet Public Library:** This Reference Center (www.ipl.org/ref) is organized around an image map. You can click on the labels in the image to find information on any of the listed subject areas. Clicking on the Reference portion of the image map takes you to the general reference section of the library, where you can find dictionaries, encyclopedias, geography, census data, and more.

- **The Virtual Reference Desk:** This site (thorplus.lib.purdue.edu/reference) includes a listing of reference books by category. The categories include Zip and International Country Codes, Phone Books and Area Codes, Information Technology, and Technical Dictionaries.

- **AOL's Reference page:** If you use America Online, you don't have to connect to the Web right away. Just sign on to AOL and enter the keyword **Reference** to go to the AOL Reference page, from which you can find more specific types of information.

- **World Factbook:** This site (www.odci.gov/cia/publications/factbook/index.html) is brought to you courtesy of the CIA! It contains up-do-date information on any country in the world, just in case you have international aspirations for your online business.

Keeping up with the news

You may never have to haul a pile of old newspapers to the recycling bin again, and you may be able to watch less television, too, because an overwhelming number of news services and resources have gone online to help you stay current.

Online versions of newspapers and broadcast news organizations sometimes offer features, such as forums, archives, and expanded background information, that aren't available in their traditional mediums.

Rather than suggesting specific online news outlets, I list two organizations that serve as clearinghouses for media sites on the Internet:

- ✔ **AJR Newslink:** This site (www.newslink.org) offers links to print and broadcast news sources, and even includes some alternative publications and college newspapers.

- ✔ **NewsIndex:** This site (www.newsindex.com) connects you to the current edition of hundred of U.S. and international newspapers.

Finding Statistics and Business Resources

Everyone needs some background information from time to time, if only to impress friends at a party by uttering clever quips like, "Did you know that 56 percent of people who shop online now use credit cards, and this number is expected to rise to 70 percent by the year 2000?"

Whether you want to be the life of the party or need to prepare an urgent request for funding, you can find the information you need online. This section shows you ways to gather statistics about online shoppers and doing business on the Internet in general.

Show me the money

You may have a brilliant idea for an online business, but you need some capital to make it all happen. The following sites can help you locate the green stuff you need:

- ✔ **America's Business Funding Directory:** This useful site (www.businessfinance.com/index.shtml) provides over 13,000 funding sources for businesses.

- ✔ **Idea Cafe's Financing Your Business:** This friendly, lighthearted site (www.ideacafe.com/getmoney/FINANCING.shtml) is devoted to getting the money you need for your online business. Pages on the site cover borrowing money, getting investors, and creative sources of financing.

The commercial online services are a rich source of online chats and other discussions related to business topics. If you use America Online, be sure to click on the button labeled Tools and Reference at the bottom of the Your Business Front Page. The Tools and Reference page has links that enable you to do company research, get stock quotes, and find other data. If you're on Prodigy, check out Your Business Bulletin Board, a forum for home-office workers. Jump (Ctrl+J) **your business** to get started.

Who's shopping online?

You may want to know just how fast the online shopping market is growing, and who is doing the shopping. Such information can help you design your Web site for maximum effect, or help you write a report for your investors. Much of this kind of data is collected by for-profit companies who charge thousands of dollars for their reports on this hot new area of market research. However, you can find some resources online for free:

- ✔ **NUA Internet Surveys:** This site (www.nua.ie/surveys) provides up-to-date articles and statistics on online shopping and the growth of e-commerce worldwide.
- ✔ **eMarketer:** This site (www.e-land.com/estats/welcome.html) hosts eStats, which, in turn, provides current articles and statistics on online shopping, e-commerce trends, and usage patterns.

General Internet and Web statistics

If you have to generate a business plan for a loan, or if you just need to convince Uncle Harry to lend you the money, you may want some general statistics on the Web and the Internet to make your presentation more professional. Look for such stats at the following sites:

- ✔ **Georgia Tech's Graphics, Visualization & Usability Centers WWW User Surveys:** The survey results are free to the public at www.cc.gatech.edu/gvu/user_surveys.
- ✔ **Cyberatlas:** This site (www.cyberatlas.com) is great for Internet and Web-related statistics and demographics.

Researching Computer and Tech Topics

As an online businessperson, you know that your computer equipment is critical. You can't afford to be off-line for an extended period due to technical difficulties. Yet you don't have a huge budget for technical support. This section suggests some places where you can find help with your technical problems.

Finding help with hardware glitches

When your computer stops working, so does your business. So it helps to have a place to turn for information and troubleshooting before you unplug the thing and take it in for repair.

- ✔ **The PC Guide:** This online resource (www.pcguide.com) is jam-packed with free information for the PC user. This site provides an introduction to the PC, a systems and components reference guide, a system care guide, a troubleshooting and repair guide, and a technical resource guide. This is a good site to bookmark and hope you never need.

- ✔ **MacFixit:** This site (macfixit.pair.com) has that little bomb we all dread in its logo, but it is indeed a wonderful place for the stressed-out Mac owner. This wonderful site, maintained by Ted Landau, offers a download library of troubleshooting-related freeware and shareware, reports on specific troubleshooting topics, and links to other sites where you can get help.

Anyone who has lost data to computer crashes, power outages, and disk failures can attest to the importance of backing up your files. Hardware failures can result in data loss, and for a business owner who maintains client records, tax files, and other important records, losing data can be disastrous. Check your particular system to find out what back-up options are available to you.

Overcoming networking dilemmas

If you have networked computers, you have your own set of unique problems. When you experience problems sharing or copying files between machines, your cabling, network cards, hubs, or networking software may be at fault.

If your network is getting you down (or, indeed, is down, as in not working), you can check out the following sites before calling in that expensive consultant. However, in my personal experience, there's no substitute for an expert technician when a network doesn't work. Don't be reluctant to call in help if you can't solve the problem yourself.

If the problem is a simple one, you may find the answer here:

- ✔ **Optimized Engineering:** This for-profit company (www.optimized. com/LIBRARY.htm) provides useful resources on its Web site. Its Library page includes an online encyclopedia of networking articles, technical information, networking tips, and a bibliography on networking.

- ✔ **Charles Spurgeon's Ethernet Web Site:** This site (wwwhost.ots. utexas.edu/ethernet) provides extensive information about Ethernet (IEEE 802.3) local area network (LAN) technology, including quick reference guides, FAQs, troubleshooting numbers, and buyers' guides.

Chapter 11

Advertising and Publicity

● ●

In This Chapter

▶ Free advertising strategies for online businesses

▶ Using newsgroups and mailing lists

▶ Keeping an electronic address book

▶ Linking and partnering with other businesses

▶ Placing banner ads

● ●

*W*hen you were very young, you raised your voice to get attention. Later, you learned to raise your hand so your teacher would call on you. Now that you're online, people can't hear your voice or see your hand. So how does a small business owner like yourself induce people to listen to what you have to say or consider what you have to offer?

The good news is that publicity on the Internet is something you can do yourself without spending lots of money. Plus, your marketing efforts can truly bring about effective results. In fact, the most successful advertising strategies often involve one individual connecting with another. Targeted, personalized public relations efforts work online because cyberspace is a personal place where intimate communication is possible. Blanketed advertising strategies of the sort you see in other media (notably, display ads, commercials, or billboards) are expensive and don't always work for online businesses.

This chapter describes cost-effective, do-it-yourself advertising techniques for the online entrepreneur with a fledgling business on a tight budget. Usually, the more effort you put into attracting attention to your business, the more visits you receive. So roll up your sleeves, raise your hand, open your mouth, and prepare to be heard!

Developing a Marketing Strategy

In case you haven't figured it out by now, half the battle with running a successful online business is developing a plan for what you want to do. The following sections describe two strategies for making your company name more visible to online customers.

Building a brand

In business-speak, branding does not refer to taking a hot iron to an animal's hide. *Branding* is the process of raising awareness of a company's name and logo through advertising, public relations, or other means.

The Web is a great place for developing a business brand. Web users tend to be fixated on their computer screens while they work. They sit only a foot or two from the screen. They interact with Web sites as they never do with television shows. A study conducted in June 1997 by MBInteractive and reported on the Internet Advertising Bureau Web site (www.iab.net) measured the impact of Web-based advertising on more than 16,000 respondents. The study found that Web advertising is "supported and liked" by consumers, and that brands advertised on the Web were seen as being "forward-thinking."

But don't rely on your Web page alone to spread your name. Make use of the whole Internet, including e-mail, online communities, contests, and promotions. Remember, on the Net, your goal is to promote your brand in many different ways.

What does this mean for a fledgling business like yours? For the most part, it means being conscious of the need to develop name awareness of your company and to realize that doing so may take a long time. You probably don't have thousands of dollars to spend on banner ads. Start with simple things, such as making sure that your signature files, your domain name, and your e-mail address all refer to your company name as closely as possible.

In some cases, "dot-com" domain names turn into effective brand names themselves, such as Amazon.com or shareware.com. Don't get creative with your spelling, though. Spellings that differ from the common English, such as niteline.com, are difficult for people to remember, and people who only hear the name spoken won't know how to type it in or search for it properly. Hyphens, such as in WBX-TV-Bozo@station.com, are another no-no because, again, their location won't be obvious.

If the perfect domain name for your business is already taken, consider adding a "cyber" prefix or suffix to your domain name. For example, if your company name is something common, like Housing Services, but housing.com and housingservices.com are both taken, try housingweb .com or housingonline.com. That way, the Web address is still easy to recall and associate with your business.

Blanketing versus targeting

The big industrial fisheries cast huge nets that snatch up all kinds of fish, including many they aren't necessarily looking for. In contrast, the old fisherman in the *Old Man in the Sea* used a single pole and hook to catch a single Big One.

Traditional broadcast advertising, like commercials or radio spots, are like the industrial fisheries' huge nets: They deliver short bits of information to huge numbers of people — everyone in their coverage areas who happens to be tuned in at a particular time. The Internet has its own form of broadcasting: getting your company mentioned or advertised on one of the sites that draws millions of visitors each day.

But where the Internet really excels is in one-to-one communication of the kind that TV and radio can't touch. I suggest that you try your own personalized forms of online advertising before you attempt to blanket cyberspace with banner ads. Often, you can reach small, *targeted* groups of people — or even one prospect at a time — through free, do-it-yourself marketing strategies.

Using Ten Free Publicity Strategies

The following sections describe some ways you can publicize your online business yourself. Your big expense is in time: It can take several hours a week to correspond by e-mail and apply to have your business listed in search services, Internet indexes, or Web sites that have a customer base similar to yours.

Building relationships, which is what many of the following strategies involve, takes energy. But the results can be great for your fledgling company. Devote some time to the care and feeding of your new business by trying these techniques before you pay to hire marketing consultants or place banner ads around the Web.

The best way to generate first-time and return visits to your business site is by providing useful information. The longer people are inclined to stay on your Web site, the more likely they are to acquire your goods or services. See Chapter 6 for some specific suggestions on generating compelling, useful content.

Getting listed in the Yahoo! index

If you want to get the most bang for your advertising buck, get your site listed on the most popular locations in cyberspace. For several years now, Yahoo! has been the number one most popular site on the Internet in a list of the "Top 25 Web Properties" published by Relevant Knowledge (www.relevantknowledge.com/Press/sdindex.html).

Aside from its steadily increasing size and popularity, one thing that sets Yahoo! apart is the way in which it evaluates sites for inclusion on its index pages. An *index page* is a list of Web sites that have been grouped together by category, much as you would find in a traditional yellow-pages phone book. Although many people think of Yahoo! primarily as a search engine, it's also a categorical index to Web sites.

For the most part, real human beings do Yahoo!'s indexing; they read your site description and your own suggested location, and determine for themselves what category to list your site under. Usually, Yahoo! lists sites in only one or two categories, but if Yahoo! editors feel that a site deserves its own special category, they create one for it.

The Yahoo! editors don't even attempt to process all the thousands of site applications they receive each week. Reports continue to circulate on the Web as to how long it takes to get listed on Yahoo!, and how difficult it is to get listed at all. The process can take weeks, months, or even years. Danny Sullivan, the editor of *Search Engine Watch,* estimates that only about a quarter of all sites that apply get listed.

Search Engine Watch (searchenginewatch.com) is a great place to go for tips on how search engines and indexes work, and how to get listed on them. The site includes an article about one company's problems getting what it considers to be adequate Yahoo! coverage (searchenginewatch.com/sereport/9801-miningco.html). Another article critical of Yahoo! was published in the February 11, 1998 issue of *HotWired* (www.wired.com/news/news/technology/story/10236.html).

What can you do to get Yahoo!-ed? I have a three-step suggestion:

1. **Make your site interesting, quirky, or somehow attention-getting.**

   You never know; you may just stand out from the sea of new Web sites and gain the attention of one of the Yahoo! editors.

2. **Go ahead and try applying to the main Yahoo! index.**

   You can at least say you tried! Go to www.yahoo.com, find the category page that you think should list your site, and click on the Add URL link. On the form that appears, provide the URL and a description for your site. Make your description as interesting as possible, while remaining within the content limit. (If you submit a description that's too long, Yahoo! asks you to revise it.)

3. **Try a local Yahoo! index.**

   Major metropolitan areas around the country, as well as in other parts of the world, have their own Yahoo! indexes. Go to the main Yahoo! page (www.yahoo.com) and click on the button labeled More Yahoo!s. Find the local index closest to you and apply as described in the preceding step. Your chances are much better of getting listed here than on the main Yahoo! site.

Yes, Virginia, there is life beyond Yahoo!. Several Web-based services are trying to compete by providing their own way of organizing and evaluating Web sites. Try submitting a listing, called a *guide,* to The Argus Clearing-house (www.clearinghouse.net), or contact one of the guides employed by The Mining Company (www.miningcompany.com).

Getting listed with search services

Search services can steer lots of business to a commercial Web site, based on how often the site appears in the list of Web pages that the user sees, and how high the site appears in the list. Your goal is to maximize your chances of being found by the search service.

The first step with any search service is to register your site. Doing so gets you in the company's database more quickly than having to wait for the "spider" program to crawl its way to you. Here's a quick example that shows how to list your site with one of the search engines. (The process is similar for all of them.)

1. **Connect to the Internet, start up your Web browser, and go to AltaVista's Web site.**

   The AltaVista home page (www.altavista.com) appears.

2. **Click on the Help link.**

   The AltaVista Help page appears.

3. **Click on the Add A Page link.**

   The Add A Page page appears.

4. **Scroll down to the bottom of the page, enter the URL for your site's home page, and then click on the Submit URL button.**

Your page is added to AltaVista's database.

Businesses on the Web can get obsessed with how high their site appears on the list of pages. They can't understand why, if someone enters the exact name of their site in, for example, Excite's text box, the site doesn't come back at the top — or even on the first page — of the list of returned sites. The fact is that, of the millions of sites listed in a search service's database, the chances are good that one has the same name, or something close to it — or that a page contains a combination of the same words that make up your organization's name. Don't be overly concerned with hitting the top of the search-hit charts. Concentrate on creating a top-notch Web site and making sales.

Embedding keywords in your pages

To maximize your Web site's chances of being listed in response to queries to the Internet search services, you can add special code to the underlying HTML (HyperText Markup Language) source code for your home page.

The *source code* for a Web page is the set of HTML commands that actually make the words, images, links, and other content appear the way they are supposed to in a Web browser window. Every Web page has HTML source code, and all Web browsers let you take a peek "behind the curtain" of a Web page to study the source code. To do so, Netscape Navigator users choose View➪Page Source; Internet Explorer users choose View➪Source.

The Collectible Exchange (a company profiled in Chapter 1) uses this strategy to draw search engines to its site. If you look at the source for the Collectible Exchange's home page, you see the following META tags:

```
<META NAME="description" content="Beanie Babies Collectible
        Exchange is the ultimate source of Beanie Babies
        on the net. We buy, sell and trade instantly
        with thousands in stock. Over 40,000 beanie
        babies traded."
<META NAME="keywords" content="beanie babies, sale, TY,
        retired, collect, Exchange, buy, sell, trade,
        instantly">
```

META is an HTML instruction, or *tag,* that contains descriptive information about the contents of a Web page or Web site. Many search services, such as Excite and AltaVista, use computer programs that scan a Web page's META tags in the course of indexing that page's contents. You can include important information in META tags to give yourself a better chance of being indexed more effectively. In the preceding example, the "description" portion of the META tag provides a standard site synopsis for search engines to display when they provide a link to your site. The "keywords" portion of the META tag includes words that users can enter into a search engine in order to find your site.

Most META tags use two attributes, NAME and CONTENT. The NAME attribute identifies the property and the CONTENT attribute specifies the property's value. Attributes are terms that provide a Web browser with more specific instructions about the command it is being given and how to act on that command.

Where to put the META Tag

Every Web page is enclosed by the two tags <HTML> and </HTML>. These tags define the page as being a HyperText Markup Language (HTML) document. The <HTML> tag goes at the beginning of the document, and </HTML> goes at the end.

Within the <HTML> and </HTML> tags reside two main subdivisions of a Web page:

- ✔ **The header section:** This section, enclosed by the tags <HEAD> and </HEAD>, is where the META tags go.

- ✔ **The body section:** This section, enclosed by the tags <BODY> and </BODY>, is where the contents of the Web page — the part you actually see on-screen — go.

You don't have to include META tags on every page on your site; in fact, your home page is the only page where doing so makes sense.

How to create a META tag

The following steps show how to add your own META tags to a Web page using FrontPage Express, the Web page editor that is bundled with the copy of Microsoft Internet Explorer included on this book's accompanying CD-ROM. These steps presume that you've already installed Internet Explorer (see the appendix), created your Web page, and saved it on your computer with a name like index.htm or index.html. To add META tags, follow these steps:

1. **Choose Start⇨Programs⇨Internet Explorer⇨FrontPage Express.**

   A blank FrontPage Express window opens.

2. **Open the Web page document to which you want to add META tags by choosing File⇨Open from FrontPage Express's menu bar.**

   The Open File dialog box appears.

3. **If the file resides on your computer's hard disk, click on the <u>B</u>rowse button in the Open File dialog box, locate the Web page file in the standard Windows navigation dialog box, and then click on <u>O</u>pen.**

   If the file resides on the Web, you can edit it by entering the URL for the page in the Location box of the Open File dialog box, and then clicking on OK.

   The Web page opens in the FrontPage Express window (see Figure 11-1). To add the META tags, you need to type them directly into the HTML source code for the page.

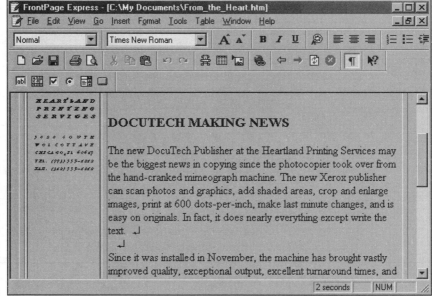

4. **Choose <u>V</u>iew⇨<u>H</u>TML from the FrontPage Express menu bar.**

   The Web page commands that tell a Web browser how to present your page on-screen appear in a separate window.

5. **Click your mouse arrow near the beginning of your page, between the <HEAD> and </HEAD> tags, and enter your keywords and description using this format:**

```
<META NAME="description" content="Your short Web site
     description goes here.">
<META NAME="keywords" content="keyword1, keyword2,
     keyword3, and so on">
```

   The output appears in the View HTML window, as shown in Figure 11-2.

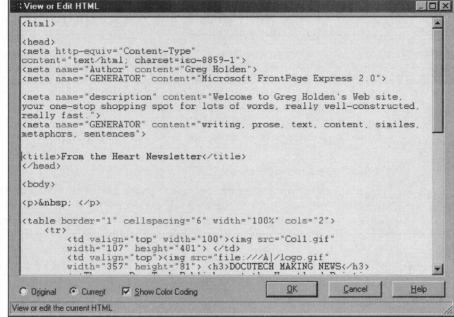

Within the figure image:

```
View or Edit HTML

<html>

<head>
<meta http-equiv="Content-Type"
content="text/html; charset=iso-8859-1">
<meta name="Author" content="Greg Holden">
<meta name="GENERATOR" content="Microsoft FrontPage Express 2.0">

<meta name="description" content="Welcome to Greg Holden's Web site,
your one-stop shopping spot for lots of words, really well-constructed,
really fast.">
<meta name="GENERATOR" content="writing, prose, text, content, similes,
metaphors, sentences">

<title>From the Heart Newsletter</title>
</head>

<body>

<p>  </p>

<table border="1" cellspacing="6" width="100%" cols="2">
   <tr>
        <td valign="top" width="100"><img src="Col1.gif"
        width="107" height="401"> </td>
        <td valign="top"><img src="file:///A|/logo.gif"
        width="357" height="81"> <h3>DOCUTECH MAKING NEWS</h3>
```

Original   Current   Show Color Coding   OK   Cancel   Help

View or edit the current HTML

Figure 11-2:
Add your META tags in the HEAD section of your HTML document.

6. **Click on OK to close the View HTML window.**

   The View HTML window closes, and you return to the FrontPage Express window. Your additions are not visible on the Web page, because they are intended for search engines, not visitors to your site.

7. **You can now make more changes to your page or choose File⇨Exit to close FrontPage Express.**

Enter the text for your META tags in exactly the format shown in the preceding steps. (FrontPage Express documents come with two META tags already inserted; you can just follow the same format for your own tags.) Be sure to insert a single blank space between the words META and NAME, and between "description" and content. Separate each keyword with a comma and a blank space. Also be sure to use straight double-quotes (double-primes) both before and after the words keywords and description. Finally, don't forget to enter the greater-than symbol (>) after each command. If you don't, the text will end up in the body of your Web page where everyone can see it.

Starting a newsletter

Back in the Dark Ages of entrepreneurship (say, four or five years ago), the only way to publish detailed information about your new business was to create a flyer or brochure. If you were on a tight budget, you could take your simple one- or two-sheet flyer to the local copy shop and get a hundred copies duplicated on neon orange paper. If you had money to burn, you could get an actual glossy brochure designed and printed for hundreds or (more likely) thousands of dollars.

Now that you're online, you can laugh at those high printing costs and publish your own online newsletter. If you've always wanted to impress people with how much you know about what you do, now's your chance. If you've been longing to say what's on your mind without being censored, you can do it in your own publication. Online newsletters also help meet your clients' customer service needs, as I discuss in Chapter 9.

Publishing considerations

The work of producing an online newsletter is offset by the benefits you get in return. You may obtain hundreds or even thousands of subscribers who find out about you and your online business. You become an authority; you're the editor in chief; you're large and in charge.

In order for your publishing venture to run smoothly, however, you have some decisions to make:

- ✔ **What will you write about?** If you run out of your own topics to write about, don't panic. Identify magazines in your field of business so you can quote articles. Get on the mailing list for any press releases you can use.

- ✔ **Who will do the work?** You're busy enough running your online business and wearing other hats (parent/spouse/full-time employee . . . take your pick). Consider assigning someone to function as editor, or line up colleagues to function as contributors.

- ✔ **What will the publication look like?** You have two choices: You can send a plain-text version that doesn't look pretty but that everyone can read easily, or you can send a formatted HTML version that looks like a Web page but that only people who can receive formatted e-mail can read. Keep in mind, though, that many users are on corporate e-mail systems that either discourage or prohibit HTML-formatted e-mail. Others don't like HTML e-mail because it takes longer to download the graphics files.

- ✔ **Whom do you want to reach?** Identify your readers and make sure that your content is useful to them.

Newsletters only work if they appear on a regular basis and if they consistently maintain a high level of quality. If you decide to create a newsletter and receive subscriptions, you're making a substantial commitment. Newsletters take a great deal of work to create and update. Whether yours comes out every week, every month, or just once a year, your subscribers will expect you to re-create your publication with every new issue. Keep your newsletter simple and make sure that you have the resources to follow through.

Fire up the presses!

After you do your planning, the actual steps involved in creating your newsletter are pretty straightforward. I suggest that, because you're just starting out, you concentrate on producing only a plain-text version of your newsletter. Later on, you can think about doing an HTML version, as well.

ASCII text isn't going to win any beauty contests, but most people who absorb information online don't care: They just want the facts and they want them as fast as possible. They're satisfied with receiving inside tips and suggestions and are happy that they don't have to wait for graphics files to download. Nancy Roebke, whose company, Profnet, Inc., is profiled in Chapter 7, uses a typical plain-text arrangement for her newsletter, *Network Ink* (see Figure 11-3).

Before you do anything, check with your ISP to make sure that a mailing-list publication is all right with them. Even if your newsletter is a simple announcement that you only send out once in a while (in contrast to a discussion list, which operates pretty much constantly), you're going to be sending a lot more e-mail messages through your ISP's machines than you otherwise would.

Keep your newsletters small in size; about 30K is the biggest e-mail file you can comfortably send to your recipients. If you absolutely must have a larger newsletter, break it into two or three separate e-mail messages. Reducing the file size of your newsletter keeps your readers from getting irritated because your message takes so long to download or to open. And keeping your customers happy should be one of your highest business priorities.

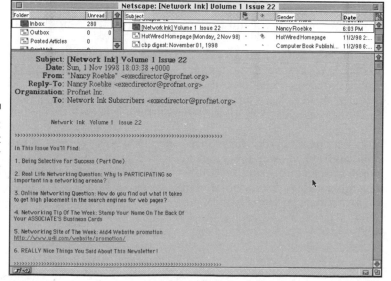

Figure 11-3:
A plain-text newsletter typically begins like this: with a heading, a rule, and a table of contents.

When you're all set with the prep work, follow these general steps for an overview of how to create and distribute your publication:

1. **Open up a plain-text editor, such as Notepad (Windows) or SimpleText (Mac).**

2. **Start typing.**

   Just because your newsletter is in plain text doesn't mean that you can't format it at all. Consider the following low-tech suggestions for emphasizing text or separating one section from another:

   - **All caps:** Using ALL CAPITAL LETTERS is always useful for distinguishing the name of the newsletter or of individual article titles.

   - **Rules:** You can create your own homemade horizontal rules by typing a row of equal signs, hyphens, or asterisks to separate sections.

   - **Blank spaces:** Used carefully, that handy-dandy spacebar on your keyboard can help you center plain text or divide it into columns.

   When you finish typing, be sure to proofread the whole newsletter before sending it out. Better yet, enlist the help of an objective viewer to read over the text for you.

3. **Save your file.**

4. **Open up your e-mail program's address book, select the mailing list of recipients, and compose a new message to them.**

5. **Attach your newsletter to the message, or paste it into the body of the message, and send it away.**

If you're sending many e-mail messages at once, be sure to do your mailing at a time when Internet traffic isn't so heavy. Many popular newsletters, such as *Netsurfer Digest* and *HotWired,* go out on weekends, for example.

Don't flood your Internet Service Provider's mail server with hundreds or thousands of messages at once; you may crash the server. Break the list into smaller batches and send them at different times. That's what Debbie Redpath Ohi does with her newsletter, *Inklings* (www.inkspot.com/inklings), which has more than 14,000 subscribers.

Be sure to mention your newsletter on your Web page, and to provide an e-mail address where people can subscribe. In the beginning, you can ask people to send subscription requests to you. If your list swells to hundreds of members, consider automated mailing-list software or a mailing-list service to manage your list.

Help with mailing list management

When you make the decision to host and run your own mailing list, you assume the responsibility of processing requests to subscribe and unsubscribe from the list. This venture can start eating into the time you need to spend on your other business activities.

You need to devote your energies to promoting and running your business online. When mailing lists get to be too much to handle yourself, you have a couple of options to make life easier.

One alternative is to purchase special mailing-list software. This type of program automatically adds or subtracts individuals from a mailing list in response to special

e-mail messages they send to you. You can usually manage the mailing list from your home computer. Look into SLMail for Windows 95 or NT users by Seattle Labs (www. seattlelabs.com/slmail). Mac users can try ListSTAR by StarNine Technologies, Inc. (www.starnine.com).

Even though mailing-list software can help reduce the work involved in maintaining a list, you still have to install and use the software on a regular basis. If you're really strapped for time, you can hire a company to run your mailing list for you. Check out SkyList.net (www.skylist.net/hosting) and Lyris (www.lyris.net) for pricing information.

Joining newsgroups and mailing lists

Many areas of the Internet can provide you with direct access to potential customers, as well as a chance to interact with them. Two of the best places to market yourself directly to individuals are mailing lists and newsgroups. Mailing lists and newsgroups are highly targeted and offer unprecedented opportunities for niche marketing. Using them takes a little creativity and time on your part, but the returns can be significant.

Get started by developing a profile of your potential customer. Then join and participate in lists and newsgroups that may provide customers for your online business. For example, if you sell TV-show items (posters, T-shirts, mugs, photos of the stars, and so on) to fans online, you may want to join some newsgroups started by the fans themselves.

Where can you find these discussion forums? Liszt (www.liszt.com) is a mailing list directory that you can search by name or topic and that includes more than 90,000 mailing lists. Reference.com (www.reference.com) enables you to easily find, browse, search, and participate in more than 150,000 newsgroups, mailing lists, and Web forums.

Mailing lists

A mailing list is a group of individuals who receive communications by e-mail. Two kinds of mailing lists are common online:

- **Discussion lists:** These are lists of people interested in a particular topic. People subscribe to the list and have messages on the topic delivered by e-mail. Each message sent to the list goes to everyone in the group. Each person can reply either to the original sender or to everyone in the group, too. The resulting series of messages on a topic is called a *thread*.

- **Announcement lists:** These lists provide only one-way communication. Recipients get a single message from the list administrator, such as an attached e-mail newsletter of the sort described earlier in this chapter.

Discussion lists are often more specific in topic than newsgroups. Some are very small and some are quite large, including thousands of people. For example, ROOTS-L is a mailing list for individuals who are pursuing genealogical quests. They exchange inquiries about ancestors they are seeking, and announce family tree information they've posted online.

By making contributions to the list, you establish a presence, and when members are looking to purchase the kind of goods or services you offer, they are likely to come to you rather than to a stranger. By participating in the lists that are right for you, you also learn invaluable information about your customers' needs and desires. Use this information to fine-tune your business so that it better meets those needs and desires.

Don't directly sell your wares on mailing lists. Blatant self-promotion is frowned upon in this arena. Marketing through lists and newsgroups requires a low-key approach. Besides, participating by answering questions or contributing your opinion to ongoing discussion topics is far more effective.

Always read the welcome message and list guidelines that you receive upon joining a mailing list. Learn the rules before you post. Lurk in the background for a few weeks to get a feel for the topics and participants before you contribute. Then introduce yourself and join the discussion. Remember to stay low-key and don't directly advertise yourself. Let your four- to six-line signature file do the work for you. Don't forget to spell-check your messages before you send them, too.

Newsgroups

Newsgroups, which are often simply called discussion groups, provide a different form of online group discussion. On the Internet, you can find discussion groups in an extensive network called Usenet. America Online and CompuServe also have their own system of discussion groups that is separate from Usenet. Large corporations and other organizations maintain their own internal discussion groups, as well. In any case, you access discussion groups with your Web browser's newsgroup software. The program that comes bundled with Netscape Communicator is called Netscape Collabra; Microsoft Outlook Express has its own newsgroup software, as well.

You can promote yourself and your business in discussion groups the same way you can make use of mailing lists: by participating in the group, providing helpful advice and comments, and answering questions. Don't forget that newsgroups are great for fun and recreation, too; they're a good way to solve problems, get support, and make new friends. For more on information on newsgroups, see Chapter 2.

Keeping an online "little black book"

If you already keep important contact information in a daily planner or other book, setting up an electronic address book on the Net will be a piece of cake. Any good e-mail program has an address book where you can quickly record the e-mail addresses of people with whom you correspond. Use it! Every time someone sends you an inquiry, save that person's address in your online address book.

Before you know it, you'll have a mailing list of customers who have contacted you. Programs like Microsoft Outlook Express, Netscape Messenger, and Eudora all let you collect a bunch of e-mail addresses into a single mailing list. You can then send an announcement or a newsletter to everyone on your list at one time.

Pssst . . . can we link?

You're probably used to exchanging businesses cards and phone or fax numbers with other businesspeople. When you go online, you can exchange something else: hypertext links to your respective Web sites. These kinds of personal recommendations can carry more weight than a banner advertisement, in my opinion.

This is another way in which tried-and-true one-to-one communication can pay off handsomely. Simply call or e-mail the owner of another Web site and ask to exchange links with that person. When you ask, be friendly, brief, and to the point. Just say, "I'll put a link to your site or your e-mail address on my home page if you put a link to my site on yours."

It's probably not good business practice to approach your fiercest competitors and ask to exchange links. Rather, try to find a complementary business or group or organization that covers every business in your field.

Striking up a business partnership

Remember the movie *Miracle on 34th Street,* in which the owners of Macy's and Gimbel's department stores decided to send customers to each other's stores when those patrons couldn't find what they were looking for? Both merchants were depicted as reaping benefits from helping one another.

You can strike up the same sort of cooperative arrangement with your own colleagues online. Notice that I said *colleagues,* not competitors. I'm not talking about approaching online businesses that do exactly the same thing you do and that target the same customers. Rather, I'm talking about teaming up with another online company whose products or services complement your own. The Big Guys do this all the time: Microsoft signs an agreement with NBC; Yahoo! joins Viacom.

On a smaller scale, the gardening site Garden.com, which is always a great place to look for examples of marketing and customer service, includes an ad for Horticulture Online and *Horticulture* magazine at the bottom of its home page (www.garden.com). Conversely, if you visit Horticulture Online (www.hortmag.com), you see the same sort of referral at the bottom of its home page (Figure 11-4).

Actually, these two businesses are more than partners; they created the Horticulture Online site together. But the principle is the same: Two related businesses help one another by promoting each other's Web sites.

Figure 11-4:
By partnering with another organization, your small business can get more attention and reach the audience you want.

Holding a contest

In Chapter 1, I describe how cartographer John Moen uses contests and other promotions to attract attention to his online business. Remember that everyone loves to receive something for free. Holding a contest can attract visitors to your Web site, where they can find out about the rest of your offerings — the ones you offer for sale, that is. (See Chapter 6 for specific details about holding a contest or sweepstakes on your Web site.)

You don't have to give away cars or trips around the world to get attention. SoftBear Shareware, a online company on America Online, gives away teddy bears and other simple items on its Web site (members.aol.com/JRSoftBEAR/bearonly.htm). As you can see in Figure 11-5, their contest has attracted at least 8,500 visitors so far. When I asked SoftBear's owner, John Raddatz, if contests had helped gain attention for his business, he responded as follows:

> "YES, YES, YES. Contests have increased traffic to my site. The re-sponse ranges anywhere from 100 to 350 entries a month! Only a few of these have actually purchased my software programs, but my site is being exposed to new surfers daily!"

You can also see in Figure 11-5 that SoftBear is enrolled in the Amazon.com Associates Program. This is another kind of cooperative link partnership you can consider for your small business. SoftBear recommends some

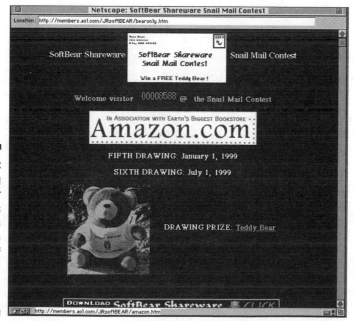

Figure 11-5:
Holding regular contests attracts attention to the rest of your online business, too.

Amazon.com books on its site and, in return, receives referral fees. Find out more by visiting www.amazon.com and clicking on the Join Associates link.

Placing banner ads

I'm not as big a booster of traditional banner ads as I am of the other strategies mentioned in this chapter, especially where small entrepreneurial businesses are concerned. Banner ads are like the traditional print ads you might take out in local newspapers. In some limited cases, banner ads are free, as long as you or a designer can create one (see the upcoming section on LinkExchange). Otherwise, you have to pay to place them on someone else's Web page, the same way you pay to take out an ad in a newspaper or magazine.

Many commercial operations *do* use banner ads successfully on the Web, however. Banner ads can be effective promotional tools under certain circumstances:

- ✔ If you pay enough money to keep them visible in cyberspace for a long period of time
- ✔ If you pay the high rates charged by the most successful Web sites, which can steer you the most traffic

Banner ads differ from other Web-specific publicity tactics in one important respect: They publicize in a one-to-many rather than a one-to-one fashion. They broadcast the name of an organization indiscriminately, without requiring the viewer to click on a link or in some respect choose to find out about the site.

Anteing up

You have to pay the piper in order to play the banner ad game. In general, Web sites have two methods of charging for banner ads:

- ✔ **CPM, or Cost Per Thousand (M):** This is a way of charging for advertising based on the number of people who visit the Web page on which your ad appears. The more visits the Web site gets, the higher the ad rates that site can charge.
- ✔ **CTR, or Clickthrough Rate:** A *clickthrough* occurs when someone clicks on a banner ad that links to your (the advertiser's) Web site. (Virtually all banner ads are linked this way.) In this case, you are billed after the ad has run for awhile and the clicks have been tallied.

Say 100,000 people visit the site on which your banner runs. If the site charges a flat $20 CPM rate, your banner ad costs $2,000 (100 × $20). If the same site charges a $1 per clickthrough rate, and 2 percent of the 100,000 visitors click through to your site (the approximate average for the industry), you pay the same: $2,000 (2,000 × $1).

Obviously, the more popular the site on which you advertise, the more your ad costs. Yahoo!, for example, charges a CPM rate of $20 to $50 for each 1,000 visits to the Yahoo! page on which the banner ad appears. If the page on which your banner runs receives 500,000 visits, such ads can cost $10,000 to $25,000. Not all advertising sites are so expensive, of course. In contrast, Mark Welch charges between $225 and $1,000 per month for ads on his site (www.markwelch.com), depending on the location of the ad.

CPM rates are difficult to calculate because of the number of repeat visitors a site typically receives. For example, a Web page designer may visit the same site a hundred times in a day when testing scripts and creating content. If the site that hosts your ad charges a rate based on CPM, make sure that they "weed out" such repeat visits. In general, you're better off advertising on sites that charge not only on a CPM basis, but on a cost-per-click basis, as well — or, better yet, *only* on a clickthrough basis. The combination of CPM and CTR is harder for the hosting site to calculate, but ultimately fairer for you, the advertiser.

Before you place any banner ads, be sure to visit a terrific resource called the Web Site Banner Advertising page (www.markwelch.com/bannerad), which presents lots of tips and advice about spending your advertising dollars wisely.

Banner ads can be a substantial investment, so be sure that your ad appears on a page whose visitors are likely to be interested in your company. If your company sells automotive parts, for example, get on one of Yahoo!'s automotive index pages.

Designing your ad

Banner ads are usually rectangular in shape (see the Amazon.com ad in Figure 11-5). However, some standard square configurations or small buttonlike shapes are common, too. The numeric measurements for ads usually appear in pixels. There are roughly 72 pixels per inch, so a 468-x-60-pixel ad (a common size) is about 6.5 inches wide and about .875 inch in height.

The rectangular ads appear most often at the top of a Web page, so they load first while other page contents have yet to appear; smaller ads may appear anywhere on a page. (It's a good idea to make sure that your ad appears at the top of a Web page.)

Many banner ads combine photographic images, type, and color in a graphically sophisticated way. However, simple ads can be effective, as well. You can create your ad yourself, if you have some experience with a graphics program like Paint Shop Pro (you can download a trial copy at www.jasc.com).

Need some help in creating your own banner ad? If you have only a simple, text-only ad in mind, and you don't have a lot of money to spend on design, try one of the online create-your-own-banner-ad services. I'm very impressed with The Banner Generator, provided for free by Prescient Code Solutions (`www.coder.com/creations/banner`). See Figure 11-6 for an ad I created using this service.

LinkExchange

One way to reduce the cost of banner advertising is by joining an ad network, a group of businesses that join together to exchange ads. One large and reputable network is LinkExchange (`www.linkexchange.com`), with about 200,000 businesses placing banner ads for free on each other's pages.

Using LinkExchange is easy. In fact, the hardest part is probably coming up with a good-quality banner ad of your own. When you have that, you can become a member of LinkExchange by filling out a form on the company's Web site and submitting your ad.

In return, you receive the ads of other members, which you have to post on your Web pages. By publishing ads for other companies, you accumulate points, which then enable you to get your own ad posted around the Internet with other LinkExchange members.

The best thing about LinkExchange is that it doesn't cost any money and that, for a small investment, you get a lot of free publicity. In other words, it's one of the resources that makes the Internet a great place to do business.

Figure 11-6:
With the right choice of type and color, a text-only banner ad can look good.

Part IV
Law, Security, and Accounting

The 5th Wave   By Rich Tennant

"Face it Vinnie— you're gonna have a hard time getting people to subscribe online with a credit card to a newsletter called 'Felons Interactive.'"

In this part . . .

Okay, so this may not be the tastiest part of the book, but it's definitely good for you.

The bad news is that doing business online has its own set of risks and dangers; the good news is that Part IV shows you strategies to protect yourself and your business. This part also includes an overview of basic accounting practices for Web businesses and suggestions of software and online accounting help that you can use to keep track of your e-commerce activities.

The following chapters take the mumble-jumble out of business law and accounting, leaving you with easy-to-read, easy-to-understand steps, definitions, and do's and don'ts to keep your business merrily humming along.

Chapter 12

Security for Your Commerce Site

*W*hen a retail store closes at the end of the business day, available cash is locked in a cash box or a safe and stock that's particularly valuable is stored in a safe area. The last employee to leave makes sure to lock the doors.

When it comes to an online store, the virtual stock that is especially valuable is data — not only your own information, but that which pertains to your customers, too.

This chapter discusses some easy-to-implement technologies and strategies that can keep your data secure. Some of these measures are easy to put into practice and especially important for home-based businesspeople. Others are technically challenging to implement yourself. But even if you have your Web host or a consultant do the work, it's good to familiarize yourself with Internet security schemes. Doing so gives you the ability to make informed decisions about how to protect your online data. You can then take steps to lock your virtual doors when you need to, and protect your cyberstock from hackers and other bad guys.

Basic Business Safety Strategies

Just because you work at home doesn't mean that your security problems are over. Working in a home office carries its own set of safety concerns for small-business owners. Luckily, these concerns tend to be easy to address. Safe Computing 101 practices, such as using password protection, making backups, and installing virus software, can go a long way toward keeping your data secure, even if you never have to get into more technical subjects like public key encryption.

Protecting your home-office privacy

Working at home is safer in many ways than driving to a remote office. You don't have to brave the highways and byways commuting from one place to another. And I probably don't need to mention that you're protected from having to deal with office politics and infighting, too.

But when your workplace is the same as your living space, you run into new challenges, not the least of which is privacy. The doorbell, the phone, and the kids all make demands on your time. Some simple steps can help you set more clearly defined boundaries so you can concentrate on your work and thus be able to focus on pets, family, and home when the work is done.

Passing the password test

To your kids and your spouse, the computer may be a place to do homework, play games, or surf the Net. But to you, it's the central tool for operating your business. The ultimate solution is to have separate machines — one for personal use and one for business use. Then set up your system so you have to log on to your business computer with a username and password. (For suggestions on how to devise a good password that's difficult to crack, see the section "Picking a good password," later in this chapter.)

If you only have one computer, passwords can still provide a measure of protection. Windows gives you the ability to set up different user profiles, each associated with its own password. You can assign a different profile to each member of your family. You can even make a game out of selecting profiles: Each person can pick his or her own background color and desktop arrangement for Windows. User profiles and passwords don't necessarily protect your business files, but they convey to your family members that they should use their own software and stick to their own directories, and not try to explore your company data.

You can also set up different user profiles for your copy of Netscape Communicator. That way, your kids won't receive your business e-mail while they're surfing the Net, because you'll have different e-mail inboxes. If you're on Windows, choose Start⇨Programs⇨Netscape Communicator⇨Setup New User Profile.

Maintaining your telephone privacy

The first step to protecting the telephone privacy of your business is to get a separate phone line for it. Not only does having a devoted phone line make your business feel more legitimate, but it also separates your business calls from your personal calls. If you need a phone line to connect to the Net, you then have a choice of which line to use for your modem.

The next step is to set up your business phone with its own answering machine, which has a different message from your personal answering machine. On your business answering machine, identify yourself with your business name. This arrangement builds credibility and makes you feel like a real business owner. You can then install privacy features like caller ID on your business line, if you feel you need to.

If you're looking for tips and news on telephone service, not only for small businesses but also for personal use, visit the Telecommunications Research & Action Center (www.trac.org). Here, you can find ways to cut your phone bills and make smart decisions on telephone service.

Watching out for icebergs

Your fledgling business is no Titanic. It wouldn't take a big iceberg to sink you before you reach your destination. A basic technique for safeguarding your data is to protect yourself against disasters. When it comes to online computing, one of the worst things that can happen is loss of data. Whether the culprit is a natural disaster, fire, theft, or computer virus or bug, you can take steps either to prevent problems in the first place, or to recover more easily should they occur.

The following sections include ways to keep from having to abandon ship and swim for the lifeboats.

Insuring against disaster

You insure your house and car, so why not protect your business investment by obtaining insurance that specifically covers you against hardware damage, theft, and loss of data? You can also go a step further and obtain a policy that covers the cost of data entry or equipment rental necessary to recover your business information. Here are some specific strategies:

 ✔ Write a list of all your hardware and software and how much each item cost, and store the list in a safe place.
 ✔ Take photos of your computer setup in case you need to make an insurance claim.

Investigate the computer hardware and software coverage provided by Data Security Insurance (www.data-security.com) and Safeware, The Insurance Agency Inc., 1-800-848-3469.

Inoculating your computers against infection

The International Computer Security Association (www.icsa.net), which keeps track of viruses circulating around the Internet, has estimated that as many as 20,000 viruses are present online at any one time. As an online businessperson, you're going to be downloading files, receiving disks from customers and vendors, and exchanging e-mail with all sorts of people you've never met before. Surf safely by installing one of the virus protection programs listed in Chapter 3.

Viruses change all the time, and new ones appear regularly. The virus program you install one day may not be able to handle the viruses that appear just a few weeks or months later. Pick a virus program that doesn't charge excessive amounts for regular upgrades. Also check the ICSA's weekly anti-virus Product Testing Reports (www.icsa.net/services/consortia/anti-virus/testing_reports.shtml).

Backing up your business treasure

Treat your business information like gold. Back up your business data two or three times a week. You can find software that automatically creates backups for you (preferably in the middle of the night, when you don't need your computer), so you don't have to spend lots of valuable business time making copies. One of the most popular packages is called Retrospect Remote (at www.dantz.com/dantz_products/retro.html).

Backup data from personal computers is most easily saved on tape drives, removable cartridges, or writeable CD-ROM drives, which I describe in Chapter 3.

Providing Public-Key Security for Your Business

Radio and TV childhood heroes used to give out "secret decoder rings" to their young audience members. They then broadcast coded messages that only the lucky ring bearers could decode.

Computers use the same process of encoding and decoding to protect information they exchange on the Internet. The schemes used online are far more complex and subtle than the ones used by kids, however. This section describes the security method used most widely on the Internet, and the one you're likely to use yourself: Secure Sockets Layer (SSL) encryption.

Are you ready for the year 2000?

No discussion of viruses and bugs would be complete without considering the millennium bug, also known as the Year 2000 (or Y2K) problem. The problem, in a nutshell, is that computers that use two, rather than four, digits to designate a year have no way of knowing that the year designated by the system as "00" is 2000, not 1900. Dates such as 02, which really designates the year 2002, may be considered by noncompliant systems as being 1902, for example. Invalid dates can wreak all kinds of havoc, including preventing computers from connecting to their networks.

Is there a real possibility that you could fire up your computer on January 1, 2000, and find that the machine thinks you are back in the days of the horseless carriage? It's a problem worth taking seriously. Especially when you consider that roughly 85 percent of all PCs are considered to be not fully compliant.

Don't panic. You can follow these steps to find out if your computer has a problem and, if necessary, determine how to deal with it:

1. **Back up all your data to an external disk before conducting the following test.**

   If you use Windows, you can make an Emergency Rescue Disk (by opening the Add/Remove Programs Control Panel and clicking on the Startup Disk tab, and then clicking on the Create Disk button). Also make sure that you don't have any unsent e-mail and that you aren't running any scheduling software that can malfunction if you reset your computer clock.

2. **Open your computer's date and time utility; set the date to December 31, 1999, and set the clock to five minutes before midnight.**

3. **Shut your computer down and wait ten minutes.**

You can use this time to put on your party hat and grab your noisemaker to stage your own pretend millennium welcome party.

4. **Restart your computer.**

   If everything works fine and your computer reports that the date is January 1, 2000, rather than January 1, 1900, pop open the champagne and celebrate. You're okay.

   If, on the other hand, your computer refuses to boot up, you have a problem. Use the startup disk to get things running again and reset your clock. If your computer does boot up but shows the date as 1900, you also have a problem. Make sure that you can connect to the Internet and use your Web browser.

Once you know that you have a problem, go to the many Y2K Web sites that are popping up all over the Net and look for any patches available for your system. Microsoft has its own Year 2000 site at www.microsoft.com/technet/topics/year2k/default.htm. Look for instructions on how to download and install the OLE Automation Library (OLEAUT32.DLL), which can convert dates with two-digit years into four-digit years. Apple Computer's Year 2000 information is at www.apple.com/macos/info/2000.html.

In addition, make sure that all your software (such as your accounting program) is Year-2000 compliant, as well. Check the manufacturer's Web site for information.

The final step is to confer with the companies you work with regularly, including financial institutions, your Web hosting service, and suppliers. Contact these support companies and ask what steps they're taking to prepare for the year 2000.

How public-key/private-key encryption works

The term *encryption* refers to the process of encoding sensitive data, such as credit card numbers. Information is encrypted by means of complex mathematical formulas called *algorithms*. Such a formula may transform a simple-looking bit of information into a huge block of seemingly incomprehensible numbers, letters, and characters. The gobbledygook can only be decoded by someone who has the right formula, called a *key*, which is itself a complex mass of encoded data.

Here's a very simple example. Suppose that my credit card number is 12345, and I encode it using an encryption formula into something like the following: `1aFgHx203gX4gLu5cy`.

The formula essentially says: "Take the first number, add x letters to it, multiply it by x numerals, take the second number, divide it by x, add x characters to it," and so on. (In reality, the formulas are far more complex than this, which is why you usually have to pay a license fee to use them. But this is the general idea.) Someone who has the same formula can run it in reverse, so to speak, in order to decrypt the encoded number and obtain the original number, 12345.

In practice, the encoded numbers generated by encryption routines and transmitted on the Internet are very large. They vary in size depending on the relative strength (or uncrackability) of the security method being used. Some methods generate keys that consist of 128 bits of data (a data bit is a single unit of digital information). These formulas are called *128-bit keys*.

Encryption is the cornerstone of security on the Internet, and the most widely used security schemes, such as the Secure Sockets Layer protocol (SSL), the Secure Electronic Transactions protocol (SET), and Pretty Good Privacy (PGP), all use some form of it.

In some security methods, the party that sends the data and the party that receives it both use the same key (this method is called *symmetrical encryption*). This approach isn't considered as secure as an asymmetrical encryption method, such as public-key encryption, however.

In public-key encryption, the originating party obtains a license to use a security method. (The following section shows you just how to do this yourself.) As part of the license, you use the encryption algorithm to generate your own private key. You never share this key with anyone. However, you use the private key to create a separate public key. This public key goes out to visitors who connect to a secure area of your Web site. As soon as they have your public key, users can encode sensitive information and send it back to you. The data can only be decoded by you using your secret, private key.

Obtaining your own certificate

Think about it: How do you know for sure whom you're dealing with on the Net? How do you know that people are whom they say they are when all you have to go on is a URL or an e-mail address? In the real world, the government issues you a passport or a state ID, and retailers use these documents to check your identity. The solution in the online world: Obtain a personal certificate that you can send to Web site visitors or append to your e-mail messages.

How certificates work

A certificate, which is also sometimes called a Digital ID, is an electronic document issued by a certification authority (CA). The certificate contains the owner's personal information as well as a public key that can be exchanged with others online. The public key is generated by the owner's private key, which the owner obtains during the process of applying for the certificate.

In issuing the certificate, the CA takes responsibility for saying that the owner of the document is the same as the person actually identified on the certificate. Although the public key helps establish the owner's identity, certificates do require you to put a level of trust in the agency that issues it.

A certificate helps both you and your customers. A certificate assures your customers that you are the person you say you are, plus it protects your e-mail communications by enabling you to encrypt them.

Obtaining a certificate from VeriSign

Considering how important a role certificates play in online security, it's remarkably easy to obtain one. You do so by applying and paying a licensing fee to a CA. One of the most popular CAs is VeriSign, Inc., which lets you apply for a certificate called a Class 1 Digital ID on its Web site (www.verisign.com).

A VeriSign personal certificate, which you can use to authenticate yourself in e-mail, news, and other interactions on the Net, costs $9.95 per year, and you can try out a free certificate for 60 days. Follow these steps to obtain your Digital ID:

1. **Connect to the Internet, launch your Web browser, and go to the VeriSign, Inc. home page at** www.verisign.com.

2. **Click on the button labeled Individual Certificates, on the left side of the page.**

   The VeriSign Digital ID Center page appears.

3. **Click on the Try It! button or on the <u>Try a Digital ID FREE for 60 days</u> link.**

   The Client Enrollment page appears.

4. **Click on <u>Class 1 Digital ID</u>.**

   An application form for a Digital ID appears. (If you use Internet Explorer, you may see an interim page when you click on Class 1 Digital ID. The interim page asks you to select either Microsoft's or Netscape's e-mail program for use with your Digital ID.)

5. **Complete the application form.**

   The application process is pretty simple. The form asks for your personal information and a challenge phrase that you can use in case anyone is trying to impersonate you. It also requires you to accept a license agreement.

6. **Click on the Accept button at the bottom of the screen.**

   A dialog box appears asking you to confirm that you want to use VeriSign's encryption technology to generate first an exchange key and then a private key for you. The private key is an essential ingredient in public-key/private-key technology.

7. **Click on OK to have your browser generate your private key.**

   A page appears asking you to check your e-mail for further instructions. In a few minutes, you receive a message that contains a Digital ID PIN.

8. **In your e-mail program, open the new message from VeriSign Digital ID Center.**

9. **Click and hold down your mouse button and scroll across the PIN to select it; then choose <u>E</u>dit⇨Copy to copy the PIN.**

10. **Go to the URL for the Digital ID Center that is included in the e-mail message, and paste your PIN in the text box next to Enter the Digital ID Personal Identification Number (PIN).**

11. **Click on Submit.**

    The certificate is generated, and the Certificate Download page appears.

12. **Click on the Install button.**

    The ID from VeriSign downloads, and you are now able to view it with your browser. Figure 12-1 shows my certificate for Microsoft Internet Explorer (copying this ID, or anyone else's, is pointless because this is only your public key; the public key is always submitted with your private key, which is secret).

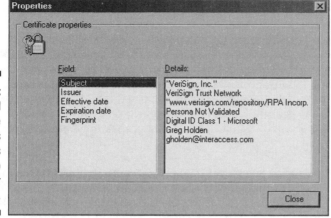

Figure 12-1:
A personal certificate ensures individuals or Web sites of your identity.

After you have your Digital ID, what do you do with it? For one thing, you can use it to ensure your identity to sites that accept certificate submissions. Some sites that require members to log in use secure servers that give you the option of submitting your certificate instead of entering the usual username and password to identify yourself. You can also attach your Digital ID to your e-mail messages to prove that your message is indeed coming from you. See your e-mail program's Help files for more specific instructions.

You can't encrypt or digitally sign messages on any computer other than the one to which your certificates are issued. If you're using a different computer than the one you used when you obtained your certificates, you must contact your certificate issuer and obtain a new certificate for the computer you're now using. Or, if your browser allows transfers, you can export your certificate to the new computer.

Keeping Your Sensitive Content Secure

Encryption isn't just for big businesses. Individuals who want to maintain their privacy, even while navigating the wilds of the Internet, can install special software or modify their existing e-mail programs in order to encode their online communications.

The Cyberangels Web site (www.cyberangels.org) presents some good tips and strategies for personal protection on the Internet.

Using personal encryption software

PGP Personal Privacy, which is owned by McAfee Associates, makes use of the popular and widely-known encryption system called Pretty Good Privacy (PGP). The program lets you protect the privacy of your e-mail messages and file attachments by encrypting them so that only those with the proper authority can decipher the information. You can also digitally sign the messages and files you exchange, which ensures the recipient that they come from you and that the information has not been tampered with on its way.

PGP Personal Privacy is a *plug-in,* an application that works with another program to provide added functionality. You can integrate the program with popular e-mail programs such as Eudora and Microsoft Outlook (although Netscape Messenger is notably absent from the list of supported applications).

In order to use PGP Personal Privacy, the first step is to obtain and install the program. During the installation process, you get the option of generating your own private-key/public-key pair. After you create a key pair, you can begin exchanging encrypted e-mail messages with other PGP users. To do so, you need to obtain a copy of their public key, and they need a copy of your public key. Because public keys are just blocks of text, trading keys with someone is really quite easy. You can include your public key in an e-mail message, copy it to a file, or post it on a public-key server where anyone can get a copy at any time.

After you have a copy of someone's public key, you can add it to your *public keyring,* which is a file on your own computer. Then you can begin to exchange encrypted and signed messages with that individual. If you're using an e-mail application supported by the PGP Personal Privacy plug-ins, you can encrypt and sign your messages by selecting the appropriate options from your application's toolbar. If your e-mail program does not have a plug-in, you can copy your e-mail message to your computer's clipboard and encrypt it there using PGP Personal Privacy's built-in functions. See the PGP Personal Privacy help files for more specific instructions.

PGP Privacy by McAfee Associates (www.mcafee.com) costs $39.95 by itself, but it is also available with a group of programs called Nuts & Bolts Deluxe — a package that includes a useful program that checks your system for Year 2000 compliance and fixes the problem, if necessary. Nuts & Bolts Deluxe costs $59.95 and runs on Windows 3.1 or higher. The program requires 8MB of RAM and 20MB of disk space. You can download and try an evaluation version from the McAfee Web site before buying the program — but be aware that this is a 6MB file!

Encrypting your e-mail messages

If you use an e-mail program that supports the S/MIME (Secure Multipurpose Internet Mail Extensions) protocol, you can use your existing software to encrypt your mail messages, rather than having to install a separate program like PCCrypto. The following sections describe the steps involved in setting up the e-mail programs that come with the Big Two browser packages, Netscape Communicator and Microsoft Internet Explorer.

Sending secure messages with Netscape Messenger

If you use Netscape Messenger, the e-mail application that comes with Netscape Communicator, you can use your Digital ID to do the following:

✔ **Send a digital signature.** You can digitally shrink-wrap your e-mail message using your certificate in order to assure the recipient that the message is really from you.

✔ **Encrypt your message.** You can digitally encode a message to ensure that only the intended party can read it.

To better understand how to keep your e-mail communications secure, read the online Secure E-Mail Reference Guide, which you can access at www.verisign.com/securemail/guide.

If you use Netscape Messenger, follow these steps to encrypt your e-mail messages or include your certificate with them:

1. **With Messenger running, click on the Security button in the toolbar of any of the Messenger windows.**

   A security information dialog box appears.

2. **Click on the word Messenger in the list of topics on the left side of the Security dialog box.**

   The following security options appear in the right half of the dialog box:

   • Encrypt your e-mail messages

   • Sign your e-mail messages with your Digital ID

   • Sign your discussion group messages with your Digital ID

3. **In order to activate Messenger's security features, check one or more of the check boxes; then click on OK.**

   The security dialog box closes. You return to the Messenger window that you were in previously.

4. **You can now address and write your message, and then click on the Send button in the Message Composition toolbar.**

   Your encrypted or digitally signed message is sent on its way.

By checking one or more of the options in the security dialog box, you activate Messenger's built-in security features for all your outgoing messages. In order to actually verify or undo those features (that is, if you want a message to be unencrypted or to be sent without a digital signature), you need to follow these additional steps:

1. **With any Messenger window (Inbox, Message Center, or Message) open, click on the New Msg toolbar button.**

   The Message Composition window appears.

2. **In the Address area of the Message Composition window, click on the Message Sending Options button, which appears at the bottom of the three buttons on the left side of the Message area.**

   The Message Sending Options appear. A check mark appears next to the Encryption or Signed options if you previously clicked on either option in the Security dialog box. (Both options have been selected in Figure 12-2.)

Figure 12-2:
When the Signed and Encryption check boxes are selected, your message goes out encrypted and with your certificate attached.

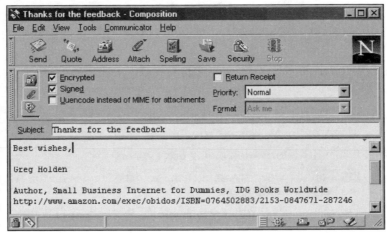

3. **If you want to undo either of these options, click on the check box to deselect it.**

4. **You can now address and write your message, and then click on the Send button in the Message Composition toolbar.**

   Your unencrypted or digitally unsigned message is sent on its way.

Sending secure messages with Outlook Express

Microsoft Outlook Express also enables you to send encrypted and digitally signed messages. The steps are similar to those for Messenger:

1. **After you obtain your own Digital ID, open Outlook Express and then click on the Address Book button in the Outlook Express toolbar.**

   The Address Book opens.

2. **Click on the name of the person whom you want to receive your Digital ID.**

   If the person is not yet included in your Address Book, you need to create a new listing.

3. **Click on the Properties toolbar button.**

   The Properties dialog box for that user appears.

4. **Click on the Certificates tab to bring it to the front, and then click on the Import button.**

   The Select Certificate File to Import dialog box appears.

5. **Locate your certificate file on your hard disk, click on its name, and then click on Open.**

   The Select Certificate File to Import dialog box closes, and you return to the Properties dialog box, where your certificate appears in the box labeled Certificates Associated with the Selected E-Mail Address.

6. **Click on OK.**

   The Properties dialog box closes and you return to the Address Book window.

7. **Select your recipient's name by clicking on it; then click on the Send Mail toolbar button.**

   The New Message dialog box appears.

8. **Click on either or both of the security buttons at the extreme right of the toolbar.**

   Digitally Sign Message enables you to add your Digital ID. Encrypt Message enables you to encrypt it.

9. **Finish writing your message and then click on the Send button.**

   Your encrypted or digitally signed message is sent on its way.

Picking a good password

Whether you're protecting your own computer, downloading software, subscribing to an online publication, or applying for a certificate (as explained earlier in this chapter), it's important to pick a password that thieves won't be able to crack.

One good method for choosing a password is to take a phrase that's easy for you to remember, and then use the first letter of each word to form the basis of a password. For example, the phrase Early to Bed and Early to Rise would be ETBAETR. Then, mix upper- and lowercase and add punctuation, and you wind up with eTb[a]ETr. If you *really* want to make a password that's hard to crack, add some numerals as well, such as the last two digits of the year you were born: eTb[a]Etr59.

Whatever you do, follow these tips for effective password etiquette:

- ✔ **Don't use passwords that are in a dictionary.** This rule should be obvious. Clever hackers can run a program that tries every word in an online dictionary as your password, until they eventually discover it.

- ✔ **Don't use the same password at more than one site.** I know this is difficult, because you tend to accumulate lots of different passwords after you've been online for a while. But if you use the same password all the time, and your password to one site on the Internet is compromised, all your password-protected accounts are in jeopardy.

- ✔ **Use at least six characters.** The more letters in your password, the more work code-crackers have to go through.

It's especially important not to re-use the same password that you enter to connect to your account on a commercial service like America Online or CompuServe as a password to an Internet site. If a hacker discovers your password on the Internet site, that person can use it to connect to your AOL or CompuServe account, too — and you'll have to pay for the time they spend online.

Protecting content with authentication

Authentication is another common security technique used on the Web. This measure simply involves assigning approved users an official username and password that they must enter before gaining access to a protected network, computer, or directory.

Most Web servers allow you to set up areas of your Web site to be protected by username and password. But not all Web hosts allow this, because it requires setting up and maintaining a special password file and storing the file in a special location on the computer that holds the Web server software. If you need to make some content on your business site (such as articles you've written) available only to registered users, talk to your Web host to see if setting up a password-protected area is possible. (Also consider setting up a micropayment system, such as MilliCent, that requires people to pay small amounts in order to access specified content. See Chapter 8 for details.)

Chapter 13
Keeping It All Legal

- -

In This Chapter

▶ Protecting your name through trademarks

▶ Paying license fees to local authorities

▶ Avoiding copyright infringement

▶ Considering the pros and cons of incorporation

▶ Avoiding major legal infractions

- -

*W*hether you're surfing the furthest reaches of the Wild Wide Web or prospecting for valuable nuggets in the frontiers of the alt newsgroups, you may get the impression that the only rule is Anything Goes. But when your business begins to contribute to the wealth of information in the cyberspace gold mine, things are hardly wide open.

In fact, what is open is the risk of getting in legal trouble of one sort or another because you lack experience in business law and you don't have lots of money with which to hire lawyers and accountants. You don't want to be learning for the first time about copyright law or the concept of intellectual property when you're in the midst of a dispute.

This chapter gives you a heads-up on legal issues you need to know about as an online businessperson, so you can head off trouble before it occurs. The good news is that you don't have to study mountains of information to cover yourself legally. And protecting yourself doesn't have to be expensive, either. Just register with the right agencies and keep the right records and, in no time, you can grow your online business in a legally secure way.

Trade Names and Trademarks

A *trade name* is the name by which a business is known in the marketplace. A trade name can also be *trademarked,* which means that a business has taken the extra step of registering its trade name so others can't use it. Big corporations protect their trade names and trademarks jealously, and sometimes court battles erupt over who can legally use a name.

What does this mean for your fledgling business? Although you may never get in a trademark battle yourself, and you may never trademark a name, you need to be careful which trade name you pick and how you use it. Choose a trade name that's easy to remember, so people can associate it with your company and return to you often when they're looking for the products or services you provide. Also, as part of taking your new business seriously and planning for success, you may want to protect your right to use your name by registering the trademark, which is a relatively easy and inexpensive process.

You can trademark any visual element that accompanies a particular tangible product or line of goods, and serves to identify and distinguish it from products sold by other sources. In other words, a trademark is not necessarily just for your business's trade name. In fact, you can trademark letters, words, names, phrases, slogans, numbers, colors, symbols, designs, or shapes. For example, take a look at the cover of the book you're reading right now. Look closely and see how many ™ or ® symbols you see. The same trademarked items are shown on the Dummies Press Web site (Figure 13-1). Even though the "...For Dummies" heading doesn't bear a symbol, it's a trademark, believe me.

The ™ mark can be used with items that may have been registered with a particular state but not with the U.S. Patent and Trademark Office. The ® symbol means the item has been registered with the aforementioned office.

Trademark symbol   Trademarked name   Trademarked logo

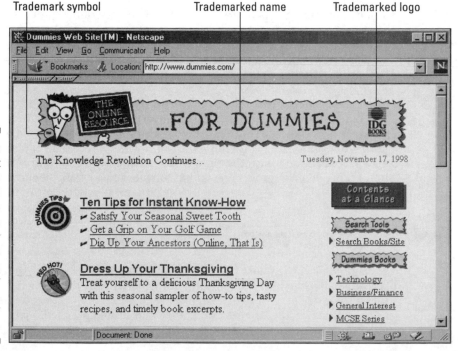

Figure 13-1:
You don't
have to use
special
symbols to
designate
logos or
phrases as
trademarks
on your
Web site,
but you may
want to.

For most small businesses, the problem with trademarks is not so much protecting your own as it is stepping on someone else's. Be sure to do research on the name you want to use to make sure that you don't run into trouble.

Researching a trademark

To avoid getting sued for trademark infringement and having to change your trade name or even pay damages if you lose, you should conduct a trademark search. A trademark search is an investigation whose goal is to discover any potential conflicts between your trade name and someone else's. Ideally, you do the search before you actually use your trade name or register for an official trademark.

You can do this search yourself the old fashioned manual way, by visiting one of the Patent and Trademark Depository Libraries (listed online at www.nolo.com/chunkPCT/PCT29.HTML). This approach can be time-consuming, but it doesn't cost anything.

You can also pay a professional search firm to research a trademark for you. Professional search firms are listed in the Yellow Pages under Trademark Consultants or Information Brokers. You can expect to pay between $25 and $50 per mark searched. More complete searches that cover registered and unregistered marks that are similar to the one you want to use can cost several hundred dollars.

Of course, you're becoming a Cyberspace Expert, and as you may expect, you can use the Web and your own computer to help you conduct a trademark search. The best place to go is the United States Patent and Trademark Office's federal trademark database. This is the same as doing a search at a depository library, only more convenient. You can search the database from the Web for free at www.uspto.gov/tmdb/index.html.

If you're on CompuServe, try searching the BizFile database of U.S. and Canadian businesses (**go:bizfile**). Also try Trademark Scan (**go:trademark**).

Cyberspace goes beyond national boundaries. A trademark search in your own country may not be enough. Most industrialized countries, including the United States, have signed international treaties that enable trademark owners in one country to enforce their rights against infringement by individuals in another country. If you are concerned about conducting business worldwide in the long term (and you should be, if you're planning for success), conduct an international trademark search. This undertaking is difficult to do yourself, so you may want to pay to have someone do the searching for you.

You may think that, just because you have a one-person business operating out of a spare room in your home, you can't possibly get in trouble by using a trademark owned by someone halfway around the world. This is dangerous thinking. The consequences of failing to conduct a reasonably thorough trademark search can be severe. In part, the consequences depend on how widely you distribute the protected item — and on the Internet, you can distribute it worldwide. If you attempt to use a trademark that has been federally registered by someone else, you could go to court and be prevented from using the mark again. You may even be liable for damages and attorney's fees. So it's best to be careful.

Protecting your trade name

In addition to a federal trademark law, each state has its own set of laws establishing when and how trademarks can be protected. You can obtain trademark rights in the states in which the mark is actually used, but you can also file an application with the United States Patent and Trademark Office.

After researching your trade name against existing trademarks, you can file an application with the Patent and Trademark Office online by following these steps:

1. **Connect to the Net, start up your browser, and go to the Trademark Electronic Application System (TEAS) page (**www.uspto.gov/teas/e-TEAS/index.html**).**

   This page includes a two-column table: The left-hand column contains instructions on how to fill out your application online and pay by credit card; the right-hand column explains how to print out the application form and mail it with a check to the Patent and Trademark Office.

2. **Click on the link for e-TEAS if you want to file online, or click on PrinTEAS if you want to mail in your application.**

   The following steps assume that you want to file online. When you click on the link for e-TEAS at the bottom of the left-hand column of the table, the Trademark/Service Mark Application Form Wizard appears (see Figure 13-2).

3. **Select the appropriate radio buttons and menu options on this page (note that you are asked whether anyone else is already using the desired trademark, so the program assumes that you've done a trademark search) and click on Next, at the bottom of the page.**

   An application form page appears.

4. **Fill out the required forms in the application, including your credit card data (so you can pay the $245 per application fee) and the electronic signature fields at the bottom of the application.**

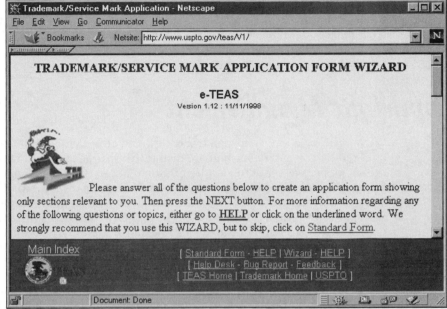

Figure 13-2:
You can
quickly
apply for
your own
federally
registered
trademark
online using
this site.

5. **You can attach a GIF or JPEG image of a symbol or logo that you want to trademark by clicking on the Attach an Image link.**

   A new page appears that lets you specify the image. Even though the image you want to trademark may be in color, the image you submit with your application must be in black-and-white form.

6. **Click on the Validation button at the bottom of the form.**

   If you filled out all the fields correctly, a Validation screen appears. If not, you return to the original form page so you can correct it.

7. **Print the special declaration to support the adoption of the electronic signature, and retain it for your records; then click on the Submit button.**

   You receive a confirmation screen if your transmission is successful. Later, you will receive an e-mail acknowledgment of your submission.

Generally, each state has its own trademark laws, which apply only to trademarks to be used within a single state. Products that may be sold in more than one state (such as those sold on the Internet) can be protected under the federal Lanham Act, which provides for protection of registered trademarks. In order to comply with the Lanham Act, you register your trademark as described in the preceding series of steps.

Trademarks are listed in the trademarks register, last for 15 years, and are renewable. You don't have to use the ™ or ® symbol when you publish your trademark, but doing so impresses upon people how seriously you take your business and its identity.

Copyright Management

What's the difference between trademark and copyright? Trademarks are covered by trademark law and are distinctive words, symbols, slogans, or other things that serve to identify products or services in the marketplace. Copyright, on the other hand, refers to the creator's ownership of creative works, such as writing, art, software, video, or cinema (but not names, titles, or short phrases). It provides the owner with redress in case someone copies the works without the owner's permission. Copyright is a legal device that enables the creator of a work the right to control how the work is to be used.

Although copyright protects the way ideas, systems, and processes are embodied in the book, record, photo, or whatever, it doesn't protect the idea, system, or process itself. In other words, if Thomas Jefferson were writing the Declaration of Independence today, the exact wording he chose to use in the Declaration would be copyrighted, but the general ideas he expressed would not.

You may or may not consider yourself to be an intellectual, but as a businessperson who produces goods and services of economic value, you may be the owner of intellectual property. *Intellectual property* refers to works of authorship, as well as certain inventions. Because intellectual property may be owned and bought and sold the same as other types of property, it's important to know something about the copyright laws governing intellectual property. Having this information maximizes the value of your products, and keeps you from throwing away potentially valuable assets or finding yourself at the wrong end of an expensive lawsuit.

What's protected by copyright

Everything you see on the Net is copyrighted, whether or not a copyright notice actually appears. For example, plenty of art is available for the taking on the Web, but look before you grab. Unless an image on the Web is specified as being copyright-free, you'll be violating copyright law if you take it. HTML tags themselves aren't copyrighted, but the content of the HTML-formatted page is. General techniques for designing Web pages are not copyrighted, but certain elements (such as logos) are.

Fair use . . . and how not to abuse it

Copyright law doesn't cover everything. One of the major limitations is the doctrine of "fair use," which is described in Section 107 of the U.S. Copyright Act. The law states that "fair use" of a work is use that does not infringe copyright "for purposes such as criticism, comment, news reporting, teaching (including multiple copies for classroom use), scholarship, or research." You can't copy text from online magazines or newsletters and call the use "fair use" because the text was originally news reporting.

"Fair use" has some big gray areas that can be traps for people who provide information on the Internet. Don't fall in. It's not difficult to shoot off a quick e-mail asking someone for permission to reproduce their work; chances are, that person will be flattered and will let you make a copy as long as you give them credit on your site.

Keep in mind that it's okay to use a work for criticism, comment, news reporting, teaching, scholarship, or research. That comes under the "fair use" limitation (see the nearby sidebar, "Fair use . . . and how not to abuse it"). However, I still contend that it's best to get permission or cite your source in these cases, just to be safe.

How to protect your copyright

A copyright, which protects original works of authorship, costs nothing, applies automatically, and lasts more than 50 years. When you affix a copyright notice to your newsletter or Web site, you make your readers think twice about unauthorized copying and put them on notice that you take copyright seriously. You can go a step further and register your work with the U.S. Copyright Office.

Create a good copyright notice

Even though any work you do is automatically protected by copyright, having some sort of notice expresses your copyright authority in a more official way. Copyright notices identify the author of a given work (such as writing or software) and then spell out the terms by which that author grants others the right (or the license) to copy that work to their computer and read it (or use it). The usual copyright notice is pretty simple, and takes this form:

```
Copyright 1999 [Your Name] All rights reserved
```

You don't have to use the © symbol, but it does make your notice look more official. In order to create a copyright symbol that appears on a Web page, you have to enter a special series of characters in the HTML source code for your page. For example, Web browsers translate the following group of characters — © — as the copyright symbol, displayed as © in the Web browser window. Most Web page creation tools provide menu options for inserting special symbols like this.

Copyright notices can also be more informal, and a personal message can have extra impact. Joseph Wu, a Canadian artist who creates some amazing origami and sells it from his Web site (www.origami.vancouver.bc.ca), includes both the usual copyright notice plus a watermark and a personal message on his home page (Figure 13-3).

Adding digital watermarks

In traditional offset printing, a *watermark* is a faint image embedded in stationery or other paper. The watermark usually bears the name of the paper manufacturer, but it can also identify an organization for whom the stationery was made.

Watermark

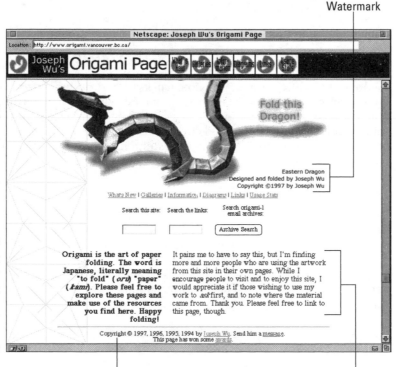

Figure 13-3: If your products are particularly precious, such as unique works of art, assert your copyright over them on your Web site.

Copyright notice   Personal message

Watermarking has its equivalent in the online world, too. Graphic artists sometimes use a technique called *digital watermarking* to protect images they create. This process involves adding copyright or other information about the image's owner to the digital image file. The information added may or may not be visible. (The image shown in Figure 13-3 has copyright information visibly added, not to the Web page, but to the image itself.)

Digimarc, which functions as a plug-in application with the popular graphics tool Adobe Photoshop (www.adobe.com), is one of the most widely used watermarking tools. Another program, OwnerMark, by Signafy, Inc. (www.signafy.com), also produces watermarks.

Making money without even trying

Joseph Wu is a perfect example of someone who operates an active Web site in his spare time and who is making extra money by providing useful online resources.

Joseph's resource is origami, the Japanese art of paper folding. He first put an origami page on the Web in its early days (1994), and being the first online has earned him a reputation as the origami authority on the Internet.

Joseph, who was born in Hong Kong and now lives in Vancouver, British Columbia, estimates that he spends five hours a week answering questions that come to him from people wanting to know about origami. (He also works full-time as a multimedia producer.) Over the years, other origami sites have placed links to his page, so he gets a lot of traffic. Because he's regarded as knowledgeable in his field, he also receives orders for his work from businesses such as advertising agencies that need paper models of various products.

Without actively marketing his site (www.origami.vancouver.bc.ca) or even regarding it as an online business, Joseph estimates that he made about $5,000 in the past year from orders that came from having his site on the Web.

Q. What is the goal of your online site?

A. To promote origami as an art form, as opposed to a child's pastime, which is the commonly-held view.

Q. Have you had problems with copyright violations?

A. Yes, people have copied my images, and some have tried to pass them off as their own. I've had to contact people on occasion to remind them of my copyright. I put watermarks on each of the images on my site.

Q. What advice would you give to someone starting an online business?

A. You have to provide something for nothing at first — something that people need. I try to answer any questions that people have about origami, or point people to places where they can find what they're looking for. I've become a clearinghouse for information.

Register your copyright

Registering your copyright is something I recommend for small businesses because it's inexpensive and easy to do, and it affords you an extra degree of protection. Having registered your copyright gives your case more weight in the event of a copyright dispute. You don't need to register, but doing so shows a court how serious you are about obtaining protection for your work.

To register your work, you can download an application form from the U.S. Copyright Office Web site at lcweb.loc.gov/copyright/forms.html. This form is in Adobe Acrobat PDF format, so you need Acrobat Reader to view it. (Adobe Acrobat Reader is a free application that you can download from the Adobe Systems Incorporated Web site at www.adobe.com.) You can then send the form by snail mail, along with a check for $20 and a printed copy of the work you are protecting, to Register of Copyrights, Library of Congress, Washington, DC 20559.

At this writing, the Copyright Office's online registration system (which is called CORDS) is being tested and is not yet available.

Licensing and Other Restrictions

Another set of legal concerns that you need to be aware of when you start an online business involves any license fees or restrictions that are levied by local agencies. (Some fees are specific to businesses that have incorporated, which brings up the question of whether you should consider incorporation for your own small business. I discuss the legal concerns and pros and cons of incorporation in the upcoming section, "Determining the Legal Form of Your Business.")

Knowing about local fees or restrictions

Before you get too far along with your online business, make sure that you have met any local licensing requirements that apply. For example, in my county in the state of Illinois, I had to pay a $10 fee to register my sole proprietorship. In return, I received a nice certificate that made everything feel official.

Other localities may have more stringent requirements, however. Check with city, county, and state licensing and/or zoning offices. Trade associations for your profession often have a wealth of information about local regulations, as well. Also, check with your local chamber of commerce. If you fail to apply for a permit or license, you may find yourself paying substantial fines.

The kinds of local regulations to which a small business may be susceptible include:

- ✔ **Zoning:** Your city or town government may have *zoning ordinances* (shudder) that prevent you from conducting business in an area that is zoned for residential use, or they may charge you a fee to operate a business out of your home. This policy varies by community; even if your Web host resides in another state, your local government may still consider your home the location of your business. Check with your local zoning department.

- ✔ **Doing Business As:** If your business name is different from your own name, you may have to file a Doing Business As (DBA) certificate and publish a notice of the filing in the local newspaper. Check with your city or county clerk's office for more information.

- ✔ **Taxes:** Some cities levy taxes on small businesses, and some even levy property tax on business assets such as office furniture and (uh-oh) computer equipment.

Keeping up with trade restrictions

If you are planning to sell your goods and services overseas, you need to be aware of any trade restrictions that may apply to your business. In particular, you need to be careful if any of the following applies:

- ✔ You trade in foodstuffs or agricultural products.
- ✔ You sell software that uses some form of encryption.
- ✔ Your clients live in countries with which your home country has imposed trade restrictions.

For more detailed suggestions of how to research international trade law, see Chapter 7.

The Arent Fox Web site, which is run by a Washington, D.C., based law firm, has lots of good legal information for people who want to do business online. Of particular interest is their International Trade Legislation Monitor (www.arentfox.com/features/tradeleg/home.html), which publishes recent trade legislation and has links to past articles about trade-related issues.

Determining the Legal Form of Your Business

Picking a legal form for your online business enables you to describe it to city and county agencies, as well as to the financial institutions with which you deal. A legal type of business is one that is recognized by taxing and licensing agencies. You have a number of options from which to choose, and the choice can affect the amount of taxes you pay and your liability in case of loss. The following sections describe your alternatives.

If you're looking for more information, Eric Tyson and Jim Schall explore the legal and financial aspects of starting up and operating a small business in *Small Business For Dummies,* published by IDG Books Worldwide, Inc.

Sole proprietorship

In a *sole proprietorship,* you're the only boss. You make all the decisions, and you get all the benefits. On the other hand, you share all the risk, too. This is the simplest and least expensive type of business because you can run it yourself. You don't need an accountant or lawyer to help you form the business, and you don't have to answer to partners or stockholders, either. To declare a sole proprietorship, you may have to file an application with your county clerk.

Partnership

In a partnership, you share the risk and profit with one or more people. Ideally, your partners bring skills to the endeavor that complement your own contributions. One obvious advantage to a partnership is that you can discuss decisions and problems with your partner. All partners are held personally liable for losses. The rate of taxes that each partner pays is based on his or her percentage of income from the partnership.

Remember that if you decide to strike a partnership with someone, it is a good idea to draw up a Partnership Agreement. Although you aren't legally required to do so, such an agreement clearly spells out the duration of the partnership and the responsibilities of each person involved. In the absence of such an agreement, the division of liabilities and assets is considered to be equal, regardless of how much more effort one person has put into the business than the other.

Incorporation

If sole proprietorships and partnerships are so simple to start up and operate, why would you consider incorporating? After all, you almost certainly need a lawyer to help you incorporate. Plus, you have to comply with the regulations made by federal and state agencies that oversee corporations. Besides that, you may undergo a type of *double taxation:* If your corporation earns profits, those profits are taxed at the corporate rate, and any shareholders have to pay income tax at the personal rate.

Despite these downsides, you may want to consider incorporation for the following sorts of reasons:

- ✔ If you have employees, you can deduct any health and disability insurance premiums you pay.
- ✔ You can raise capital by offering stock for sale.
- ✔ It's easier to transfer ownership from one shareholder to another.
- ✔ The company's principals are shielded from liability in case of lawsuits.

If you offer services that may be susceptible to costly lawsuits, incorporation may be the way to go. You then have two options: a C corporation or a subchapter S corporation. The latter is the most likely choice for small businesses.

Subchapter S corporations

One benefit of forming a subchapter S corporation is liability protection. This form or incorporation enables start-up businesses that encounter losses early on to offset those losses against their personal income. Subchapter S is intended for businesses with fewer than 75 shareholders. The income gained by an S corporation is subject only to personal tax, not corporate tax.

Sounds great, doesn't it? Before you start looking for a lawyer to get you started, consider the following:

- ✔ Incorporation typically costs several hundred dollars.
- ✔ Corporations must pay an annual tax.
- ✔ Attorneys' fees can be expensive.
- ✔ Filing for S corporation status can take weeks or months to be received and approved.

All these facts can be daunting for a lone entrepreneur who's just starting out and has only a few customers. I recommend that you wait until you have enough income to hire an attorney and pay incorporation fees before you seriously consider incorporating, even as an S corporation.

C corporations

Many big businesses choose to become C corporations. In fact, everything about C corporations tends to be big — including profits, which are taxed at the corporate level — so I mention this legal designation only in passing, because it's probably not for your small entrepreneurial business. C corporations tend to be large and have lots of shareholders. In order to incorporate, all stockholders and shareholders must agree on the name of the company, the choice of the people who will manage it, and many other issues.

Limited liability corporations

The limited liability corporation (LLC) is a relatively new type of corporation that combines aspects of both S and C corporations. Limited liability corporations have a number of attractive options that make them good candidates for small businesses (such as the Collectible Exchange, LLC, which is profiled in Chapter 1). Benefits include the following:

- ✔ Members have limited liability for debts and obligations of the LLC.
- ✔ LLCs receive favorable tax treatment.
- ✔ Income and losses are shared by the individual investors, who are called members.

The responsibilities of LLC members are spelled out in an operating agreement, an often complex document that should be prepared by a knowledgeable attorney.

Steering Clear of Legal Trouble

A big part of keeping your online business legal is steering clear of so-called business opportunities that can turn into big problems. You can run into trouble both at the federal or the local level. Here are some areas to watch out for:

Be wary of multilevel marketing

Be careful if you undertake multilevel marketing. Multilevel marketing (MLM) is a strategy used by many reputable firms, such as Amway. But other companies (many of which you can find online) use MLM to run an old-fashioned pyramid scheme in which the participants recruit other investors.

The U.S. Postal Service treats MLM businesses as lotteries and has a Web page warning about them (www.usps.gov/websites/depart/inspect/pyramid.htm). Fraudulent pyramid schemes typically violate the Postal Lottery Statute (Title 18, United States Code, Section 1302). Yahoo! also maintains a list of Web pages that warn against MLM schemes (dir.yahoo.com/Business_and_Economy/Business_Opportunities/Multi_Level_Marketing/Anti_Multi_Level_Marketing/). Don't be taken in yourself by someone who wants you to participate in an questionable MLM-type scheme.

Be aware of risks with adult content

Be careful if you provide so-called adult content. There's no doubt about it: Cyberspace is full of X-rated sites, some of which do make money. But this is a risky area. Congress continues to debate legislation that may legally require online vendors of adult material to restrict access to sites by persons less than 17 years of age. And many ISPs prohibit you from publishing Web pages that contain adult content.

If you do sell adult items online, consider working with a blocking company, such as SurfWatch (www.surfwatch.com) or Net Nanny (www.netnanny.com), that can prevent minors from visiting your site.

Know about acceptable use policies

Be aware of acceptable use policies set up by agencies that control what goes out online. Usually, the company that hosts your Web set has a set of acceptable use guidelines spelling out what kind of material you can and can't publish. For example, America Online has its own policies for its members who create home pages through AOL.

Another important kind of acceptable use policy that you need to know about is the acceptable use policy issued by your Internet Service Provider. The most common restriction is one against *spamming* (sending out unsolicited bulk mailings).

Not following your Web host's or your ISP's guidelines can get you kicked off the Net. So make sure that you're aware of any restrictions by reading the guidelines posted on your ISP's or Web host's site.

Pay your state sales taxes

Sales tax varies from state to state. Your job, as an online store owner, is to charge the sales tax rate applicable in the state in which the purchase is made — that is, the state where your customer lives, not where you live.

Luckily, computer software is available to help you calculate sales taxes for every state. Many Web hosting services or ISPs also help with sales tax collection, among their other services. Shopping cart programs and some electronic storefront programs, such as the ones mentioned in Chapter 4, help you calculate sales tax, too.

If you're on your own, however, you can download a shareware sales tax program. The following steps show how to install and use Tax It!, a shareware application created by John Toalson for Windows 95/98/NT users.

1. **Connect to the Internet, launch your Web browser, and go to the Tax It! home page** (`ourworld.compuserve.com/homepages/ Two_Oceans_Studio/download.htm`).

   The Two Oceans Recording Studio – Download Page appears.

2. **Click on the <u>Tax it!</u> link.**

   The TaxIt!.zip archive file downloads to your computer. If your browser isn't configured to automatically download and open .zip compressed file archives, you get a dialog box asking what to do with the file. Click on the Save File button, locate the directory on your computer where you want to save the file, and click on Save.

3. **You must have the Visual Basic 5 runtime application installed on your computer in order to operate Tax It!: If you already have this application, skip ahead to Step 8, if not, click on the <u>msvbvm50.zip</u> link.**

   The Save File dialog box appears. Locate a directory where you want to download the file, which is in the form of a .zip archive. (You need WinZip to extract the archive; visit `www.winzip.com` if you don't yet have this indispensable Internet application.)

4. **When you locate the directory where you want to save the file, click on the Save button.**

   The file is downloaded to your computer.

5. **Double-click on the msvbvm50.zip file you just downloaded.**

   The WinZip application launches.

6. **Click on the Extract button in the WinZip toolbar.**

   A dialog box appears, prompting you for the location where you want to download the file.

7. **Locate the directory C:\Windows\System and then click on the Extract button to extract the file MSVBVM50.DLL there.**

8. **Double-click on the TaxIt.exe application you downloaded in Step 2.**

   The program launches, and the Tax It! window appears, as shown in Figure 13-4.

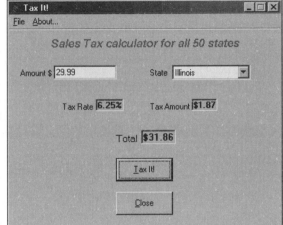

Figure 13-4:
Tax It!
calculates
sales tax for
individual
states.

9. **Enter the amount of the purchase in the Amount $ text box.**

10. **Click on the triangle next to the State box and choose a state from the drop-down menu.**

    The tax rate for the selected state appears in the Tax Rate box, and the program automatically calculates the Tax Amount and Total.

11. **If the selected state is your own state, choose File⇨Save current state as default.**

    The next time you start Tax It!, the default state appears in the State box.

Be sure to verify the tax rate for the state you choose. The rate shown for Illinois in Figure 13-4 has since increased to 8 percent.

Chapter 14

Online Business Accounting Tools

Some people have a gift for keeping track of expenses, recording financial information, and performing other fiscal functions. Unfortunately, I'm not one of those people. Yet I know well the value of accounting procedures, especially those that relate to an online business.

Without having at least some minimal records of your day-to-day operations, you won't have any way — other than the proverbial "gut feeling" — of knowing whether or not your business is truly successful. Besides that, banks and taxing authorities don't put much stock in gut feelings. When the time comes to ask for a loan or to pay taxes, you'll regret not having the records close at hand.

This chapter introduces you to some simple, straightforward ways to handle your online business's financial information. Read on to discover the most important accounting practices, get pointers on where to find accounting help online, and find out about software that can help you tackle the essential fiscal tasks you need to undertake to keep your new business viable.

Basic Accounting Practices

The most important accounting practices for your online business can be summarized as follows:

  ✔ **Deciding what type of business you're going to be.** Are you going to be a sole proprietorship, partnership, or corporation? (See Chapter 13.)

> ✔ **Establishing good record-keeping practices.** Record expenses and income in ways that will help you at tax time.
>
> ✔ **Obtaining financing when you need it.** Although getting started in business online doesn't cost a lot, you may want to expand someday, and good accounting can help you do it.

There's nothing sexy about accounting (unless, of course, you're married to an accountant; in that case, you have a financial expert at hand and can skip this chapter anyway!). Then again, there's nothing enjoyable about unexpected cash shortages or other problems that can result from bad record-keeping.

Good accounting is the key to order and good management for your business. How else can you know how you're doing? Yet many new business-people are intimidated by the numbers game. Use the tool at hand — your computer — to help you overcome your fear: Start keeping those books!

Choosing an accounting method

Accepting that you have to keep track of your business's accounting is only half the battle; next, you need to decide how to do it. The point at which you make note of each transaction in your books and the period of time over which you record the data make a difference not only to your accountant but also to agencies like the Internal Revenue Service. Even if you hire someone to keep the books for you, it's good to know what options are open to you.

Cash-basis versus accrual-basis accounting

Don't be intimidated by these terms: They are simply two methods of totting up income and expenses. Exactly where and how you do the recording is up to you. You can take a piece of paper, divide it into two columns labeled *Income* and *Expenses,* and do it that way. (I describe some more high-tech tools later in this chapter.) These are just two standard ways of deciding when to report them:

> ✔ **Cash-basis accounting:** You report income when you actually receive it and write off expenses when you pay them. This is the easy way to report income and expenses, and probably the way most new small businesses do it.
>
> ✔ **Accrual-basis accounting:** This method is more complicated than the cash-basis method, but if your online business maintains an inventory, you must use the accrual method. You report income when you actually receive the payment; you write down expenses *when services are rendered* (even though you may not have made the cash payment yet). For example, if a payment is due on December 1, but you send the check

out on December 8, you record the bill as being paid on December 1, when the payment was originally due. Accrual-basis accounting creates a more accurate picture of a business's financial situation. If a business is experiencing cash flow problems and is extending payment on some of its bills, cash-basis accounting provides an unduly rosy financial picture, whereas the accrual-basis method would be more accurate.

Choosing an accounting period

The other choice you need to make when it comes to deciding how to keep your books is the accounting period you're going to use. Here, again, you have two choices:

- ✔ **Calendar year:** The fiscal year ends on December 31. This is the period with which you're probably most familiar, and the one most small or home-based businesses choose, because it's the easiest to work with.

- ✔ **Fiscal year:** In this case, the business picks a date other than December 31 to function as the end of the fiscal year. Many large organizations pick a date that coincides with the end of their business cycle. Some pick March 31 as the end, others June 30, and still others September 30.

If you use the fiscal-year method of accounting, you must file your tax return three and a half months after the end of the fiscal year. If the fiscal year ends on June 30, for example, you must file by October 15.

Knowing what records to keep

When you run your own business, it pays to be meticulous about recording everything that pertains to your commercial activities. The more you understand what you have to record, the more accurate your records will be — and the more deductions you can take, too.

Tracking income

Receiving checks for your goods or services is the fun part of doing business, and so income is probably the kind of data that you'll be happiest about recording.

You need to keep track of your company's income (or, as it is sometimes called, your *gross receipts*) carefully. Not all the income your business receives is taxable. What you receive as a result of sales (your *revenue*) is taxable, but loans that you receive are not. Be sure to separate the two and pay tax only on the sales income. But keep good records: If you cannot accurately report the source of income that you didn't pay taxes on, the IRS will label it *unreported income,* and you will have to pay taxes and possibly fines and penalties on it.

Just how should you record your revenue? For each item, write down a brief, informal statement. This is a personal record that you may make on a slip of paper or even on the back of a canceled check. Be sure to include the following information:

- ✔ Amount you received
- ✔ Type of payment (credit card, electronic cash, or check)
- ✔ Date of the transaction
- ✔ Name of the client or customer
- ✔ Goods or services you provided in exchange for the payment

Collect all your check stubs and revenue statements in a folder labeled *Income,* so you can find them easily at tax time.

Assessing your assets

Assets are resources that your business owns, such as your office and computer equipment. *Equity* refers to your remaining assets after you pay your creditors.

Any equipment you have that contributes to your business activities constitutes your assets. Equipment that has a life span of more than a year is expected to help you generate income over its useful life; therefore, you must spread out (or, in other words, *expense*) the original cost of the equipment over its life span. Expensing the cost of an asset over the period of its useful life is called *depreciation.* In order to depreciate an item, you estimate how many years you're going to use it, and then divide the original cost by the number of years. The result is the amount that you report in any given year. For example, if you purchase a computer that costs $3,000 and you expect to use it in your business for five years, you expense $600 of the cost each year.

You need to keep records of your assets that include the following information:

- ✔ Name, model number, and description
- ✔ Purchase date
- ✔ Purchase price, including fees
- ✔ Date the item went into service
- ✔ Amount of time the item is put to personal (as opposed to business) use

File these records in a safe location along with your other tax-related information.

Recording payments

Even a lone entrepreneur doesn't work in a vacuum. An online business owner needs to pay a Web host, an ISP, and possibly Web page designers and other consultants. If you take on partners or employees, things get more complicated. But in general, you need to record all payments such as these in detail, as well.

Your accountant is likely to bring up the question of how you pay the people who work for you. You have two options: You can treat them either as full-time employees or as independent contractors. The IRS uses a stringent series of guidelines to determine who is a contractor and who is a full-time employee. Refer to the IRS Publication 15A (www.irs.ustreas.gov/prod/forms_pubs/pubs/p15a02.htm), which discusses the employee/independent contractor subject in detail.

Hiring independent contractors rather than salaried workers is far simpler for you: You don't have to pay benefits to independent contractors, and you don't have to withhold federal and state taxes. Just be sure to get invoices from any independent contractor who works for you. If you have full-time employees whom you pay an hourly wage, things get more complicated, and you had best consult an accountant to help you set up the salary payments.

Listing expenses

In general, business expenses include travel, business meals, advertisements, postage, and other costs that you incur in order to *produce revenue.* This is in contrast to instances when you're just exchanging one asset (cash) for another (a printer or modem, for example). That is not an expense. The difference is that in the second case, the act of spending the money does not directly result in more revenue for you — even though the equipment being purchased will *eventually* help you produce revenue.

Get a big folder and use it to hold any receipts, contracts, canceled checks, credit card statements, or invoices that represent expenses. It's also a great idea to maintain a record of expenses that includes the following information:

- Date the expense occurred
- Name of the person or company that received payment from you
- Type of expense incurred (equipment, utilities, supplies, and so on)

Recalling exactly what some receipts were for is often difficult a year or even just a month after the fact. Be sure to jot down a quick note on all canceled checks and copies of receipts to remind you of what the expense involved.

Should you hire an accountant?

Hiring someone at least to help you with your taxes and advise you from time to time on financial planning may be a good idea. Enlisting the help of an accountant can be particularly helpful if you're self-employed and don't have sources of financial advice through your place of employment.

How do you find an accountant? I found mine through a personal recommendation, which is always a good way to find professionals. Here are some things to look for:

✔ **Look for a CPA.** Of the two groups of accountants — Public Accountants and Certified Public Accountants (CPAs) — CPAs are the best-qualified candidates.

✔ **Try a small accounting firm rather than going to a big corporate firm.** The small players probably have more experience with small business concerns, and they tend to charge lower fees, too.

✔ **Get recommendations.** If you can't find a personal recommendation, ask your state CPA society for a list of accountants in your area.

When you interview accountants, ask about any small business clients they have and especially any online businesses they may handle.

Understanding the Ps and Qs of P&Ls

You're likely to hear the term *profit-and-loss statement* (also called a P&L) thrown around when discussing your online business with financial people. A P&L is a report that measures the operation of a business over a given period of time, such as a week, a month, or a year. The person who prepares the P&L (either you or your accountant) adds up your business revenues and subtracts the operating expenses. What's left are either the profits or the losses.

Most of the programs listed later, in the "Accounting Software for Your Business" section of this chapter, include some way of presenting profit-and-loss statements and enable you to customize the statements to fit your needs.

Accounting Software for Your Business

The well-known commercial accounting packages, such as QuickBooks and M.Y.O.B., let you prepare statements and reports, and even tie into a tax preparation system. Stick with these programs if you like setting up systems such as databases on your computer. Otherwise, go for a simpler method, and hire an accountant to help you.

Whatever program you choose, make sure that you're able to do the following:

- ✔ Keep accurate books.
- ✔ Set up privacy schemes that prevent your kids from zapping your business records.

If your business is a relatively simple sole proprietorship, you can record expenses and income by hand and add them up at tax time. Then carry them through to Schedule C or IRS Form 1040. Alternatively, you can record your entries and turn them over to a tax advisor who will prepare a profit-and-loss statement and tell you the balance due on your tax payment.

Nothing's wrong with keeping the books by buying an old-fashioned ledger or journal and recording the data by hand. But if you want to file your taxes electronically or generate profit-and-loss statements yourself, accounting software can make that part of your financial life easier. And besides, you're starting an online business that you basically run through your computer, so why not get in the habit of regarding the computer as a tool that can make your life easier? Check out the programs on this book's CD-ROM before you start loading up on office supplies.

The big commercial programs

A good software package can help save time when it comes to accounting and tax preparation for small businesses. The well-known packages described in this section have plenty of features and add-ons. Programs like Microsoft Money and Quicken, for example, let you create customizable home pages that you can configure to provide up-to-the minute reports on your stock holdings. They also help you with financial planning. All let you record income and expenses and prepare business reports.

As a small-business owner on a budget, you're better off shopping around to get the best package for your individual needs. It also pays to try out inexpensive shareware accounting programs that you can download from the Web, some of which are included on this book's CD-ROM.

Easy personal finance packages

Two well-known software packages from Microsoft and Intuit are easy to use but mainly suitable for financial planning, checkbook balancing, and stock watching. They aren't primarily for small business owners. However, if you have a small-scale business and need to manage a simple set of income and expenses, these programs may be good enough for you.

- **Microsoft Money 99 Financial Suite** (`www.microsoft.com/products/prodref/699_ov.htm`): One of Microsoft Money's distinguishing features is its level of integration with the Internet. You can get automatic updates on stock prices and other information, as well as suggestions of online resources. The program has a list price of $64.95 but comes with a $25 rebate.

- **Quicken Home and Business 99** (`www.quicken99.com`): The program is available for Windows 95 or 98. A separate program, Quicken 98 (`www.intuit.com/quicken98`), is available for Macintosh users. The business features that come with the program include invoicing, business reports, basic accounts payable and receivable, and other features. The list price is $89.95, but you can get a $20 mail-in rebate.

Accounting and small business software

Whereas the aforementioned programs are primarily personal checkbook managers, the following three programs are more useful if your needs include managing an inventory or dealing with payroll issues.

Often, these programs work by requiring the user to fill out simple business forms. After you enter the data, the software assumes the role of accountant and crunches numbers in the background in order to prepare reports of your business activities.

You can find an in-depth comparison of ten accounting packages at `www.smalloffice.com/expert/archive/tebuyer30.htm`.

- **QuickBooks Pro 5.0** (`www.quickbooks.com`): This program, which comes in both Macintosh and Windows versions, is frequently praised as being one of the simplest and easiest-to-learn accounting programs, especially for those with no prior accounting experience. Online businesses that provide services to clients can make use of the QuickBooks time-tracking system. Small businesses that provide items for sale can benefit from the program's inventory features.

- **M.Y.O.B. Accounting Plus** (`www.bestware.com`): This program, by BestWare, also comes in versions for the Mac and Windows. It is intuitive and uses flowcharts rather than forms to help you organize data, as shown in Figure 14-1. The program's estimated retail price is $179 for the Windows version and $199 for the Macintosh version. You can order a trial CD-ROM version that you can use for 25 sessions only. You can view the system requirements for all versions at `www.bestware.com/sysreq.htm`.

- **Peachtree Office Accounting** (`www.peachtree.com`): This is a powerful program full of very strong features for a complex business operation. Sole proprietors who are afraid of accounting and are looking for the simplest possible interface may well find that Peachtree has more features than they need; on the other hand, this is a $99 program that you and your business can grow into.

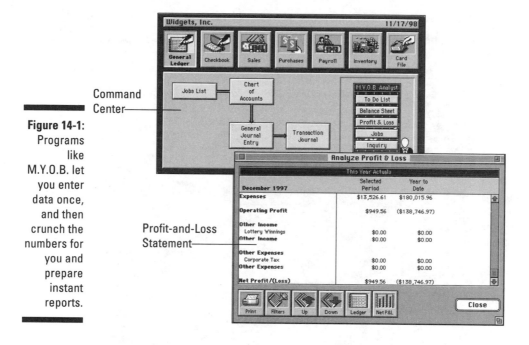

Command Center—

Figure 14-1:
Programs like M.Y.O.B. let you enter data once, and then crunch the numbers for you and prepare instant reports.

Profit-and-Loss Statement—

Shareware programs for the budget-conscious

Many of the commercial accounting packages listed in the previous sections are not available in trial versions. You can't always go to a Web site, download the program, and try it out. (Although a CD-ROM-based trial version of M.Y.O.B. is available, and this book's CD includes a copy.) If you're in a hurry and are looking for an accounting program that you can set up right now, look no farther than the programs included on this very book's CD-ROM, including Owl Simple Business Accounting and Easy Account.

Owl Simple Business Accounting

Simple Business Accounting, by Owl Software (www.owlsoftware.com), really lives up to its name. It's so simple that even a financially impaired person like yours truly can pick it up quickly. Owl Simple Business Accounting (SBA) is designed to let people with no prior accounting experience keep track of income and expenses, and it uses the single-entry accounting system favored by the IRS.

The following steps illustrate how easy it is to start keeping books with SBA. They assume that you have installed the software from the CD-ROM by following the steps described in the appendix.

1. **Choose Start⇨Programs⇨Owl Business Apps⇨SB Accounting.**

   The main Owl Simple Business Accounting window appears (see Figure 14-2).

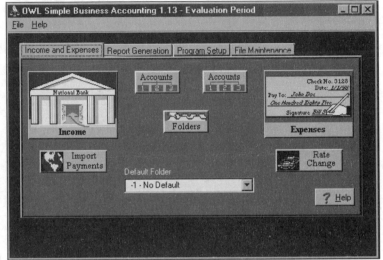

Figure 14-2: Owl Simple Business Accounting uses folders to contain income and expense data that you report.

The program comes with a set of sample data already entered to help you learn its features. Choose Help⇨Help to open the SBA User's Guide help files and click on the topic Getting Started, if you want an overview of how the program operates.

2. **Click on the Program Setup tab to bring it to the front, and make any custom changes you may want:**

   • If you want to operate in a different fiscal year than the pre-entered January 1, enter the number for a new month or year opening.

   • If you want your on-screen and printed reports to be in a different font than the preselected one (MS Sans Serif), click on the Report Font button, choose the font you want, and then click on OK to close the Font dialog box. Times New Roman is usually a good choice, because it's relatively compact.

3. **Click on the File Maintenance tab to bring it to the front, and then click on the Erase Data Files button.**

   This step erases the sample data that was pre-entered to show you how the program works.

4. Select the Income and Expenses tab to bring it to the front, and then click on the Folders button to create folders for your business data.

The PickFol dialog box appears, as shown in Figure 14-3. This dialog box lists any folders that have been created. One sample folder called BUSINESS is already entered.

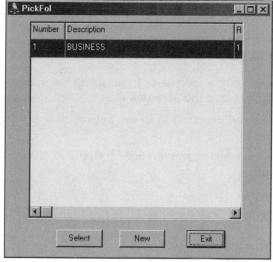

Figure 14-3: Use this dialog box to add, delete, or edit folders that hold your business data.

5. You can change the sample folder name to something more specific by clicking on Select.

The Folder Definition dialog box appears with the word BUSINESS pre-entered in the Description box.

6. Enter a new name in the Description box and click on Save.

The Folder Definition dialog box closes, and you return to the PickFol dialog box, where your folder appears with its new name.

7. To create a new folder, click on the New button at the bottom of the PickFol dialog box.

The Folder Definition dialog box appears.

8. Enter the new name in the Description box and click on Save.

A dialog box appears asking you to confirm that you want to add a new folder.

9. Click on OK.

The Folder Definition dialog box closes, but then immediately reopens so that you can enter a new folder name if you want to.

10. **Click on Cancel and you return to the PickFol dialog box, where your folder is listed.**

    You may want to create separate folders for your personal or business finances, for example. After your folders are set up, you can record data as described in the following steps.

11. **Select the Income and Expenses tab to bring it to the front, and then click on either the Income button or the Expense button, depending on the type of data you want to enter.**

    In either case, the Select Item dialog box appears.

12. **Click on New to enter a new item.**

    A dialog box named either Income or Expense appears, depending on the button you selected in the previous step.

13. **Enter the amount and description in the appropriate fields, and click on Save.**

    A dialog box appears asking you to confirm that you either want to add or delete a record.

14. **Click on OK.**

    You return to the Income or Expense dialog box, where you can make more entries.

15. **When you finish, click on Save.**

    You return to the Select Item dialog box, where you can review your changes.

16. **Click on Exit.**

    You return to the Income and Expenses options.

17. **When you're all finished, choose File⇨Exit to exit the program until your next accounting session.**

After entering some data, you can select the Report Generation tab, run each of the reports provided by SBA, and examine the output. SBA can generate the following reports: Expense Reports, Income Reports, Profit Reports, and a General Ledger Report. When running the reports, be sure to select a reporting period within the current calendar year.

Easy Account

For Macintosh users, Easy Account by Edwin de Leur provides an intuitive, user-friendly way to record basic income and expense records. The program's main operating window (see Figure 14-4) contains all the buttons you need to set up records and enter data.

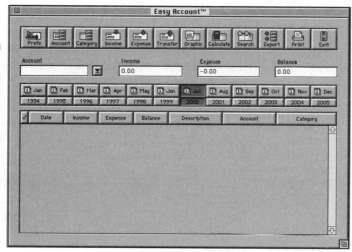

Figure 14-4:
With Easy
Account,
you click on
a data field,
press the
Income or
Expense
button to
enter data,
and away
you go.

The version of Easy Account that's included on this book's CD-ROM includes Readme files and other documentation to help you get going, too. See the appendix for instructions on how to install the program.

Finding accounting help online

In a survey taken by American Express that involved 300 small-business owners (www.smalloffice.com/miser/taxpage/taxnews4.htm), nearly three-quarters of all participants reported that they pass tax work on to professional accountants. You may well decide to secure professional help, too, so you can concentrate on running and promoting your online business.

Keep in mind, however, that anyone you hire to keep your books, prepare profit-and-loss statements, or prepare your tax returns will have access to virtually all your financial information. If you're reluctant to entrust someone with that level of responsibility, look for some free instruction and support on the Web itself. Here are a few sites you can visit that provide good starter information for budding cyberaccountants:

✔ **Entrepreneur's Help Page:** This Web site, which is full of useful information for online entrepreneurs, includes a Financial Records page (www.tannedfeet.com/html/financial_records.htm) that discusses the basics of small business accounting.

✔ **Accounting Over Easy:** A CPA created this Web site (www.ezaccounting.com) devoted to making accounting easy to learn for small business owners. He charges $9.95 for access to most of the content. You can view a preview page for free, however.

Small Business Tax Concerns

After you make it through the start-up phase of your business, it's time to be concerned with taxes. Here, too, a little preparation up front can save you lots of headaches down the road. But as a hard-working entrepreneur, time is your biggest obstacle.

In an American Express survey, 26 percent reported that they wait until the last minute to start preparing their taxes, and 13.9 percent said that they usually ask for an extension. Yet advance planning is really important for taxes. In fact, Internal Revenue Code Section 6001 mandates that businesses must keep records appropriate to their trade or business. The IRS has the right to view these records if they want to audit your business's (or your personal) tax return. If your records aren't to the IRS's satisfaction, the penalties can be serious.

One good piece of news is that in October 1998, Congress passed and sent to the president a tax package that includes a three-year freeze on new taxes on Internet access and e-commerce. Your legislators are trying to help you; your job is to get educated on tax requirements so you can help yourself when it comes to taxes.

The Smalloffice.com Web site maintains an excellent Tax Page among its many resources for small businesses. It's full of tips on taking all the deductions for which you are eligible, filing electronically, and more. Check it out at www.smalloffice.com/miser/taxpage/index1.htm.

Federal and state taxes

Although operating a business does complicate your tax return, it's something you can handle if your business is a simple one-person operation, if you are willing to expend the time, and, finally, if you have kept the proper business records.

If you have a sole proprietorship, you need to file IRS form Schedule C along with your regular form 1040 tax return. If your sole proprietorship has net income, you are also required to file Schedule SE to determine any Social Security and FICA taxes that are due.

State taxes vary depending on where you live. You most likely need to file sales tax and income tax. If you have employees, you also need to pay employee withholding tax. Contact a local accountant in order to find out what you have to file, or contact the state tax department yourself. Most state tax offices provide guide books to help you understand state tax requirements.

Paying quarterly estimates

When you start making money for yourself independently, rather than depending on a regular paycheck from an employer, you have to start doing something you've probably never done before: You have to start estimating the tax you will have to pay based on the income from your own business. You are then required to pay this tax on a quarterly basis, both to the IRS and to your state taxing agency. Estimating and paying quarterly taxes is an important part of meeting your tax obligations as a self-employed person.

The IRS provides you with instructions for calculating how much tax you have to pay, as does your state taxing office. (If you have an accountant, that person can also help you determine how much to pay.) You file a Form 1040-ES every quarter, along with a check for the required amount. You have to do the same on the state level, but the required forms vary by state. Check out IRS publication 505 (`www.irs.ustreas.gov/prod/forms_pubs/pubs/p5050205.htm`) for the official word on the subject.

A page full of links to state tax agencies is available at `www.tannedfeet.com/html/state_tax_agencies.htm`.

Deducing your business deductions

One of the benefits of starting a new business, even if the business isn't profitable in the beginning, is the opportunity to take business deductions and reduce your tax payments. Always keep receipts from any purchases or expenses associated with your business activities. Make sure that you're taking all the deductions for which you are eligible. I mention some of these deductions in the following sections.

Don't overdo it when it comes to entertainment and travel expenses. Only 50 percent of your business entertainment and travel expenses are deductible. Health club and other club dues aren't deductible at all.

Your home office

If you work at home (and I'm assuming that, as an entrepreneur, you probably do), set aside some space for a home office. This isn't just a territorial thing. It can result in some nifty business deductions too.

Taking a home office deduction used to be difficult, because a 1993 Supreme Court decision stated that, unless you met with clients, customers, or patients on a regular basis in your home office, you couldn't claim the home-office deduction. However, the 1997 tax law eliminates the client requirement and requires only that the office be used "regularly and exclusively" for business. You can read more about the change at `www.dtonline.com/promises/chap8.htm`.

What you deduct depends on the amount of space in your home that is used for your business. If your office is one room in a four-room house, you can deduct 25 percent of your utilities, for example. If you have a separate phone line that is solely for business use, you are able to deduct 100 percent of that expense, however.

Your computer equipment

Computer equipment is probably the biggest expense related to your online business. But taking tax deductions can help offset the cost substantially. The key is showing the IRS (by reporting your income from your online business on your tax return) that your PC and related items, such as modems or printers, were used for business purposes.

In case you are ever audited, be sure to keep some sort of record detailing all the ways in which you have put your computer equipment to use for business purposes. If less than half of your computer use is for your business, consider depreciating its cost over several years.

Other common business deductions

Many of the business-related expenses that you can deduct are listed on IRS form Schedule C. The following is a brief list of some of the deductions you can look for:

- ✔ **Advertising:** Not just online advertising, but any newspaper, magazine, or other promotional fees are eligible.

- ✔ **Internet access charges:** You may be able to deduct monthly fees you pay to your ISP or Web host.

- ✔ **Computer supplies:** All the equipment you use to operate your online business count.

- ✔ **Shipping and delivery:** You can deduct any costs associated with shipping and postage.

- ✔ **Interest expenses:** Include the interest you pay on bank loans that you used for business purposes.

- ✔ **Office supplies:** Your paper, toner, paper-clip, and other costs can be counted too.

- ✔ **Utilities:** You can deduct the light, electricity, and telephone costs that pertain to your home office.

- ✔ **Accountants' fees:** Any fees you pay to the person who adds up your deductions are themselves deductible, too.

Using online tax resources

The best place on the Internet for tax information (and one of the best resources online) is the IRS's own Web site. The home page is at www.irs.ustreas.gov, but check out its index of pages specifically for businesses (www.irs.ustreas.gov/prod/bus_info/index.html), and a page full of tax tips aimed at small businesses (www.irs.ustreas.gov/prod/bus_info/bus_help.html).

Here are two other tax-resource sites you can visit:

- ✔ **1040.com** (www.1040.com): This site, operated by Drake Software, contains some resources that you won't find on the IRS's Web site, including a tax-related bulletin board, a database of tax preparers, and links to state tax agencies.

- ✔ **Tax News and Views** (www.dtonline.com/tnv/tnv.htm): If a question arises about the latest tax provisions, and you need to look up the answer quickly, try this publication, which is produced by Deloitte & Touche LLP.

The Starting an Online Business For Dummies Internet Directory

The 5th Wave

By Rich Tennant

©RICHTENNANT

"Just how accurately should my Web site reflect my place of business?"

In this directory . . .

Trying to find a Web site or Internet resource can be like trying to get a drink out of a fire hydrant. You're sure that what you want is out there in cyberspace somewhere, but every time you try to find it, you get deluged.

The following directory does the sorting for you. The flood of choices has been quality-tested, labeled, and organized, just like rows of bottled water neatly arranged and just waiting for your enjoyment. My research assistant and I scouted out hundreds of possibilities in order to provide for you the definitive collection of online resources especially for online entrepreneurs.

One thing on the Web leads to another, and you're sure to find plenty on your own when you get started. The following directory is intended to serve as a set of starting points. So jump in whenever you're ready. The water's fine!

The Starting an Online Business For Dummies Internet Directory

. . . .

In This Directory

▶ Downloading software to help you construct your commercial site

▶ Finding out about Web design and e-commerce

▶ Marketing and advertising your business online

▶ Finding business networks and groups you can join

▶ Using Internet resources designed for start-ups like yours

. . . .

*W*hen it comes to finding sources of support as you start your new business, the best place to turn is the Internet itself. The Starting an Online Business For Dummies Internet Directory is a comprehensive Yellow Pages-style list of Web sites and other resources to give you a jump start.

To help you judge at a glance whether a site may be useful for you, this directory includes some handy miniature icons (otherwise known as *micons*). Here's an explanation of what each micon means:

$ You have to pay a fee to access some services at this site.

This site gives you a chance to talk to fellow entrepreneurs, business authorities, or potential customers online.

You can download software or other files at this site.

Information about electronic commerce or shopping-cart software is available at this site.

This site has particularly good hyperlinks, which can be very useful for business research.

Turn up the volume; this site contains audio files.

This site is truly worthy of a four-star rating. It's a particularly valuable resource due to its content, links, free software, or all of these.

Accounting Software

"You mean I have to keep *track* of all this stuff?" Yes, my entrepreneurial friend, owning and managing a small business, whether it's located online or not, requires good accounting practices and record-keeping. Here are some powerful, yet user-friendly, accounting software programs that can help you organize and control your finances.

Quicken 99

www.quicken99.com

www.intuit.com/quicken98

From this site, you can order Quicken Home and Business 99, which enables you to manage both your personal and business finances; create business invoices, reports, and graphs; and take advantage of financial services, including online banking and online payment and investment tracking. Quicken Home and Business 99 is for Windows users only; Quicken Deluxe 98 (also available at this site) has similar features and is available for Macintosh users. This site also contains links to the Intuit Online Financial Services site, where current users can do online banking, pay bills, and track investments. The Quicken Support Network area (www.intuit.com/ofs) contains information on how Quicken users can join user communities and obtain technical support.

QuickBooks

www.quickbooks.com

QuickBooks and QuickBooks Pro, like Quicken, are produced by Intuit, Inc. Whereas Quicken has personal finance features that you can use to manage your

home accounts, QuickBooks is more of a straight business product. Another difference is that you can download a trial version (which you can use for free for up to 25 uses) of QuickBooks or QuickBooks Pro from Intuit's Web site. Current users of QuickBooks can find plenty of support on this site, including user discussion forums, ways to contact QuickBooks Professional Advisors, free e-mail newsletters, a set of Frequently Asked Questions, and tips, tools, and advice designed for specific types of industries.

Peachtree Office Accounting

www.peachtree.com

If you're looking for accounting software that's specifically designed for a small business, Peachtree Software's products may just be right for you. Peachtree Office Accounting and Peachtree Complete Accounting allow you to work seamlessly with Microsoft Office products such as Excel and Word. This company also offers a variety of business services built around their software, including payroll and tax filing, bill payment, banking, and Web site building. Through a program called PeachLink (www.peachtree.com/adpbiz2), Peachtree helps users of its products to develop and host a Web site (in less than an hour). You can export product inventory directly from your Peachtree accounting program into your Web site catalog and process orders and customer information from your Web site into your accounting software. (Peachtree Office Accounting and Peachtree Complete Accounting are available for Windows users only.)

Microsoft Money 99 Web Site

www.microsoft.com/money

One of Microsoft Money's distinguishing features is its level of integration with the Internet. It gives you automatic updates on stock prices and other information, as well as suggestions of online resources. Many of those resources are accessible through this Web site. You can also download a 90-day trial version of Microsoft Money 99 Financial Suite from this site. For current users of Microsoft Money, this site includes a set of Frequently Asked Questions, an offer for a year of free online data backups, and links to financial institutions that support Microsoft money bill payments.

M.Y.O.B. Accounting Plus Web Site

www.bestware.com

From this site, you can order a version of M.Y.O.B. on CD-ROM that will be shipped to you. This program, by BestWare, comes in versions for Macintosh and Windows. Accountants who use M.Y.O.B. can join the M.Y.O.B. Accountant Club, a group that provides products and services to help them advise and support their clients. Other users can find technical support in the Support Services area of the site (`www.bestware.com/suppserv.htm`).

Other Stuff to Check Out

www.owlsoftware.com
www.smalloffice.com/miser/taxpage/
     index1.htm
www.palo-alto.com
www.1040.com

Advertising Your Site on the Web

Advertising on the Web is a broad subject that encompasses traditional banner advertising, the use of search engines and linking, as well as a variety of combined approaches that are unique to online business. What follows is a list of

sample sites related to the use of two of the most important Web advertising methods — banners and linking. I also include a reference page that provides a well-maintained list of Web advertising resources.

Advertising Resources on the WWW

www.uconect.net/~gmik

This well maintained and frequently updated page offers links to banner exchanges, classifieds, link pages, and other kinds of advertising resources. The page is part of a larger site owned by an ISP called UcoNects, which hosts a number of business Web sites.

AutoLink

www.career-pro.com

$

CareerPro, a resume- and career-development business, provides several services to help businesses promote themselves online. For a fee, you can use CareerPro's AutoLink and MasterLink programs to broadcast your Web site's URL twice a day to more than 500 locations on the Internet. You can also add your URL to CareerPro's Free For All Link Page.

Best Way! Banner Exchange

www.bestwayimaging.com/ads

Best Way! Banner Exchange represents one common technique for advertising Web sites. You create a banner ad for your site and join a banner exchange program. Other members of the program post your ad on their Web sites; in return, you agree to display the advertising banners for other members on your Web site. Best Way! lets you choose the types of sites you'll advertise on your site and the types of sites that will promote you in return. (Where, you ask, do you get your own banner ad? See the listing for Media Builder, later in this section.)

LinkExchange

www.linkexchange.com

★ ★
★ ★

LinkExchange's massive site is a must-stop for the Web entrepreneur. It contains extensive resources for advertising and promoting your online business. These include the Banner Network for promoting your site and getting stats, SiteInpector for checking your site's quality, ListBot for creating your own mailing list, FastCounter for keeping track of visits, Daily Digest for discussing site promotion issues, Submit It! for registering with more than 400 search engines, and much, much more. In addition, the Link Exchange Web Resource Center offers a wealth of background information that you can use to develop your site.

MediaBuilder

www.mediabuilder.com/abm.html

With Media Builder, you can create your own custom animated banner for free. After choosing the animation effects and the type of text, you click on the Make Banner button. You can then save the banner to your own computer. This site also offers a button-maker and a host of image files, fonts, and software tools.

Other Stuff to Check Out

www.iab.net
www.markwelch.com/bannerad
www.coder.com/creations/banner
www.exchange-it.com

Auctions

One increasingly popular way to sell or buy something is through an online auction. The obvious advantage over listing or buying through your local newspaper is that these auctions give you access to the entire international Web community. Making a bid or offering something for sale usually requires a registration process. Trading is public, which adds interest and keeps the forum honest. One of the larger auction sites listed below has a feedback forum, where users can indicate whether a trade was a positive or negative experience.

eBay

www.ebay.com

$

eBay is certainly one of the largest person-to-person trading areas on the Internet, offering over 750,000 items in 300 categories of auction classifieds. eBay claims that tens of thousands of transactions take place on its site each week, and those of us who regularly scan the listings know this to be true when a particularly precious or collectible item goes up for auction. You can browse the listings or search by specific item, bid on anything, or offer something for sale. Viewing, bidding, and buying items are free; listing and selling items incur insertion fees and final value fees.

Yahoo! Auctions

auctions.yahoo.com

Yahoo! allows you to browse its auction categories in order to identify auction

Web sites or search for a particular item available at a current auction site. It doesn't cost a thing to sell, bid on, or purchase an item.

Other Stuff to Check Out

www.onsale.com
www.auction-sales.com
dir.yahoo.com/Business_and_Economy/
   Companies/Auctions/Online_auctions

Business Resources on the Web

The Web offers a vast resource for the entrepreneur. An overwhelming amount of information is available on every conceivable topic related to the starting and growing of a small business. So the question isn't "Does the Web have useful information for me?" but rather "Where on the Web do I find the best information for my needs?" The following sites are either guides to small-business sites on the Web or are themselves some of the better business sites available.

BizProWeb

www.bizproweb.com

BizProWeb is a searchable site offering 675 pages of business links, information, and resources for small-business owners, professionals, and home office entrepreneurs.

Bloomberg Small Business

www.bloomberg.com/smallbiz

This is a great multimedia site that includes a feature story, a tip of the month, and video and audio interviews with experts on aspects of small business. Past interviews are archived and available.

CCH Business Owners Toolkit

www.toolkit.cch.com

This site offers model business plans and other business documents you can download and use, an "Ask Alice" advice column, and useful articles about starting and running a small business.

The Mining Company Guide to Small Business Information

sbinformation.miningco.com

A great guide to small-business information on the Web, The Mining Company Guide presents links to a comprehensive list of topics, a bulletin board, a free newsletter, and a chat room that's always open.

Netscape Small Business Source

home.netscape.com/netcenter/
   smallbusiness/index.html

Netscape provides a jam-packed page full of links and other resources including a free service that helps you create a Web site. You can also host your business site with Netscape for free. One unusual feature, Netscape Online Backup, gives you a place to back up your files online for $14.95 per month.

smallbizNet

www.lowe.org/smallbiznet

Sponsored by the Edward Lowe Foundation, smallbizNet claims to have "the answers you need for starting, running, and growing your small business." This is a well-designed, searchable site loaded with useful information for the small-business owner.

smalloffice.com

www.smalloffice.com

★ ★
★ ★

This is one of my very favorite small-business resources. The editors of the magazines *Home Office Computing* and *Small Business Computing* offer reviews of small-business Web sites and software packages, tips on running an online business, and much more information of use to the online entrepreneur. The site includes a "How To" department with advice on start-up, sales and marketing, and finance, as well as message boards and a link allowing you to conduct a trademark search.

Yahoo! Small Business

smallbusiness.yahoo.com

Yahoo! Small Business topics include Starting a Business, Finance, Office Supplies, Technology, Communications, Government Services, Legal, Taxes, Sales and Marketing, Human Resources, and International Business and Trade. Other resources on this page include links to Package Tracking, Business Tools, Communications Tools, Featured Articles, News, Local Events, and other Yahoo! business-related categories.

Other Stuff to Check Out

www.office.com/biztools
www.entrepreneurmag.com
www.fastcompany.com

Classifieds

The Web offers countless sources for advertising via classified ads. Included here are guides to the many sites that offer this service, some of which are free and some require payment. Obviously, the beauty of the Web is that you reach a lot more people than you would by advertising in your local newspaper. On the Web, the whole world of online users can be your potential buyers.

America Online Business Directory

$

downtown.web.aol.com

This is a great resource if you are already a customer of PrimeHost, America Online's Web site hosting service. PrimeHost customers can list their business in this searchable classified ad database for free. All you have to do is fill out a simple online form with your PrimeHost customer number, e-mail address, URL, and site category. Noncustomers must pay $125 to place an ad in the directory.

The Grandfather of All Links Free Advertising Directory

ecki.com/links/oclass.shtml

This huge listing of free classified advertising sites takes forever to load but is updated and current. Sites are sorted alphabetically and grouped by how long you can run the ad and whether the ad is city- or state-specific. The Grandfather of All Links also includes a directory of non-English sites.

Yahoo! Classifieds

www.yahoo.com/
Business_and_Economy/Classifieds

As usual, Yahoo! is a great starting point if you're looking for just about anything — in this case, sites where you can place your classified ads online. Yahoo! allows you to browse by region or by category. Also listed are general classified sites that can include additional services such as chat rooms, personal ads, and auctions.

Other Stuff to Check Out

www.villagesclassified.com
www.classifieds2000.com
classifieds.imall.com/ads.shtml
www.trade-direct.com

Developing Compelling Content

As a fledgling Web entrepreneur, you may find yourself preoccupied with the technical issues of this relatively new medium — page design, layout, graphic elements, icons, browsers, ease of navigation, animation — but when it comes to the user, content is king. Bottom line: People go to the Web to find information. Studies show that users don't read, but rather *scan* the page, and that they prefer scannable, objective writing to the promotional and over-hyped language that is tolerated and expected in other media. The following sites contain guidance to help you create Web content that is concise and effective.

"Concise, Scannable, and Objective: How to Write for the Web"

www.useit.com/papers/webwriting/
writing.html

John Morkes and Jakob Nielsen of Sun Microsystems provide this scholarly but very readable article on how to write effectively for the Web. Their studies suggest that effective Web writing has to be *scannable,* that users want to be able to pick out what they need in a few sentences, that the writing has to be short and to the point, and that it must provide factual information rather than marketing fluff.

Contentious

www.contentious.com

Contentious is a monthly Web-zine primarily intended for professional writers and editors who create content for the Web and other online media. It regularly examines key content-related issues, such as the differences between writing for the Web and writing for print, and what rules are emerging for the editorial aspects of online media. However, the readers of this journal are not just writers but all kinds of online publishers, from e-zines to business Web sites, and anyone interested in effective online writing.

E-write

www.ewriteonline.com

The owners started E-write when they realized that e-mail and the Internet were reinventing the way people communicate with their customers, coworkers, and suppliers. They understand that good writing is key to using e-mail effectively, as well as developing user-friendly Web content. Their site includes articles for the small-business entrepreneur on writing competitive e-mail that allows you to communicate quickly and frequently with your customer.

Web Central

www.cio.com/central/style.html

Web Central, the Web site affiliated with *CIO Magazine,* is a rich resource for anyone involved in online business, whether you're a Fortune 500 company or a small-business owner. In one little corner of this large site, you can find "Web Writing Style Resources," a collection of articles that provide various writing style guides for developing the written content of your Web site. Most of the articles combine the discussion of effective written communication with tips for user-friendly Web design.

"Writing for the Web, Parts I & II"

www.electric-pages.com/articles/ wftw1.htm

Electric-Pages is the Development Journal of the Graphics Research Laboratory. Sounds pretty intimidating, but this down-to-earth, nuts-and-bolts article by Jack Powers explains why text on the Web cannot just be "re-purposed print material squirted out through an HTML word processor." He explains very clearly why print and the Web are entirely different mediums requiring entirely different writing strategies.

Domain Names

Your domain name is really an alias that functions as the online version of your street address and phone number. In the URL http://www.idgbooks.com, for example, idgbooks.com is the domain name. The *suffix,* or filename extension at the end of a domain name — that is, the part that comes after the dot — identifies the type of organization that owns the domain name. Dot-com (.com) usually means a commercial enterprise, and dot-org (.org) often means a not-for-profit organization.

Your domain name may or may not be the same as your actual company name, although most businesspeople like the two to be identical so customers can remember the URL more easily. If someone already owns the name you want, you may explore buying that name through a broker.

BestDomains

www.bestdomains.com

$

BestDomains claims to be the largest Internet name- and asset-trading site and acts as a broker and agency in the sale of cyberspace assets, including domain names, rights, and assets. If you're interested in a name that is already taken, consider contacting a company like this one.

InterNIC

www.internic.net

$

As Chapter 17 explains, the domain-name system under which the Internet has operated for the past several years is in flux. InterNIC, which has been responsible for registering sites in the .com, .org, and .net domains, may not be performing that function by the time you read this. However, you can still search for your domain name here and see whether it's available. You can also get the latest information on the domain-name registration controversy.

E-Commerce Service Providers

A growing number of companies are offering packaged services and software to entrepreneurs who want to get their business online quickly and with the support of experts. They provide a broad range of services, from the simple to the complex, that can include site hosting, shopping cart and credit card services, consultation on design, content, and marketing, and anything else you may need.

iCat.com

www.icat.com

iCat is a great resource for the small-business person who wants to start a business online quickly and inexpensively. This company enables you to build your store online, helps you manage it, provides marketing services, hosts an e-commerce forum, and offers guidance and support for the fledgling online business person. iCat also hosts a cybermall, with over 1,000 online merchants.

Merchant Planet Network

www.merchantplanet.com

Merchant Planet Network offers "the easiest way to add electronic commerce functionality to your Web site." There's no software to install; you can keep your current Web host while still taking advantage of Merchant Planet's e-commerce solutions. Options include a real-time credit card authorization package, which provides an online merchant account from Cardservice International; the ability to import a product list from your accounting application; and the capacity to sell downloadable software online.

Open Market

www.openmarket.com

$

Open Market, Inc. is a provider of Internet commerce software products that perform order management, security, authentication, and online merchandising and marketing. Check out ShopSite Express, which you can use for free to add e-commerce capability to your site. This company also offers training and consulting services.

Yahoo! Store

store.yahoo.com/index.html

$

Yahoo! bills itself as the fastest, easiest way to open an online store. You create your site on their server using nothing more than the browser you're using to read their page. This isn't a free service; hosting costs are based on the number of items you sell per month. However, it's a good solution for those of us who are non-technical and want to get a presence on the Web in a quick, affordable way. Yahoo! Store has built-in searches, statistical tools, and flexible pricing options.

Other Stuff to Check Out

www.icverify.com
www.intershop.com
hometown.aol.com
www.verifone.com
www.awa.com

Finance

You say you're brimming with great ideas but have no money with which to turn them into reality? Never fear. The Web has some resources to help you find the capital you need for your online business.

Idea Cafe's Financing Your Business

**www.ideacafe.com/getmoney/
FINANCING.shtml**

★★ ★★

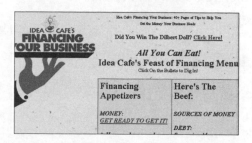

Idea Cafe offers 40-plus Web pages full of tips to help you secure the money your business needs. This site provides a vast range of information on finance. Topics include how to borrow money, attract investors, or find alternate funding sources. It also holds moderated forums on credit card use, bank financing, government funding, borrowing from family and friends, women and money, and much more. Try the All-in-One Budget Calculator to find out how much money you really need. A must-visit site!

Quicken.com: Small Business: Starting a Business: Funding Your Business

**www.quicken.com/small_business/
answers/
?channel=0&topic=1&subtopic=22**

The URL above might look odd, but give it a try. If you're looking for funding for your

fledgling company, you'll be glad you did. This site provides answers to questions such as: How can I find a lender that's right for my business? What types of alternative financing can I pursue? How do lenders evaluate loan applications? Is it harder for women to get a small-business loan? What is inventory financing, and can it help my business? This is a terrific site for anyone looking for small-business funding.

Small Business Administration

www.sba.gov/financing

The SBA site offers extensive information on financing your business, including tips on taking out a loan and working with lenders. You can download an online library full of shareware programs designed to help you manage your small business. You can even enroll in an online workshop called "Financing Options: What You, as a Loan Applicant, Should Know."

Other Stuff to Check Out

www.businessfinance.com
www.garage.com
www.cfol.com/framehome.htm
www.moneyhunter.com
www.entrepreneurmag.com/resource/
rm_intro.hts

Glossaries, Dictionaries, and Encyclopedias

You may want to bookmark these handy reference sites for those times when you find yourself knee-deep in computer, Internet, or Web terms you have never heard before. Rest assured: New terms are being created even as we speak.

Computing Dictionary

wombat.doc.ic.ac.uk/foldoc/index.html

Enter a computer word or phrase in the box at the top of the page and click on Search for free access to this online dictionary of computing.

New York Times Glossary of Internet Terms

www.nytimes.com/library/cyber/ reference/glossary.html

From Archie and ARPAnet to Zine, this list of techy terms is a resource for the Web entrepreneur. Terms are listed alphabetically and cross-referenced. Entries are thorough and up-to-date. You have to register to use the site by choosing a username and password, but registration is free.

The Webmaster's Lexicon

www.Stars.com/Reference/Index

An easy-to-use alphabetical listing of key words and phrases that you will inevitably come across in your new role as online business owner.

Government

As an online businessperson, you will at times have need of government information. The following are a few useful sites in this area. Be sure to check out the Small Business Administration site and the site run by the Secretariat for Electronic Commerce.

Internal Revenue Service: Forms

www.irs.ustreas.gov/prod/forms_pubs/ forms.html

The new-and-improved IRS provides this Web site, where you can download any form you want in a choice of four different file formats — or simply output them to your laser printer.

SCORE: Service Corps of Retired Executives

www.score.org

The SCORE Association, a resource partner with the U.S. Small Business Administration, provides confidential business counseling free of charge by e-mail. SCORE also offers workshops and free satellite conferences. The SCORE Web site provides many additional resources worth exploring.

State and Local Government on the Net

www.piperinfo.com/state/states.html

This up-to-date site has extensive lists of links to state and local government sites, multi-state sites, and some federal resources. It also includes listings of national organizations related to government and other miscellaneous government resources.

United States Government Electronic Commerce Policy

www.ecommerce.gov

This site is maintained by the Secretariat for Electronic Commerce, U.S. Department of Commerce. The reports and documents available for reading and download provide an important framework for understanding the phenomenal growth of online business and the emerging digital economy, both globally and nationally. This site also includes links to related international sites and links to examples of electronic commerce.

U.S. Small Business Administration

www.sba.gov

The U.S. Small Business Administration site offers a huge amount of information useful to the small-business person, as well as a listing of programs offering various kinds of assistance and an online library.

HTML and Link-Checking Tools

Even though you don't have to actually learn HTML in order to create a Web page — in fact, precisely *because* you may not know HTML — it pays to have a Web-based service do an evaluation of your pages to make sure that they're written correctly. Here are some Web page "tune-up" sites you can try.

Doctor HTML

www2.imagiware.com/RxHTML

Doctor HTML is a Web page analysis tool that retrieves an HTML page and reports any problems that it finds. The online version of Doctor HTML is free, but you may also purchase a license to use the program on an internal intranet.

Link Check

netmechanic.com/link_check.htm

NetMechanic's Link Check is a free online verification and validation tool that can help you find the broken links in your site. The Link Check robot searches your Web site — testing, verifying, and validating each link — and then reports the status of each link tested.

Web Site Garage

www.websitegarage.com

$

Tune Up Your Web Site!

Run critical performance diagnostics on your entire Web site, ensure browser compatibility by seeing your site as viewed by 18 different browsers, speed up your site by optimizing your images. All services are available for a fee.

Other Stuff to Check Out

www.linkexchange.com
watson.addy.com
www.cs.dartmouth.edu/~crow/lvrfy.html
www.tiac.net/users/zach1/htmlcheck/
htmlcheck.shtml

Legal Resources

You don't need to be in legal trouble in order to research the many legal resources in cyberspace. Small-business owners often need to know about copyright and trademark issues, as well as international trade law and state laws.

The Copyright Website

www.benedict.com

This site endeavors to inject a measure of humor into the sometimes-dry subject of copyright. It has a section on Fair Use and Public Domain, and a chat group on copyright issues.

The Internet Legal Resource Guide

www.ilrg.com

This is a good general starting point if you're looking for legal information. The ILRG includes an index of lawyers and law firms, in case you're in need of help. It also has extensive databases of legal information, articles, and links.

Nolo Press

**www.nolo.com/chunkPCT/
    PCT.index.html**

Nolo Press is a well-known publisher in the field of self-help law. This page on patent, copyright, and trademark resources points you to lots of good information on intellectual property terminology, as well. Scroll down the page and explore the links called <u>Conducting A Trademark Search</u> and <u>Registering A Trademark</u>, subjects that can be especially important to your small business.

Piper Resources Guide to State and Local Government

www.piperinfo.com/state/states.html

This Piper Resources site is regarded as one of the best legal resources online when it comes to state law. This directory is a quick index to state and local government sites online.

THOMAS

thomas.loc.gov

THOMAS (which is named after Thomas Jefferson) is the official Web site of the U.S. Congress. Administered by the Library of Congress, THOMAS lets you check on the status of pending legislation before the Congress. You can search by bill number, title, or keyword.

The United States Copyright Office

lcweb.loc.gov/copyright

★ ★
★ ★

An outstanding resource on a topic of interest to everyone who wants to start an online business, this is the place to go if you want to apply to register for copyright for your Web site. Registering your copyright gives you an extra level of protection for your business site contents, even though copyright law provides for online material to be protected as soon as it is published.

Other Stuff to Check Out

www.doc.gov
www.yahoo.com/Government/Law/Federal
www.eff.org
www.findlaw.com/01topics/10cyberspace
www.findlaw.com
www.globalcontact.com

Search Engines

You're probably already familiar with search engines from the standpoint of a consumer: You can find information on just about any topic by using an Internet search service. When it comes to running an online business, your perspective is different. You need to visit these sites to find out how to get your business listed so that customers can find you more easily. Each site has information that explains how to include your site on its index.

AltaVista

www.altavista.com

AltaVista, which is maintained by Digital Equipment Corporation (DEC), is the search engine I use most often. It's fast, and it provides users with a wide range of shortcuts to narrow down the information you want. Like other search services, AltaVista presents a directory of Internet sites on a topic-by-topic basis. Its Business and Finance category includes sites for Regulation and Government and Small Businesses.

DejaNews

www.dejanews.com

DejaNews specializes in searching through the thousands of newsgroups that make up the wild, wild world of Usenet. DejaNews can help you locate a group that's related to your area of business. Or you can enter a topic in the Search text box at the top of the DejaNews home page, click on Find, and after a short time, a page appears with links to individual newsgroup messages that are related to your query.

Excite

www.excite.com

Excite lets users create their own personalized Web pages so they can receive the news and business information of their choice. Excite's home page contains lots of current news, weather, and stock information.

HotBot

www.hotbot.com

HotBot's colorful artwork reflects its creator, Wired Digital, which is now part of the Lycos Network. HotBot is especially good if you are searching for links to your own Web site: Enter your own URL in the search text box, and select "links to this site" from the first drop-down menu under Options. If you're looking for your own free home page or e-mail address, HotBot even provides hosting, too.

Infoseek

www.infoseek.com

InfoSeek lets you search not only Web sites but also news outlets, corporations, and newsgroups. It has an especially rich selection of international Web directories in different languages. Among other things, Infoseek has a topic heading for small businesses, which may be of particular interest to you.

Lycos

www.lycos.com

Lycos is one of the oldest search engines on the Web, which means that it's more than a few years old. Like Infoseek, Lycos has a category listing for small-business resources that you may find useful. It lets you search not only the usual categories like the Web and newsgroups, but also stocks, weather, and even recipes. Its Top 5 Percent rating system attempts to separate higher-quality Web sites from those of the ho-hum variety.

WebCrawler

www.webcrawler.com

WebCrawler began as a student project in 1994 and has since turned into a mini-industry of its own. One good thing about WebCrawler is that it lets you (or your customers) search through Internet classifieds for particular items. Look at the fine print at the bottom of the page for a surprise: WebCrawler is owned by another search engine's owner, Excite, Inc.

Yahoo!

www.yahoo.com

★★
★★

Yahoo! is probably the most popular and best-known site on the Web. It's the place to go if you want to find information about almost anything. Yahoo! is at once a search engine that helps you find sites on the Web and a well-organized index to Web sites arranged by topic. In addition, Yahoo! Store is a good place to create a business Web site. I probably end up turning to Yahoo! once or twice on almost every surfing session, and I always seem to find something of interest.

Small Business Associations

There's nothing like a little help when you're sitting all alone at your kitchen table or in your office, wondering how to make your business a success. The following organizations provide information, support, and much needed health insurance and other benefits for the self-employed.

American Home Business Association, Inc.

www.homebusiness.com

★★
★★

This is a friendly site from a friendly organization offering home-based business resources. Everything from information on starting up your business, to business finance, and even personal finance is here. Don't forget to subscribe to the free weekly home-business newsletter, *Tips For the Lone Entrepreneur.*

American Association of Home-Based Businesses

www.aahbb.org

AAHBB is a not-for-profit organization offering a variety of benefits to members, including discounts on long-distance service, discounted prepaid legal services, access to merchant banking services, discounted cellular phone services, and health and business insurance.

Home Office Association of America

www.hoaa.com

HOAA offers health insurance, UPS discounts, a newsletter that monitors new equipment and software developments, help with improving your business skills, low-cost long-distance service, home-business equipment insurance, airline discounts, a collection agency for bad accounts, and free or discounted software.

National Association for the Self-Employed

www.nase.org

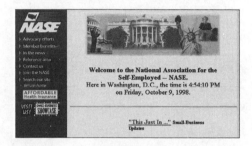

NASE provides a variety of member benefits and advocacy efforts for the self-employed person, including health insurance, discounted delivery services, and tax advice.

SOHO America

www.soho.org

According to SOHO (Small Office/Home Office), 43 million people work from their homes. SOHO was founded to provide reference tools and technical support, benefits, and news affecting small and home offices, and to represent your interests as a small-business owner.

Yahoo! Guide to Small Business Organizations

dir.yahoo.com/Business_and_Economy/ Small_Business_Information/ Organizations

If you want to take the wide view, Yahoo! provides you with a huge listing of

small-business support organizations you can join. Note that some are regional or for specific ethnic or age groups.

Tutorials and Online Classes

It's never too late to learn something new, especially when it comes to creating Web pages or discovering how the Internet works (that's why you're reading this book, after all). A variety of Web sites provide tutorials in Web design, HTML, and Web graphics. And for a small fee, you can attend online classes at one of several virtual universities.

The Bare Bones Guide to HTML

werbach.com/barebones

The Bare Bones Guide to HTML lists every official HTML tag in common usage plus the Netscape extensions. This guide has been translated into over 30 languages, and you can access those translations from this site. The current version conforms to HTML 3.2, and author Kevin Werbach is currently working on the HTML 4.0 specification.

How a Web Page Works

www.howstuffworks.com/ web-page.htm

Marshall Brian's "How Stuff Works" site provides a simple, easy to read explanation of how Web pages end up on your computer screen. He even gives you a little experiment in HTML that you can open in your own browser.

The NSCA Beginners Guide to HTML

www.ncsa.uiuc.edu/General/Internet/ WWW/HTMLPrimer.html

★ ★
★ ★

The University of Illinois provides this well-respected and useful introduction to HTML. The disclaimer notes that this is only an introduction and does not pretend to offer instructions on every aspect of HTML. Links to additional Web resources about HTML are listed at the end of the guide.

Spectrum Virtual U

www.vu.org

 $

Spectrum Virtual U offers online courses in computers and Internet technology, journalism and writing, and other topics, and claims to be the largest online learning community on the Internet, with over half a million people from 128 countries having attended their classes to date. Enrollment opens on the first Monday of December, March, June, and September. You may take up to three classes for a fee of $15.00.

Web Design Tutorials

**www.mediabuilder.com/
    webdesigntutor.html**

Mediabuilder provides links to tutorials in HTML. Sites are rated for beginners and more advanced students, and include tutorials for forms and frames.

Web Authoring Tools

New WYSIWYG (what-you-see-is-what-you-get) Web authoring tools are making it easier to produce your own Web page. Check out The Web Tools Guide for a comprehensive list of every conceivable Web tool, authoring, and more. The most

recent authoring products on the market are similar to print page-layout programs and allow you to design a Web page without knowing HTML coding. If you want to learn HTML, you have the option of using an HTML editor such as BBEdit. Most of these companies allow you to download a preview copy from their site before you buy their product.

BBEdit

www.barebones.com

Bare Bones Software's motto has always been "It doesn't suck." Recently, they revised it to "It still doesn't suck." BBEdit is a high performance text and HTML editor for the Macintosh. It is designed for the editing, searching, transformation, and manipulation of text. Features are too many to list but include a Web-safe color palette, drag-and-drop HTML tools, PageMill cleaner tool, and one-button preview in any browser. The Bare Bones Web site provides you with ways to download, purchase, and update the software. You'll also find extensive technical support links, including links to discussion groups related to Bare Bones products, plus a searchable archive of past discussion group comments.

CyberStudio Go Live

www.golive.com

CyberStudio, a sophisticated program for Macintosh users only, is a WYSIWYG HTML editor with all the capabilities and feel of desktop publishing software. Floating toolbars place and control elements on a page, and icons on the Palette toolbar denote various page elements. This program includes support for cascading style sheets, Java, and dynamic HTML. The Go Live Web site lets you download a trial version of the

D-20 Web Authoring Tools

program or purchase and register the program online. The GoLearnIt section of the site includes links to tutorials you can either view online or download to your computer, plus listings of classes where you can learn how to use CyberStudio in a more formal setting. There's also an extensive customer service/technical support area for current users of the program.

Dreamweaver

www.macromedia.com/software/ dreamweaver

Dreamweaver is a powerful (and expensive) professional design tool that includes a customizable interface and support for dynamic HTML. Dreamweaver's source code features color syntax highlighting and appears in a separate window so that you can tile your WYSIWYG and source views and watch the code appear as you add elements visually. The Macromedia Web site leads you to a "feature tour" illustrating the program's features, areas to download a trial version or purchase a version of the program, and a set of extensions that extend Dreamweaver's functionality. These extensions let you add connectivity to databases, create music and sound, and perform many other useful tasks.

FrontPage 98

www.microsoft.com/products/prodref/ 571_ov.htm

FrontPage 98 is an inexpensive yet very complete WYSIWYG tool that works well with other Microsoft products. However, to really get the most out of FrontPage, you need a Microsoft Web server and your users need to have the latest Microsoft browser. This FrontPage includes ways to order the product online, links to Web site hosting services, and instructions on how to use FrontPage on an internal intranet, among other things.

Home Page

www.filemaker.com

Like Adobe PageMill, Home Page is a fine beginner's tool, but when used in conjunction with FileMaker Pro, it delivers some advanced features allowing you to create pages connected to a FileMaker Pro database. It includes built-in clip art and site templates. From this site, you can download a trial version of Home Page or purchase a fully registered version of the program.

PageMill

www.adobe.com./prodindex/pagemill/ main.html

Here is another inexpensive, easy-to-use tool from Adobe for beginners with minimal HTML skills. To help get your business online, you can use PageMill to lay out a simple page with graphics, text, image maps, and Java applets. This site includes links to tips for current PageMill users, a download site for the trial version of PageMill, a registration area for users who have purchased the program, and case studies showing how both profit and nonprofit organizations have used PageMill to create their Web sites.

The Web Tools Guide

webreview.com/wr/pub/webtools

Webreview.com's guide to Web tools covers every aspect of Web design and development. This is a great place to start to get the lay of the land for authoring tools and more.

Other Stuff to Check Out

www.sausage.com
www.miracleinc.com

Web and Business Publications Online

If you're relatively new to the online world, you'll want to know about the latest news and developments so you can keep up with both your competitors and your customers. The following cybermedia outlets provide you with daily business news, as well as the latest technological developments.

ChannelSeven.com

www.channelseven.com

Channel Seven is a networking source for Internet development, marketing, and advertising executives. This site may not be aimed expressly toward the small-business owner, but it pays to learn from watching what the "big boys and girls" are doing. The news coverage is excellent, and the site has departments called eMarketer and Ad/Insight, which present advertising case studies.

CIO WebBusiness

webbusiness.cio.com

This print publication with an online presence provides substantive articles and resources for larger companies, but it also has much for the small-business entrepreneur to use. Previous articles included "Designing Principles: An online catalog is only as good as its design," and "Flash is Trash: Forget the spinning logos and blinking lights. Real people want real information, and they want it fast."

Down To Business

206.100.116.136/dtb.html

Down To Business is a no-frills online magazine for entrepreneurs and marketers.

It's published by Shel Horowitz, author and publisher of *Marketing Without Megabucks: How to Sell Anything on a Shoestring*. It offers articles from some of the leading lights in the entrepreneurial niche and is a gold mine for the small operator. You will find articles on the use of e-mail, Internet strategies, the World Wide Web, technologies and trends, speaking in person and on the media, marketing and sales, and interpersonal relationships and family business. Bookmark this site.

Inc. Online

www.inc.com

The online version of the print magazine *Inc.* provides great reading for the small-business person. Expect good reporting on Web businesses and Web marketing, as well as solid articles on all aspects of business.

Internet World

www.iw.com

★ ★
★ ★

Internet World is one of the best online publications for the online entrepreneur. All articles in this daily e-zine are geared toward electronic business or Web development. *Internet World* deserves a bookmark and frequent visits.

New York Times: Technolology: Cybertimes

www.nytimes.com/yr/mo/day/tech/ indexcyber.html

One of the best daily sources of current information on all aspects of the Web and the Internet, this section features original columns and articles produced expressly for the Web. The five special weekly columns include Education, Travel Log, Eurobytes, arts@large, and CyberLaw Journal.

D-22 Web Design

Web Developers Journal

www.webdevelopersjournal.com

Web Developers Journal is a great publication that promises to have something for everyone, whether you are "a suit, ponytail, or prophead." This journal is primarily for people who create Web sites, but it does have an e-commerce department and a discussion group, as well as a book-review section and good feature articles.

Wired

www.wired.com/wired

Wired offers an irreverent and hip look at new media, online economy, new technology, and policy regarding the Internet and the World Wide Web. You can browse the archives of past issues on these topics. Wired News, HotWired, LiveWired HotBot, and Suck.com are all linked from this site.

Other Stuff to Check Out

www.eweekly.com
enews.com
www.webtechniques.com

Web Design

If you're planning to design and create your own Web site, this section is for you. But even if you're planning to hire someone to do the job for you, it's still useful to find out as much as you can about Web page design. Understanding what goes into making an attractive and compelling site is crucial for anyone hoping to have a successful online business. Knowing some of the technical and design issues involved in the production of a Web site goes a long way in helping you communicate effectively with a designer.

BigNoseBird

www.bignosebird.com

A fantastic Web authoring resources site with a strange name and a great sense of humor, BigNoseBird offers tutorials on a huge range of subjects. This site boasts an overwhelming amount of information and is worth many visits. If you get lost, try the search engine.

Designing a Business Web Site

www.wilsonweb.com/webmarket/
design.htm

Wilson Internet Services provides a collection of articles specifically on business Web site design and useful for the Web entrepreneur.

The Design and Publishing Center

www.graphic-design.com/default.html

An accessible and friendly site that includes information for both print and Web design, The Design and Publishing Center offers discussion forums, letters from readers, and special sections for Web designers. Be sure to check out the Web Design Reader Reviews section.

Microsoft Site Builder Network

www.microsoft.com/sitebuilder

Microsoft Site Builder Network is a one-stop resource for Web professionals, including designers, programmers, authors, and administrators. This searchable site includes in-depth technical articles and downloadables, a magazine, and a gallery of free Web components. This is a huge resource worth bookmarking. Registration is encouraged but not required.

Netscape's Open Studio

developer.netscape.com/openstudio/
home2.html

Netscape's Open Studio, "Your Resource for Building Websites," offers a vast array of resources for the Web designer/developer, including sections on HTML, scripting, support and newsgroups, products and downloads, software discounts for members, and articles on every aspect of Web development. Registration is encouraged but not required.

useit.com

www.useit.com

Jacob Nielsen, author of *Designing Excellent Websites: Secrets of an Information Architect,* presents some excellent advice about the art of Web design with an emphasis on usability.

Web Design List

designlist.internet.com

If you're looking for a professional Web designer to create your Web site, check out the more than 700 professional designers listed in Internet.com's Web Design List. You can browse the entire database or select by location and professional services you need.

Webmonkey

www.hotwired.com/webmonkey

Hotwired's Webmonkey is a "How-to Guide for Web Developers." A well-designed, very hip site that offers information on e-business, design, HTML, dynamic HTML, stylesheets, graphics and fonts, multimedia, browsers, Java, Javascript, Perl, and Backend. This site pulls relevant articles from Wired News. You have the option to have the front page of this site delivered to your

mailbox everyday, subscribe to a weekly newsletter, and/or join a mailing list for Web designers.

Web Pages That Suck

www.webpagesthatsuck.com

★ ★
★ ★

One of the best-known Web design sites gets its name and fame from the book with the same title. This site invites you to learn good design by looking at bad design. The authors provide substantive and useful information about what to do and not to do when designing your Web site, and they deliver this information with a great sense of humor.

Web Review

★ ★
★ ★

webreview.com

Web Review is a huge and important site for the Web designer/developer. Visiting the site is free, but you are asked to register to receive additional benefits, including a free weekly newsletter and special offers on new Web products. Web Review offers 30 different departments, all loaded with up-to-date, valuable information. An absolute must visit.

D-24 **Web Graphics** _____

Other Stuff to Check Out

webdesign.miningco.com
www.webdeveloper.com
usableweb.com
www.killersites.com/core.html
www.builder.com
www.webreference.com

Web Graphics

Its ability to display visual imagery and animation makes the Web an exciting medium for business communication. The following sites give some insight into the development of graphics for the Web. If you don't want to create your own graphics, check out the sites where you can download graphic elements — including backgrounds, icons, and animation — for free.

Lynda.com

www.lynda.com

Lynda Weinman, author of *Designing Web Graphics: How to Prepare Images and Media for the Web*, hosts this site. In addition to promoting her books and workshops, she provides information and links related to the use of graphics and color on Web pages. If you plan to develop your own graphics, her books are well worth reading.

Reallybig.com

reallybig.com/default.shtml

This great site offers more than 3,000 resources for Web builders, including clip art, hit counters, fonts, HTML, animations, backgrounds, icons, and buttons. Whew! Besides these Web page goodies, this site also offers a selection of WYSIWYG Web page editors. On top of this, you can get help with promoting your Web site here, too.

Tudogs

www.tudogs.com

Tudogs claims to be the ultimate directory of gratis software. Help yourself to free Web tools, graphics software, clip art, animation, music, games, and a host of other resources. Tudogs says it has tested every software application and visited every graphics and service site on its pages.

Yahoo Listing of Stock Photo Companies

**search.yahoo.com/bin/
search?p=stock+Photos**

$

If you need photos for your site, Yahoo lists more than 225 stock photo companies that allow you to download whatever you want, for a fee.

Yale C/AIM Web Style Guide

**info.med.yale.edu/caim/manual/
graphics/graphics.html**

This comprehensive resource guide can help you optimize the look and efficiency of your Web page graphics. The Style Guide covers color displays, graphic file formats, GIFs, JPEG graphics, information on optimizing graphics, colored backgrounds, and image maps.

Web Graphics Tools

Graphics tools enable you to create the visual elements on your Web page. Some of the applications listed in this section were traditionally used for print media and were adopted by Web designers for Web use. The latest versions of these older programs may include Web enhancements. Some newer products have been designed specifically for creating graphics for the Web. Because most of these programs are on the expensive side, I recommend downloading a preview copy before you buy.

DeBabelizer

www.equilibrium.com/ProductInfo/ solutions.html

DeBabelizer enables you to re-purpose digital content that may have been intended for print or a CD-ROM and optimize it for use on your Web site. It allows color reduction and optimization of GIFs, JPEGs, and PNGs for the highest image quality and quickest download times; HTML parsing for quick access; processing and updating of Web graphics; and the creation and optimization of GIFs and QuickTime movies for Web delivery. At this Web site, you can download a trial version, purchase a registered version, and obtain support for DeBabelizer.

Fireworks

www.macromedia.com/software/ fireworks

Fireworks combines design, illustration, image editing, JavaScript, and animation tools to enable you to create professional vector graphics for your Web site. Everything is editable all the time. You can draw using organic brush strokes and create unlimited shapes and objects. You can then go back and edit the strokes at any time. The Fireworks area of the Macromedia Web site includes a tutorial on the program, instructions on how to use the program with the popular presentation tool Macromedia Director, as well as links to pages where you can download a trial version or purchase the program.

Freehand

www.macromedia.com/software/ freehand

Freehand is another professional tool for designers creating and producing illustrations and layouts for print and the Web. Create mixed-media pieces that combine line art with bitmaps and typography, as well as graphic elements, interfaces, and animations for the Internet. The Freehand area of the Macromedia Web site contains links to a trial version of the program and a tutorial you can download, as well as a version of Freehand that you can purchase and a gallery showing examples of how big-name companies use Freehand to create graphics.

Illustrator

www.adobe.com./prodindex/illustrator/ main.html

A professional illustration tool for graphic artists and technical illustrators, Illustrator was primarily designed for print but can also be used to create Web graphics. You can easily use it with Photoshop and ImageReady. This Web page is full of links that explain Illustrator's key features, tips on using the program, information about where to download and/or purchase the software, and much more.

ImageReady

www.adobe.com/prodindex/ imageready/main.html

ImageReady is a professional Web tool for preparing graphics for use on the Web. Key features include an optimized colors palette, image slicing, image maps, animation, tiled backgrounds, and seamless integration with Photoshop and

Illustrator. This Web page includes links to tips on using the program, case studies that show how various companies use ImageReady, and detailed information about the program's features. You can either purchase the program or download a trial version online.

ImageStyler

**www.adobe.com/prodindex/
imagestyler/main.html**

ImageStyler is marketed to the "creative business user" or non-design professional to "instantly add style to your Web site." It enables you to apply dazzling effects to text, shapes, and images; to create JavaScript rollover effects without writing code; to generate precise Web-ready HTML layouts and image maps; and to quickly change the look and feel of your site with Batch graphic-creation features. This Web page provides you with tips and information about the program's features; you can download a trial version or purchase ImageStyler online.

Painter

**www.metacreations.com/products/
painter55**

Painter is a professional natural-media image-creation tool that was originally used for print. Painter 5.5 includes Web authoring enhancements, including image slicing, the ability to design tiled background patterns, JavaScript rollovers, and dynamic text insert. This Web site includes a customer service area for current users. In addition, the technical support area provides assistance with installation and configuration, including a set of Frequently Asked Questions.

Photoshop

**www.adobe.com./prodindex/
photoshop/main.html**

Photoshop software is the professional standard for digital image enhancement, photo retouching, and image composition. This program is widely used by Web and print designers alike to create compelling photographic imagery. This Web page includes links to tips on using the program, case studies that show how various companies use Photoshop, and detailed information about the program's features. You can either purchase the program or download a trial version online.

Web Marketing

Marketing and advertising are two different activities, to my mind, at least. Advertising involves spreading your URL and banner ads around the Web, either to a wide variety of sites or a narrowly selected audience. Marketing involves building credibility for yourself and your site through content, participation in newsgroups, effective e-mail use, and a number of other strategies. The following sites either market your online business for you or suggest ways you can spread the word yourself.

CyberAtlas

cyberatlas.internet.com

CyberAtlas is the reference desk for Web marketers that provides valuable statistics and demographic information, as well as advertising, e-commerce, and site-building resources. This is a well-organized site for the online entrepreneur who wants an edge in understanding Web marketing.

eMarketer

www.e-land.com

A handsome, well-organized site that inspires with its design as well as its content, eMarketer offers an impressive menu of resources and information and boasts having the best online statistics available. One of the most valuable parts of the site is eCommunity, a variety of discussion groups where you can meet other online marketers and compare notes.

Guerrilla Marketing Online

www.gmarketing.com/tactics/
    weekly.html

Guerrilla Marketing is a weekly online magazine for small businesses, entrepreneurs, sales people, and marketers of all kinds. Though not limited to Web marketing, this a site full of good ideas. The general philosophy of Guerrilla Marketing is achieving conventional goals, such as profits and joy, with unconventional methods, such as investing energy instead of money.

MMG: The Online Agency

www.mmgco.com

MMG is an example of a growing number of online advertising and marketing agencies that you can hire to do your marketing for you. This site prominently displays an "MMG E-Commerce Clock," a

real-time clock ticking way the billions of dollars spent online to date. Even if you don't plan to hire MMG, this site is worth the visit just for the clock.

Promotion 101

www.promotion101.com

Promotion 101 is a Web site marketing and promotion information center with some unique offerings, including a search engine placement guide and a META tag builder. Also available are articles on banner advertising, branding, e-mail marking, public relations, and Usenet newsgroups.

SearchZ.com

www.searchz.com/index.shtml

SearchZ is the only dedicated search engine covering online advertising, marketing, and commerce. A place to start if you are looking for information on a particular Web marketing topic.

Web Marketing Today

www.wilsonweb.com/webmarket

Wilson Internet Services is a Web consulting firm that provides a free and substantial Internet marketing resource with links to hundreds of online articles. This site offers a clickable index and a keyword search and claims that its E-Commerce Research Room is the Internet's largest and most comprehensive e-commerce resource and portal site. This is an excellent, not-to-be missed site.

Who's Marketing Online?

www.wmo.com/index.shtml

Who's Marketing Online? Is an online publication that looks at online marketing as a phenomena in its own right and as a tool to help online businesses achieve success on the Web. Besides reading articles on marketing, you can explore an impressive and unusual list of links, particularly in the area of site launch and public relations, areas not usually well-covered on other resource sites.

Web Statistics and Demographics

The phenomenal and revolutionary growth of the Internet and the World Wide Web has major implications for the entrepreneur who wants to take advantage of this new way to market goods and services. Some folks are trying to keep track of Internet use and demographics. If you're curious about such matters, check out the following sites.

Domainstats

www.domainstats.com

A company called NetNames Ltd. provides daily statistics on the total domains registered worldwide. Further statistics include a breakdown of InterNIC domains by suffix, a listing of ISO and country-level domains, and a look at new country suffix names to watch (such as .tm, .nu, and .to). At the time that I write this, 4,882,025 domain names are registered worldwide, and current weekly growth is 71,232. Makes you want to hurry up and get your domain name, doesn't it?

Dr. Bruce Klopfenstein's Links to WWW User Research

www.bgsu.edu/departments/tcom/users.html

Dr. Klopfenstein has compiled a comprehensive and up-to-date listing of articles about Web use; demographics, papers, and proceedings from conferences; graphs; and links to market research firms and their reports.

Part V
The Part of Tens

The 5th Wave   By Rich Tennant

"Come on Walt—time to freshen the company Web page."

In this part . . .

If you're like me, you have one drawer in the kitchen filled with utensils and other assorted objects that don't belong anywhere else. Strangely enough, that's the place I can almost always find something to perform the task at hand.

Part V of this book is called The Part of Tens because it's an oddball collection of miscellaneous secrets arranged in sets of ten. Filled with tips, cautions, suggestions, and examples, The Part of Tens presents many kinds of information that can help you plan and create your own business presence on the Internet.

Chapter 15

Ten Ways to Boost Your Online Business

In This Chapter

▶ Planning for success and getting off to a good start

▶ Networking through effective e-mail techniques

▶ Revising and improving your business Web site

*T*he Internet may seem like a place for loners, but it's not. Sure, you sit at your computer by yourself (or possibly with a family member or partner) and create your Web pages. You answer your e-mail by yourself. But you aren't in a vacuum, not by a long shot. Just open your eyes and look around at what other *ontrepreneurs* (online entrepreneurs) have done and are doing, ask a few questions, and suddenly, you have plenty of advice and support. You're networking!

In the course of writing this and other books, I've accumulated many tips from individuals who are conducting successful online businesses. In this chapter, I reveal the secrets they've passed on to me about what separates an exciting, money-making project from one that induces a great big virtual yawn. Many of these tips aren't really secrets at all, but just commonsense practices that you may overlook while you're hooking up modems, dialing access numbers, filling out Web page forms, and doing other nuts-and-bolts things.

This chapter omits some of the obvious tips and tips that I include elsewhere in this book, and concentrates instead on strategies that may not occur to you right away. If you can add even just a few of these strategies to your fuel tank, you'll be boosting your business (that is, getting more visits and inquiries, receiving more positive feedback, and making more sales) faster than you can say, "How many of those do you want to order?"

Think Positive!

Seem obvious? I don't think so. In fact, this one didn't occur to me until I interviewed Dan Podraza, the head of the family of ontrepreneurs who started the super-successful Beanie Baby site, the Collectible Exchange (see Chapter 1).

When I asked Dan about the problems he encountered starting the online business, he told me, "We operated on a low budget in the beginning, and we didn't have the inventory that people wanted. People need to plan to be successful, and they need to be confident in what they are doing. We weren't exactly as confident as we could have been, but we were lucky because Beanie Babies are so popular."

Although choosing a product to sell that is eagerly desired by a passionately committed group of users is certainly important, what's really important is your frame of mind going into your online business project. If you have a positive frame of mind, you can sell just about anything. If you plan ahead to be successful, you *will* be successful.

How, exactly, do you plan to be successful? If you've never been terribly successful before, this is a good question. Here are some strategies for success that are based on my own experience and on what online business owners have told me over the years:

- **Believe in what you have to sell.** Love your product and promote it energetically and enthusiastically. Come up with catchy slogans and put them into your e-mail signature file. Take humorous photos of yourself and your product; these imply that you're confident enough to have fun with your business. Your own enthusiasm will radiate to your prospective customers or clients.

- **Order sufficient inventory.** You may not be able to go overboard in this area, especially on a limited budget, but don't be caught short in case you start getting tons of orders. Keep a modest surplus on hand in case of success. If necessary, you can always give extra products away as promotions.

- **Don't skimp on your computer setup.** Time and time again, I've tried to cut corners by buying a bargain computer with a small storage area (500MB is small these days) and ended up regretting it less than a year later. Some of the people I interviewed for this book (like Dr. Werner Steurenburg in Chapter 2) also tried to get the least expensive Internet connection they could find, and ended up changing to a faster connection with better services later on. Plan for success by paying a little extra up front for the most memory, the fastest processor, the speediest modem, and the Web hosting service with the most features. A year from now, you'll be thanking yourself instead of kicking yourself!

Get Your Ducks in a Row Before You Start

Before you can make a big splash, you have to test the waters. Ask around and find the best beach in which to swim. Attend a class with other novice swimmers who can encourage you to get into the water gradually and then move around efficiently rather than stirring up the surf.

The same tips apply to starting an online business. As Nancy Roebke says in Chapter 7, she spent six months getting herself known and learning about her market before starting her online business, Profnet, Inc.

Try these strategies:

- ✔ Research your competition by visiting their Web sites. Make a list of things they do that you can do better.
- ✔ Join mailing lists and get to know the authorities in your field.
- ✔ Look through Usenet newsgroups where people in your market hang out. Find out what they like and dislike — and more importantly, what they need that they aren't getting now.

Don't be in a hurry to jump into cyberspace. It will be waiting there for you when you are ready. Chances are, the longer you wait, the less expensive the computer software and hardware you need will be. And later on, new software tools and online resources may be available to help you create business Web sites, set up shopping carts and online catalogs, and so on.

The important thing is not to rush online with an idea that isn't well thought-out. The danger is that your good idea will drop like the proverbial lead balloon, and you'll get discouraged and give up on it. If you have a business plan ready, a line-up of the strategies you need to carry it through, and personal contacts with people who will help you along, you're more likely to stay with your business project through any ups and downs you may encounter.

Make It Easy on Your Customers

Your chances of receiving orders and making transactions go up in direct proportion to how easily visitors can browse through your site and then locate and order what they want.

Most Web site consultants agree that you have to attract a visitor's attention and get your message across in less than a minute — in fact, I would say in less than 20 seconds. At the point of making a sale, your site needs to be easy enough to use so that an impulse buyer can follow his or her immediate desire and make an order or purchase instantly.

How do you do it? Follow these basic rules:

- **Remember the KISS principle.** That's Keep It Simple, Stupid. A music file that plays in the background while your Web page is loading may seem clever, but save it for your personal home page, not your business site. Stay away from Java applets and complex image files that users with slow connections will have to wait for precious seconds (or minutes) to download. Concentrate on your content first, and let the graphics support it.

- **Tell all up front.** Explain who you are, what you do, why you do it, and how you can be contacted right on your home page.

- **Make shopping easy.** Find a Web host that lets you create a shopping-cart system that customers can use to pick out items. Provide a simple Web form that visitors can fill out quickly.

- **Make shoppers feel safe.** Sign up with a host that has a secure server that can protect customers' credit card information. Stress security and integrity on your site. Provide a low-tech alternative, such as mailing in a check, for people who don't want to use a credit card. Many shoppers are still squeamish about ordering over the Internet, so making them feel safe is essential.

If you do decide to accept credit card purchases from your customers, you need to set up a merchant account with a bank (see Chapter 8). A secure server (see Chapter 12) is also essential, and most Web hosts charge extra for this. And to protect yourself from someone submitting false credit card information, pay a little more to have a company such as Octagon (www.otginc.com) verify your credit card transactions.

Keep Your Information Fresh

Nothing says "Don't Shop Here!" louder than a site with a "last updated" date that's a year or two old, or a site that still advertises products for sale that have been unavailable for months.

One way to avoid being out-of-date is not to use dates on your site at all, unless you plan to update your content regularly. The better way to appear fresh and current is to provide a Web page devoted to Breaking News, Weekly Specials, or some other type of timely information.

Consider sending a newsletter or simple e-mail announcement to individuals who have visited your site informing them of new content. Even if you only send out such messages monthly or quarterly, they make people aware that you work on your online business regularly and that your site has new content that they should check out.

Give Something Away for Free!

Nothing drums up business inquiries for an online company like freebies. Shoppers on the Web love getting something for nothing, and, in fact, I think that they're so used to the convenience of finding freebies online that they *expect* to get something for free when they visit a commercial Web site.

Don't disappoint your customers. Give 'em what they want. If your online business provides products for sale, set aside one or two items to give away in a contest. You can use the e-mail addresses you receive with entries for future mailings.

If you're in the business of providing information or services online, consider doing some work for free. Share your expertise freely on mailing lists, and offer to let people try out your services for nothing if they say that they're "on the fence" and aren't sure about contracting with you.

Keep Rehabbing This Old Web Site

You don't have to come up with the perfect Web site design or the ideal catalog system all at once. In fact, tackling the organization and design of your Web site in stages is often easier to manage.

Consider starting with only three to six Web pages for your online business. Concentrate on providing a few good products or services for sale. Begin to promote yourself online.

After a few months, move to Phase Two of your online business project. Add six to ten more Web pages. These can describe such topics as

✔ Who you are and why you love what you do

✔ How people can get customer service information if they need it

✔ Testimonials from satisfied customers

✔ Links to related resources online where people can find out more about your field

Phase Two can also involve a redesign of your Web pages. Turn your headings into graphic images that use striking typefaces. Scan more photos of your work or your items for sale. After six months, you can then move on to Phase Three, which may include an expansion of your online sales catalog. The important thing is to regard your online business as an ongoing project that you continually revise and improve.

Master the Art of Effective E-Mail

E-mail is right up there with Web sites as the most important part of an online business. In fact, if I were asked to say which is more important, I don't think I could pick one or the other. If you learn to use these two parts of the Internet to communicate, you'll find that they complement one another beautifully.

Don't throw away your old e-mail messages; rather, organize the most important messages into folders so you can track correspondence with your Very Important People later on. Also, be sure to use your e-mail software's Address Book function to save e-mail addresses of people with whom you correspond frequently.

Get into the habit of checking your e-mail every day. If work or other responsibilities prevent you from checking your e-mail daily, this can be a good job for a spouse, an assistant, or an older son or daughter. Don't let e-mail inquiries sit for days on end. Each day you wait increases the likelihood that people who were interested will find another resource.

Even if you don't have the product or service that someone is looking for, send a message back informing that person of that fact and encouraging him or her to check back in the future. You may even consider suggesting the URL of another site that may be useful to people you can't help. The goodwill you generate might bring them back to you for a future transaction.

Reaching Out through Newsgroups, Mailing Lists, and Offline Media

Time and time again, I've discovered that the most successful businesspeople are the ones who devote the most energy into connecting with other individuals. It never fails: If I sent out ten e-mails requesting interviews or other information, the ones who get back to me the quickest are the ones who are also the busiest and most successful businesspeople.

The contact you make doesn't necessarily have to be on the Internet. It can also be through trade shows, conferences, classified ads in newspapers or magazines, or simply getting back to people on the phone.

Don't stick solely to the Web or search engines for your Web site promotion. Use the whole Internet, including subscribing to mailing lists, posting on bulletin boards, contributing to discussions on Usenet, and participating in online chats. The more frequently you drop your name and voice your comments out there in cyberspace, the better your chances of making a sale or closing a business deal. (Chapters 9 and 11 contain more ways to promote your business on the Internet.)

Get Your Business Listed in All the Right Places

This is one of those online business tips that gets mentioned all the time, not only in books like this, but by companies that want to host your Web site. So I won't belabor the point. But it is an important one: In order to boost your business, you have to make sure that people can find you easily. This means

- Listing yourself with as many search engines, indexes, and Internet Yellow Pages services as possible

- Adding META keywords to your Web pages, making your site more likely to turn up on search engine pages (see Chapter 11)

- Making sure that your site is listed on both local and national versions of Yahoo!

Don't spend hundreds of dollars to have a company promote your site online for you. Save your money to spend on more inventory or better Web page design. Spend an evening or weekend filling out the search sites' submission forms and then use a free service like the limited trial version of !Register-It! (www.register-it.com), which allows you to hit 11 resources at once.

Be Patient, Be Committed, and Don't Give Up

The lucky entrepreneur is the one whose site gets a thousand hits the first week and starts making sales on the first day. Most online businesses don't have such luck. Don't be discouraged if yours is one of the many online businesses that takes weeks or even months to start making sales.

Be prepared to spend a good deal of time cultivating your business before you actually start turning a profit. Some people may tell you that this process takes six months, others say a year, and still others say two years.

If you're working on your online business on evenings or weekends away from your "day job," you can afford to keep at it for months at a time. And the cost of keeping a Web site business online is minimal compared to the rents and other overhead costs that physical stores face in the offline world. Look to mailing lists, such as the excellent Biz Discussion List, for support in case you get discouraged. (Send an e-mail message to `majordomo@talkbiz.com`, with *subscribe biz-digest* as the body of the message.) Appreciate any small bit of attention you get. Whatever you do, don't give up!

Chapter 16

Ten Online Commerce Pitfalls to Avoid

● ●

In This Chapter

▶ Avoiding overdesigned or overly complex Web sites

▶ Preparing a business plan and marketing strategy

▶ Learning how not to offend e-mail correspondents

▶ Testing and proofreading to prevent embarrassing mistakes

● ●

Sometimes, navigating the road to success is as much a matter of avoiding potholes, traffic slowdowns, and fender-benders as it is of driving the quickest or shortest way.

Speed bumps and accidents can detract from your online business's chances of success, too. Because you're just starting out in business for yourself, even a minor problem can jeopardize your project's future. This chapter provides a road map that you can use to steer clear of trouble, so you can focus on the positive things you can do to boost your business (such as the tips provided in Chapter 15).

Not Having a Business Strategy

So you say you have a bright idea for a business, and the Internet would be a cool place to start it? Whoa there, pa'dner. Having an inspiration is only half the battle. In fact, too many people try to start an online commerce site with only a hunch or rough idea of what they plan to do. Unless they're extremely lucky, these would-be Rockefellers are asking for trouble.

Before you sign up with a Web host and start to make Web pages, sit down for a moment and discuss (with your family, your friends, your partners, or yourself) exactly what you want to do. Specifically:

- ✔ Know whom you want to reach.
- ✔ Be clear about the goal(s) of your online business.
- ✔ Map out and organize your Web site, and determine whether you want to develop your site in stages or all at once.
- ✔ Make a list of the goods and/or services you plan to provide.

It's been said that, if you have no idea where you're going, you are guaranteed to get there. Don't end up with your cyberbusiness going nowhere. Have a clear idea of your goal and develop the strategies to reach it.

Not Having a Marketing Plan

As Dan Padroza of the Collectible Exchange says in Chapter 1: "Figure out how you're going to attract people to your site."

First, determine whom you want to attract. Draw up descriptions of two or three typical customers, complete with their ages, their occupations, their mode of dress, and so on.

Then, figure out a plan for how to get the attention of your likely customers and get people to come to your site through e-mail, promotions, or advertisements. Be sure to include a plan for getting listed on the search engines and indexes, as described in Chapter 11.

Beginning your marketing efforts before your business goes online never hurts. Although it's true that you can't advertise your site before it is available, you can market yourself by participating in online discussions as well as trade shows and conferences.

Pushing Products or Services People Don't Need

You can create a terrific Web site, you can offer your wares at reasonable rates, and you can do everything else right, but if people don't need what you have to offer, your business will fall short of your expectations.

Half the battle with starting a business is identifying a clear need that many individuals share. Often, this idea comes from your own experience. You yourself encounter something that you or your family needs, and you realize that lots of other people need it, too.

For example, an article in the online *New York Times* (`www.nytimes.com/ library/tech/98/10/circuits/articles/22mate.html`) profiled Maralyn Facey, who, following her divorce, discovered that plenty of parale-gals, lawyers, and judges needed software to make drawing up visitation schedules easier. Her product, Kidmate (`www.kidmate.com`), made $100,000 in the first year.

Overdesigning Your Web Pages

Making your Web site state-of-the art is certainly tempting. Many sites use high-tech tricks like Shockwave animations, Java applets, video clips, and more. The problem is that many of these goodies require special software programs or browser add-ons, called *plug-ins,* in order to show up. Users who haven't downloaded and installed the proper software can't see any of your special effects. Rather, they see generic image icons or gaping blank spaces on the Web page. Even if they do have the correct software, the special features (especially Java applets) take a lo-o-o-ng time to download, and you run the risk of losing some visitors to boredom.

Are your customers technically savvy types like software engineers? Are you sure that they have fast connections and plenty of plug-ins? If not, don't bother with the high-tech goodies.

Not only that, but overusing more common techno-tricks like Web page frames can cause problems, too. The best Web pages take the largest number of users into account. They have content that most browsers on most computer platforms can view. The point is to know your audience, keep your objectives in mind, and don't let technical requirements obscure your basic message.

Making Too Many Links to Other Sites

You're in a hurry. You need pretty images for your Web site. What do you do? Well, here's what *not* to do:

1. Surf around to a number of clip-art sites that provide drawings and photos for people to copy.

2. Rather than download an image file to your computer, you copy the link that leads to the image.

3. Add the link to your Web page. *Voilà!* You have instant images without having to use up disk space to contain them.

4. Do the same for utilities such as guestbook scripts that exist on other sites and that let you add to your site by inserting some HTML into the source code for one of your Web pages. (Chapter 6 describes this process, by the way.)

The result of following the preceding steps is that you end up with Web pages that load s-l-o-w-l-y while the visitor's browser labors to access site after site and download file after file. Don't depend on your prospects to be patient as they wait for images to crawl onto their computer screens. If you're going to copy someone else's clip art, copy the image to your computer and upload the image to your Web server along with your Web pages.

Read the permissions requirements before you copy; many clip-art sites ask for fees or credits, and they often restrict image copying to noncommercial sites.

Typos, Boo-Boos, and Broken Images — Oh My!

Publishing your golden prose and your images on the Web is easy. Just click your mouse button a couple of times, wait a few seconds, and, *bingo,* you're published.

But wait — if you haven't proofread your pages and checked your images and links to make sure that they all work correctly, you can just as easily go online with Web pages full of mistakes that can embarrass you and hurt your business's credibility.

Before you go online, take the time to test your pages on your own computer by opening your home page in your browser window. You do this by choosing File⇨Open or File⇨Open Page from your browser's toolbar, and then navigating to the file on your computer's hard disk. When the page opens, read the text carefully, click on all your links, and make sure that your images appear in their entirety and aren't distorted.

People who do proofreading for a living, as part of their editorial work, know that a second pair of eyes can catch many mistakes that go unnoticed by someone who has read the text many times. If you can't find someone to look over your text for you, try scanning it from back to front in order to get a fresh look at your contents.

Trying to Do It All Yourself

Part of being a good businessperson is knowing how to spend your time efficiently. Concentrate on the important things and leave the technical details to experts who can save you time.

People who think that they have no money to spend try to do all the work themselves. They spend hours learning HTML and scripting languages. They spend days trying to get networked computers to talk to one another. I know, because I used to be one of those people.

Over the years, I've realized that it doesn't pay to learn an entirely new technology just to perform one function that isn't directly related to your area of business. Time and again, I've discovered other successful businesspeople who knew the value of hiring a good designer or technician.

Even if your budget is severely limited, strongly consider spending a few bucks on a competent designer, Webmaster, or computer technician who can get your site up and running smoothly in a fraction of the time that it would take to do everything yourself. You'll be less frustrated, you'll get online more quickly, and you'll be able to concentrate on selling and promoting your business.

Spamming or Flaming

If you really want to torpedo your chances of success in a hurry, send unwanted e-mail messages to a list of people who didn't ask for it. Worse yet, post advertisements to all the newsgroups you can find that are even barely related to your online work.

Why stop there? Send press releases or huge graphics files as attachments to your newsgroup or mailing list postings. Then, when people complain (as they inevitably will), fire back an angry e-mail message called a *flame*. Who knows? You may be able to ignite a *flame war*, in which the participants engage in cutting one another down, usually with offensive and abusive language.

How can these kinds of tactics hurt a business? The denizens of the Internet have plenty of ways to make life miserable for someone who offends the code of behavior called Netiquette. They can send *mail bombs,* in which your e-mail address is flooded with mail messages that clog your ISP's mail server. They can spread the bad word about you throughout the Net. They can complain to your ISP and get your account canceled. The list goes on. . . .

Providing Slow Customer Service

Get back to people as fast as you can. Many things in cyberspace seem to happen more quickly than they do in the offline world. That applies to a fickle Internet shopper's time frame for decision-making, too. It's a very narrow window.

Remember that Web surfers are used to instant gratification. If they want to know the answer to a homework or trivia question, they have only to turn to some search services or online encyclopedias, and the answer appears in a few minutes. If they want a software program, they can probably find something available immediately in the shareware archives.

What does this mean for you, the provider of goods and services to these hungry, impatient consumers? It means that you need to do the following:

- Check your e-mail daily, or once every couple of days.

- Sign up with a Web hosting service that provides you with *autoresponders*. These are e-mail addresses (such as `info@company.com`) that automatically respond to e-mail inquiries by sending back a standard response to the effect of, "We have received your request, and we'll be getting back to you right away." You can also set up autoresponders to send an attached text file that provides information about your company or a particular line of products.

- Provide some sort of customer service information on your site. This can be as simple as a single page that instructs customers on how to contact you if they have problems, complaints, or questions. Or you can create individual pages that provide background information about specific items or services.

If you're the type of person who loves to keep in touch by telephone and hates to miss messages, look into the Internet paging options from PageNet (`www.pagenet.com`). You can forward e-mail messages to your pager rather than your e-mail inbox. If you know how to create Web page forms, you can set up a simple form that does the same thing. My friend John Casler has one of these on his Web page (`www.manaburger.com`).

Treating your customers well means respecting their privacy as well as responding to them in a timely way. Don't give out information about your customers without permission. And don't sell your mailing list without your customers' knowledge. If you protect your customers' interests, they'll respond with loyalty (that is, return business).

Letting Your Business Sell Itself

"My stuff is so good, people are bound to love it," the unwise business-person proclaims. "They're bound to find me online!"

Don't count on it. Marketing is essential to making your Web site stand out from the millions of others that are crowding cyberspace. Follow the many options described in Chapters 7 and 11 in order to attract visitors.

A site that you allow to sit there on your host's server after you do the initial work of putting it together is going to do just that — sit there. The more energy you put into promoting yourself, the better your business will do. Also, be sure to change your site's contents regularly. For example, you can add a weekly special sale item or highlight a new service or client. Even a small change lets people know that your site is worthy of revisiting.

Chapter 17

Ten Online Business Secrets

*O*ne of the nice things about writing books like this is that it gives me a chance to share tips I've learned over the years, both as a user of computers and as an owner of a small business. The tidbits collected in this Part of Tens chapter aren't all secrets, exactly, but they may not be immediately obvious to you as you develop your online business.

Some of these little-known facts are advanced technical tricks that you may want to try yourself, after you've been online for a while. Others are facts about running a business that people don't tend to bring up in casual conversation. Still others are hints I didn't have a chance to mention elsewhere but that I wanted to be sure to pass along.

You Can Interpret Your Log Files

A *log file* is a computer document that records data related to the operation of a Web server. (A *Web server,* for its part, is a program that lets people access files with a Web browser, FTP program, or other software.)

Log files aren't pretty. In fact, they're so "techy" in appearance that novice users are likely to scratch their heads and wonder what the contents mean. Nevertheless, log files can provide you with lots of useful information.

Log files aren't something you have to create yourself; the server can compile them automatically. The key is to make sure that your Web host will provide you with regular log-file reports. Better yet, sign up with a host that uses log-file analyzer software, which makes the data in the log files easier to understand. Some of the flashier programs, likeWebTrends (www.webtrends. com), provide data in graphs and pie charts that are great to print out and show to your business colleagues.

You Can Keep Track of Your Referrers

Log files have their limitations. They can't tell you the exact names or e-mail addresses of your visitors. But they *can* tell you how many visits your site has received, what countries they are from, and more.

For example, you can obtain a log file that tracks the sites that contained the hypertext links on which visitors clicked in order to reach *your* site. In the language of Web servers, this is called a *referer log file* (with one *r*, not two). These files are also sometimes called *backlinks*. Tracking these links helps you evaluate the effectiveness of any advertisements you have placed that are linked to your site.

One of the more popular search services, HotBot (www.hotbot.com), has a great utility that lets you track backlinks to your site. Type in the name of your site and then choose Look for⇨links to this site.

You Can Create Your Own Animations

You don't have to be a cartoonist to make an animated GIF image. GIF (Graphics Interchange Format) is one of the most popular graphics formats in use on the Web. One quality of the GIF format is that you can compile a series of separate GIF images into a single image file. When the combined file appears on the Web, the images within it play in succession.

You just need two things to create your own animated GIFs:

✔ **A computer graphics program to create the images that comprise the animated GIF:** One of the best programs for Windows users is Paint Shop Pro, which is included on this book's CD. On the Macintosh side, the preeminent program is Adobe Photoshop, but it's complex. Look into Adobe ImageStyler, a beginning-level program that's available in a 30-day trial version. Both the Adobe programs are available in Windows versions as well; visit the Adobe Systems Incorporated Web site (www.adobe.com) for more information.

✔ **A special program for creating animated GIFs:** GIF Construction Set for Windows is available as shareware for $20 from Alchemy Mindworks, Inc. (`www.mindworkshop.com/alchemy/gifcon.html`). If you use a Mac, you can install a $49 shareware version of GIFmation by Box Top Software (`www.boxtopsoft.com`). You also have an online alternative: After preparing your individual images, you can use the Animate Page online utility (`www.vrl.com/Imaging/animate.html`) to assemble them into an animated GIF file.

You can save yourself the work of putting GIF images into an animation by making use of the animated GIFs at AGL, the Animated GIFs Library (`www.arosnet.se/agl`). You can search a database of animated GIFs to find the one you want. All the images included on the site are free for commercial and noncommercial use. You don't need any software programs to use the images, because they've already been created: All you need to do is copy them onto your Web page.

Dynamic Pages Don't Get Indexed

Web pages come in many varieties. Some use simple HTML to present the contents. Others get flashy with computer scripts called CGIs that generate pages dynamically — that is, when you connect to a Web site, the script creates the page for you containing up-to-the-minute information. The important thing to remember is that, if you or your Web page designer use a CGI or another form of *dynamic HTML* to create your pages, those pages may or may not be indexed by the search services that you want to publicize your business.

A Web page that is divided into two or more frames actually consists of two or more HTML documents. However, some search engines don't index framed content. As the search service Excite suggests (`www.excitecom/info/listing.html`), including a <NOFRAMES> section in the HTML source code for your Web page allows its search program to index the page. A <NOFRAMES> section is enclosed by the HTML commands <NOFRAMES> and </NOFRAMES>, and provides an alternate, conventional layout for a Web page. See Chapters 5 and 6 for more information on HTML. For a really in-depth look at the subject, check out *HTML 4 For Dummies Quick Reference,* by Deborah S. Ray and Eric J. Ray, published by IDG Books Worldwide, Inc.

Be Careful with Your Customers' Information

Treat your database of customers' e-mail addresses, credit card numbers, and other personal information like gold. Remember, you're trying to build loyalty among your customers, many of whom are probably concerned about privacy issues on the Internet. Don't sell or give out information unless you have permission from your customers to do so.

If you provide a feedback or subscription form on your site, include a check box that asks people to answer Yes or No to the question, "May we share this information with others?" You can then develop a secondary list of customers who have given you permission to give out their information.

Some Domain Names Aren't Regulated

The "dot-com" (.com) you see in the Internet addresses of so many commercial Web sites is one of several top-level domains. (Other top-level domains are .edu, .net, .org, .gov, and .mil.) The theory is that top-level domains are organized on the Internet according to the content and mission of the sites to which they are assigned. However, you may be able to secure a name like www.company.org or www.company.net for your business if www.company.com (where "company" is the name of your business) is not available.

The reason is that InterNIC, which has been responsible for registering domains, receives too many requests to check them all. Nowadays, many for-profit businesses have domain names that end with .org (which is supposed to be for nonprofit organizations) or .net (which is supposed to be for networks, such as Internet Service Providers).

In fact, the .com sites are being used up so fast that a new set of domains is under consideration. If www.yourname.com is not available because someone else is using it, there is hope: New names like www.company.firm, www.company.info, and www.company.shop have been proposed and (hopefully) will be available in 1999.

Unfortunately, as I write this, the outcome is not crystal-clear. Network Solutions' InterNIC Registration Services, the organization that has been keeping track of top-level Internet domain names, saw its contract with the U.S. government end in late 1998. The government has proposed that Network Solutions remain the registrar for these domains. But it's likely you can still go to the InterNIC Web site (rs.internic.net) and fill out the domain name you want to research.

Chat Events Can Promote Your Business

Not long ago, I helped organize a chat event on the Internet for a large nonprofit institution. In the course of setting things up, I discovered that chat is becoming widespread in the business world. Chat, which is short for Internet Relay Chat (IRC), gives computer users around the world a chance to gather in groups and conduct real-time discussions by typing messages to one another online. Chat is probably best-known as a forum for young people to gab online about their problems and common interests, but it's fast becoming a respectable business tool, as well.

You can promote yourself and your business by setting up your own chat room and linking it to your site. Look into TalkCity (www.talkcitycom), which provides this service for free. Click on the <u>Set Up Your Own Chat Room</u> link to find out more.

You Can Become an FTP Resource

If you are in the business of providing your own shareware programs over the Internet, consider setting up an FTP server so that people can download your files. (FTP, which stands for File Transfer Protocol, is a system for transferring data from one computer to another on the Internet. See Chapter 3 for more information about using FTP.)

Any computer that's connected to the Net can be set up to operate as an FTP server. The machine itself can either be located in your home office or at your hosting service's location. Either way, the FTP computer should be connected to the Net all the time. (For home users, a cable modem or ADSL connection is ideal; see Chapter 3.)

Inexpensive software is available to help you serve files by FTP. On the Macintosh side, the easiest FTP server software is NetPresenz by Peter N. Lewis, which is available as shareware for $10 from www.stairways.com. Windows users can try WFTPD by Alun Jones (www.wftpd.com/wftpd.htm).

If You Go X-Rated, Do It Right

Whether or not you or I personally approve of X- or R-rated content in cyberspace, entrepreneurs do make money creating adult sites on the Internet. There are, however, two major considerations to look at seriously:

✔ Tons of adult sites are online already. You'll have plenty of competition. Web surfers don't really *need* any more X-rated places to visit, in my opinion.

✔ Many Internet users are under the legal age to view adult content. If you do decide to go this way, take steps to get your site a rating so parents like me can protect our kids. Check out SurfWatch (`www.surfwatch.com`), Net Nanny (`www.netnanny.com`), or standards like the Platform for Internet Content Selection (PICS) to find out how you can be a responsible member of the Internet community.

You Can Operate Your Own Web Server

True, it's far easier to sign up with a Web hosting service that serves your Web pages and other files for you. Also, a direct connection is pretty much mandatory to operate a Web server. But it's also true that functioning as your own Web host lets you experience the Web to the fullest by giving you ultimate control over your site. You can set up areas that only users who have an approved name and password can access, and areas that customers can access anonymously to download software. You can even redirect visitors to specific pages based on what browser they use. Operating your own server not only gives you constant access to your log files (see Chapter 16), but it also enables you to customize those files so you get just the information you want about visits to your site.

Here, too, software is becoming easier to use. The most popular Web server program available, Apache, was recently released in a Windows version, and a Macintosh version is expected soon. Visit the Apache Web site (`www.apache.org`) to find out more.

You can find lots of information on setting up your own business Web server in *Selling Online For Dummies,* by Leslie Heeter Lundquist, published by IDG Books Worldwide, Inc.

Appendix

About the CD

*A*s an entrepreneur just starting your own business, you're bound to be on a tight budget when it comes to purchasing software. In deciding to go online, you've come to the right place. The ability to obtain low-cost trial software or no-cost demo software is one of your advantages.

The CD-ROM that accompanies *Starting an Online Business For Dummies* provides you with software you don't have to wait minutes (or sometimes even hours) to download. You can install and use the programs right away. I've gathered programs that are geared toward the needs of someone who's starting a new Web-based business. Here's some of what you can find on the disc:

- ✓ **MindSpring Internet Access:** A popular Internet Service Provider
- ✓ **Paint Shop Pro:** A great shareware graphics program for Windows
- ✓ **HotDog Professional 5 Webmaster Suite:** A popular and full-featured Web page creation program for Windows
- ✓ **Trial versions of QuickBooks and QuickBooks Pro:** Two of the most popular accounting programs around
- ✓ **Maximizer:** A program that helps businesses manage customer contacts and conduct electronic commerce
- ✓ **ecBuilder:** Software that helps you develop your own commerce-capable business Web site

System Requirements

Make sure that your computer meets the minimum system requirements listed below. If your computer doesn't match up to most of these requirements, you may have problems using the contents of the CD.

- ✓ A PC with a 486 or faster processor, or a Mac OS computer with a 68,030 or faster processor
- ✓ Microsoft Windows 3.1 or later, or Windows NT 4.0 (If you use NT, you need to have Service Pack 3 installed.)

> ✔ At least 8MB of total RAM installed on your computer (This is a bare minimum. For best performance, I recommend that Windows 95-equipped PCs and Mac OS computers with PowerPC processors have at least 16MB of RAM installed. In my experience, Windows 98 works best with 32MB or more of RAM.)
>
> ✔ At least 60MB of hard drive space available to install all the software from this CD (You need less space if you don't install every program.)
>
> ✔ A CD-ROM drive — double-speed (2x) or faster
>
> ✔ A sound card for PCs
>
> ✔ A monitor capable of displaying at least 256 colors or grayscale
>
> ✔ A modem with a speed of at least 14,400 bps

For more information about what all these requirements mean, consult Chapter 3 of this book. Or check out *PCs For Dummies,* 6th Edition, by Dan Gookin; *Macs For Dummies,* 6th Edition, by David Pogue; *Windows 95 For Dummies,* 2nd Edition, by Andy Rathbone; or *Windows 3.11 For Dummies,* 4th Edition, by Andy Rathbone (all published by IDG Books Worldwide, Inc.).

Using the CD

The following sections tell you how to install the software on the CD-ROM and use the links page to visit the URLs listed in the *Starting an Online Business For Dummies* Internet Directory.

In order to run some of the programs on the CD, you may need to keep the disc inside your CD-ROM drive. This is a good thing. Otherwise, you would have to install a very large chunk of the program to your hard drive, which may have kept you from being able to install other software.

Installing the CD with Microsoft Windows

If you use Microsoft Windows, follow these steps to install the items from the CD to your hard drive:

1. **Insert the CD into your computer's CD-ROM drive.**

2. **Windows 95/98/NT users: Choose Start⇨Run.**

   Windows 3.1 or 3.11 users: From Program Manger, choose File⇨Run.

3. **In the dialog box that appears, type** D:\SETUP.EXE.

If your CD-ROM drive uses a different letter, replace *D* with the proper drive letter. (If you don't know what letter your CD-ROM drive uses, look under My Computer in Windows 95/98/NT or File Manager in Windows 3.1.)

4. **Click on OK.**

   A License Agreement window appears.

5. **Read through the License Agreement, nod your head, and then click the Accept button if you want to use the CD — after you click Accept, you'll never be bothered by the License Agreement window again.**

   The CD interface Welcome screen appears. The interface is a little program that shows you what's on the CD and coordinates installing the programs and running the demos. The interface basically enables you to click a button or two to make things happen.

6. **Click anywhere on the Welcome screen to enter the interface.**

   Now you are getting to the action. This next screen lists categories for the software on the CD.

7. **To view the items within a category, just click the category's name.**

   A list of programs in the category appears.

8. **For more information about a program, click the program's name.**

   Be sure to read the information that appears. Sometimes, a program has its own system requirements or requires you to do a few tricks on your computer before you can install or run the program, and this screen tells you anything special you may need to do.

9. **To install a program, click on the appropriate Install button.**

   The CD interface drops to the background while the CD installs the program you chose.

If you don't want to install the program, click the Go Back button to return to the previous screen. You can always return to the previous screen by clicking the Go Back button. This feature allows you to browse the different categories and products and decide what you want to install.

10. **To install other items, repeat Steps 7, 8, and 9.**

11. **When you finish installing programs, click on the Quit button to close the interface.**

    You can eject the CD now. Carefully place it back in the plastic jacket of the book for safekeeping.

Installing the CD with a Macintosh

To install the items from the CD to your Mac hard drive, follow these steps:

1. **Insert the CD into your computer's CD-ROM drive.**

   In a moment, an icon representing the CD you just inserted appears on your Mac desktop. Chances are, the icon looks like a CD-ROM.

2. **Double-click on the CD icon to show the CD's contents.**

3. **Double-click on the License Agreement icon.**

   This is the End-User License that you are agreeing to by using the CD. You should look it over at least once.

4. **Double-click on the Read Me First icon.**

   This text file contains information about the CD's programs and any last-minute instructions you need to know about installing the programs on the CD that we don't cover in this appendix.

5. **To install most programs, just drag the program's folder from the CD window and drop it on your hard drive icon.**

6. **Some programs come with installer programs; to install these programs, you simply open the program's folder on the CD and double-click on the icon with the word "Install" or "Installer."**

   After you install the programs you want, you can eject the CD. Carefully place it back in the plastic jacket of the book for safekeeping.

Using the directory links

For your convenience, I have put all the URLs that are listed in the *Starting an Online Business For Dummies* Internet Directory on the CD. You can open the links in your Web browser with a simple mouse click.

To use these links pages, follow these steps:

1. **With the CD-ROM in your drive, connect to the Internet and launch your Web browser.**

2. **Choose your brower's Open File command.**

   If you use Microsoft Internet Explorer, choose File⇨Open File. If you use Netscape Navigator, choose File⇨Open. An Open dialog box appears.

3. **Select the Links.htm file.**

   If you're using Windows, type **D:\LINKS.HTM**. (If your CD-ROM drive is not D:\, be sure to use the correct letter for your drive.)

If you're using the Mac OS, use the Open dialog box to display the contents of the CD-ROM. Select the Links.htm file and press Return.

4. Click on a link for any site that you want to visit.

Doing so opens a second browser window that takes you to the Web site you've selected. The links page remains open in the original browser window so that you can toggle back to it to select another link. Each time you select a new link, the Web site selected pops up in that second browser window — so don't worry that you're going to end up with several browser windows open at one time.

What's on the CD

Here's a summary of the software on this CD. If you use Windows, the CD interface helps you install software easily. (If you have no idea what I mean by *CD interface*, flip back to the section called "Installing the CD with Microsoft Windows.") If you use a Mac OS computer, you can enjoy the ease of the Mac interface to quickly install the programs.

Getting your site online

✔ **BBEdit 5.0 Demo and BBEdit Lite by Bare Bones Software, Inc.:** *For Mac OS.* BBEdit Lite is a Macintosh freeware text editor. BBEdit 5.0 is not free, but as the free demo version attests, it comes with powerful features that make creating HTML for your Web pages easy. If you're familiar with HTML already, BBEdit is a good program to use. BBEdit is ideally suited for marking up text. When you're ready to design a Web page, you can use another program, such as HotDog, to combine your text with images, colors, and other graphic elements. You can find out more about BBEdit at www.barebones.com.

✔ **ecBuilder by Multiactive Technologies, Inc.:** *For Windows 95/98/NT.* ecBuilder software leads you through the process of creating a commercial Web site in ten easy steps. The program helps you create a Web site consisting of interlinked pages, as well as an online catalog to which you can add product images, company logos, and other graphics. To find out more, visit www.ecbuilder.com.

✔ **Fusion 3.0 by NetObjects, Inc.:** *For Windows 95/98/NT and Mac OS.* Fusion is powerful software for creating complex business Web sites. What makes Fusion special is that it enables you to create Web pages visually by dragging and dropping content into a Web page in progress. Fusion is also notable because it provides a visual interface so you can view the organization of an entire Web site. It also helps you link database content to your Web pages. Find out more at www.netobjects.com.

✔ **HotDog Professional 5 Webmaster Suite by Sausage Software:** *For Windows 95/98/NT.* HotDog Professional 5 is a dramatically upgraded version of HotDog from Sausage Software, which for several years has been one of the most popular Web page editing tools around. The Professional version includes Web site management features in addition to the more basic utilities you need to create HTML Web pages. To find out more about HotDog, visit www.sausage.com.

Note: If you get a "Class not registered" error when you try to run HotDog the first time, please see the D:\online\hotdogp\error.txt file for the steps to correct the error.

✔ **Internet Explorer 4.0 by Microsoft Corporation:** *For Windows 3.1, Windows 95/98/NT, and Mac OS.* This is full-featured Web browser from Microsoft includes a Web page creation tool called FrontPage Express. You can use the version on the CD for all your Web surfing needs, as well as for creating your Web site. For more information, check out www.microsoft.com/ie.

✔ **MindSpring Internet Access by MindSpring Enterprises Inc.:** *For Windows 3.1, Windows 95/98/NT, and Mac OS.* MindSpring Internet Access is a free commercial product that you can use to sign up to the MindSpring Internet Service Provider. If you don't already have Internet access, MindSpring is an excellent ISP that offers Internet access for a low monthly fee. MindSpring also has different Web hosting options, depending on the kind of account you have. If you're already on the Internet but want to find out more about MindSpring and the different service options it offers, visit www.mindspring.com.

Please note that the versions for Mac and Windows 3.1 offer to install Internet Explorer 3.0. If you already have Internet Explorer 4.0 on your computer, you will not be able to install the earlier version. Also, when you install MindSpring on Windows 3.1 and Mac, the installation program asks you for a key code. Enter **DUMY8579** into the dialog box. Be sure to use all capital letters, just as it's shown here.

If you already have an Internet Service Provider, installing MindSpring may replace your current settings. You may no longer be able to access the Internet through your original provider.

✔ **Paint Shop Pro by Jasc Inc.:** *For Windows 3.1 and Windows 95/98/NT.* Paint Shop Pro is a powerful shareware graphics editing and viewing tool. The program lets you create original computer graphics or edit existing graphics files. Check out www.jasc.com on the World Wide Web for full descriptions and the updated versions.

✔ **Netscape Communicator 4.5 by Netscape Communications:** *For Windows 3.1 (version 4.07 is the latest available for this platform), Windows 95/98/NT, and Mac OS.* Netscape Communicator is a sophisticated suite of Web browsing and Internet tools. Communicator includes e-mail, newsgroup, and address-book software that you're sure to find useful in your daily online business activities. For more information and the latest version, visit www.netscape.com.

Taking care of business

✔ **Acrobat Reader 3.01 by Adobe Systems Inc.:** *For Windows 3.1, Windows 95/98/NT, and Mac OS.* Adobe Acrobat Reader is a free program that opens portable document format (PDF) files. PDFs are handy ways to publish electronic documents that contain the same formatting and graphics of a printed document. To find out more, check out the Adobe Web site at www.adobe.com.

✔ **Business Plan Pro by Palo Alto Software, Inc.:** *For Windows 95/98/NT.* Business Plan Pro is a frequently praised program that helps you develop your own official-looking business plan based on templates that you customize. The resulting business plan combines your own textual descriptions with automatically generated charts and graphs. Developing a business plan is an important process if you're looking for funding from financial institutions. Visit www.palo-alto.com to find out more about Business Plan Pro and the soon-to-be-released version for Macintosh, Business Planning Toolkit.

✔ **EasyAccount 2.2 by Edwin deLeur:** *For Mac OS.* EasyAccount, a shareware accounting program by Edwin de Leur, provides an intuitive, user-friendly way to record basic income and expense records. The program's main operating window contains all the buttons you need to set up records and enter data.

✔ **Maximizer 5.0 by Multiactive Software, Inc.:** *For Windows 95/98/NT.* Maximizer helps you compile an electronic database of customer contacts. You can then use your customer list to send out mailings announcing new products and services. Maximizer enables you to e-mail individual customers instantly and to set up schedules so you can manage your business time more effectively. To find out more, check out www.maximizer.com.

✔ **MyMailList by MySoftware Company:** *For Windows 95/98.* MyMailList is software designed to help with mailings (such as newsletters, product updates, or other announcements) that you want to send to many customers at once. The program provides a simple interface so you can keep track of customer contact information. After you assemble this customer database, MyMailList helps you find individuals right away through an address book, print out labels or envelopes, or send e-mail to list members. To find out more about MyMailList and related business products, check out www.mysoftware.com.

✔ **M.Y.O.B. Accounting Plus by BestWare USA:** *For Windows 95/98.* This intuitive accounting program includes general ledger, checkbook, sales, purchase, payroll, time-billing, inventory, and card-file functions, as well as on-screen analysis, jobs and sub-jobs management, and over 100 financial and management reports. In addition, the M.Y.O.B. OfficeLink feature allows for expanded analysis and marketing capabilities through direct, one-click access to Excel, Word, and WordPerfect. To find out more about this program, visit www.bestware.com.

Unlike most other computer software, accounting programs require more than just the occasional language translation to work across country borders. In fact, through international republishers, BestWare has nine distinct English-language versions of M.Y.O.B. — each localized for the country or area in which it is distributed: United States, Canada, United Kingdom, Southern Africa, Australia, New Zealand, Malaysia, Singapore, and Hong Kong. In each case, specific changes must be made because of the accountancy and/or taxation standards of the country in which it is distributed.

✔ **Norton Utilities 3.0 by Symantec:** *For Windows 95/98.* Norton Utilities is a suite of programs that enable you to speed up disks, repair disks, recover lost files, and much more. It's an indispensable set of tools for business owners whose data represents income. To find out more, visit the Symantec Web site at www.symantec.com/nu/index.html.

✔ **QuickBooks and QuickBooks Pro by Intuit Inc.:** *For Windows 95/98.* This program is frequently praised as being one of the simplest and easiest-to-learn accounting programs, especially for those with no prior accounting experience. Online businesses that provide services to clients can make use of QuickBooks' time-tracking system. Small businesses that provide items for sale can benefit from the program's inventory features. To find out more, visit the Intuit Web site at www.intuit.com.

('QuickBooks' is a registered trademark of Intuit, Inc. *Starting an Online Business For Dummies* has not been reviewed or approved by Intuit, and Intuit expressly disclaims any responsibility for its content or accuracy.)

✔ **Simple Business Invoicing & Inventory and Simple Business Accounting by OWL Software:** *For Windows95/98.* Simple Business Accounting is designed to let people with no prior accounting experience keep track of income and expenses, and it uses the single-entry accounting system favored by the IRS. Simple Business Invoicing & Inventory is a complete sales management system that helps you with inventory tracking, invoicing and billing, and mailing list management. For more information, visit www.owlsoftware.com.

✔ **WhereDidAllMyMoneyGo? By Bert Torfs:** *For Mac OS.* WhereDidAllMyMoneyGo? is shareware for the Macintosh that helps you set up simple accounts and manage transactions. It's especially good if you need to convert one type of currency to another. For more information, visit ourworld.compuserve.com/homepages/bert_torfs.

✔ **WinFax PRO 9.0 by Symantec:** *For Windows 95/98/NT.* WinFax is software that lets you use your computer to exchange faxes with someone else's computer or fax machine. You don't have to purchase a separate hardware fax device if you have this software. I've used the program myself; it's easy to set up and frequently recommended by software reviewers. Your Windows computer needs to be equipped with a modem in order to send or receive faxes with WinFax. To find out more about the program, visit www.symentec.com/winfax/index.html.

If You Have Problems (Of the CD Kind)

I tried my best to compile programs that work on most computers with the minimum system requirements. Alas, your computer may differ, and some programs may not work properly for some reason.

The two likeliest problems are that you don't have enough memory (RAM) for the programs you want to use, or you have other programs running that are affecting the installation or running of a program. If you get error messages such as Not enough memory or Setup cannot continue, try one or more of the following and then try using the software again:

- **Turn off any antivirus software that you have on your computer.** Installers sometimes mimic virus activity and may make your computer incorrectly believe that it is being infected by a virus.

- **Close all running programs.** The more programs you're running, the less memory is available to other programs. Installers also typically update files and programs; if you keep other programs running, installation may not work properly.

- **In Windows, close the CD interface and run demos or installations directly from Windows Explorer.** The interface itself can tie up system memory, or even conflict with certain kinds of interactive demos. Use Windows Explorer to browse the files on the CD and launch installers or demos.

- **Have your local computer store add more RAM to your computer.** This is, admittedly, a drastic and somewhat expensive step. However, if you have a Windows 95/98 PC or a Macintosh with a PowerPC chip, adding more memory can really help the speed of your computer and enable more programs to run at the same time.

If you still have trouble installing the items from the CD, please call the IDG Books Worldwide Customer Service line: 800-762-2974 (outside the U.S.: 317-596-5430).

Index

• **J** •

• **K** •

• **L** •

IDG Books Worldwide, Inc., End-User License Agreement

READ THIS. You should carefully read these terms and conditions before opening the software packet(s) included with this book ("Book"). This is a license agreement ("Agreement") between you and IDG Books Worldwide, Inc. ("IDGB"). By opening the accompanying software packet(s), you acknowledge that you have read and accept the following terms and conditions. If you do not agree and do not want to be bound by such terms and conditions, promptly return the Book and the unopened software packet(s) to the place you obtained them for a full refund.

1. **License Grant.** IDGB grants to you (either an individual or entity) a nonexclusive license to use one copy of the enclosed software program(s) (collectively, the "Software") solely for your own personal or business purposes on a single computer (whether a standard computer or a workstation component of a multiuser network). The Software is in use on a computer when it is loaded into temporary memory (RAM) or installed into permanent memory (hard disk, CD-ROM, or other storage device). IDGB reserves all rights not expressly granted herein.

2. **Ownership.** IDGB is the owner of all right, title, and interest, including copyright, in and to the compilation of the Software recorded on the disk(s) or CD-ROM ("Software Media"). Copyright to the individual programs recorded on the Software Media is owned by the author or other authorized copyright owner of each program. Ownership of the Software and all proprietary rights relating thereto remain with IDGB and its licensers.

3. **Restrictions on Use and Transfer.**

    (a) You may only (i) make one copy of the Software for backup or archival purposes, or (ii) transfer the Software to a single hard disk, provided that you keep the original for backup or archival purposes. You may not (i) rent or lease the Software, (ii) copy or reproduce the Software through a LAN or other network system or through any computer subscriber system or bulletin-board system, or (iii) modify, adapt, or create derivative works based on the Software.

    (b) You may not reverse engineer, decompile, or disassemble the Software. You may transfer the Software and user documentation on a permanent basis, provided that the transferee agrees to accept the terms and conditions of this Agreement and you retain no copies. If the Software is an update or has been updated, any transfer must include the most recent update and all prior versions.

4. **Restrictions on Use of Individual Programs.** You must follow the individual requirements and restrictions detailed for each individual program in the "About the CD" appendix of this Book. These limitations are also contained in the individual license agreements recorded on the Software Media. These limitations may include a requirement that after using the program for a specified period of time, the user must pay a registration fee or discontinue use. By opening the Software packet(s), you will be agreeing to abide by the licenses and restrictions for these individual programs that are detailed in the "About the CD" appendix and on the Software Media. None of the material on this Software Media or listed in this Book may ever be redistributed, in original or modified form, for commercial purposes.

5. **Limited Warranty.**

    (a) IDGB warrants that the Software and Software Media are free from defects in materials and workmanship under normal use for a period of sixty (60) days from the date of purchase of this Book. If IDGB receives notification within the warranty period of defects in materials or workmanship, IDGB will replace the defective Software Media.

    (b) **IDGB AND THE AUTHOR OF THE BOOK DISCLAIM ALL OTHER WARRANTIES, EXPRESS OR IMPLIED, INCLUDING WITHOUT LIMITATION IMPLIED WARRANTIES OF MERCHANTABILITY AND FITNESS FOR A PARTICULAR PURPOSE, WITH RESPECT TO THE SOFTWARE, THE PROGRAMS, THE SOURCE CODE CONTAINED THEREIN, AND/OR THE TECHNIQUES DESCRIBED IN THIS BOOK. IDGB DOES NOT WARRANT THAT THE FUNCTIONS CONTAINED IN THE SOFTWARE WILL MEET YOUR REQUIREMENTS OR THAT THE OPERATION OF THE SOFTWARE WILL BE ERROR FREE.**

    (c) This limited warranty gives you specific legal rights, and you may have other rights that vary from jurisdiction to jurisdiction.

6. **Remedies.**

    (a) IDGB's entire liability and your exclusive remedy for defects in materials and workmanship shall be limited to replacement of the Software Media, which may be returned to IDGB with a copy of your receipt at the following address: Software Media Fulfillment Department, Attn.: *Starting an Online Business For Dummies,* IDG Books Worldwide, Inc., 7260 Shadeland Station, Ste. 100, Indianapolis, IN 46256, or call 800-762-2974. Please allow three to four weeks for delivery. This Limited Warranty is void if failure of the Software Media has resulted from accident, abuse, or misapplication. Any replacement Software Media will be warranted for the remainder of the original warranty period or thirty (30) days, whichever is longer.

    (b) In no event shall IDGB or the author be liable for any damages whatsoever (including without limitation damages for loss of business profits, business interruption, loss of business information, or any other pecuniary loss) arising from the use of or inability to use the Book or the Software, even if IDGB has been advised of the possibility of such damages.

    (c) Because some jurisdictions do not allow the exclusion or limitation of liability for consequential or incidental damages, the above limitation or exclusion may not apply to you.

7. **U.S. Government Restricted Rights.** Use, duplication, or disclosure of the Software by the U.S. Government is subject to restrictions stated in paragraph (c)(1)(ii) of the Rights in Technical Data and Computer Software clause of DFARS 252.227-7013, and in subparagraphs (a) through (d) of the Commercial Computer–Restricted Rights clause at FAR 52.227-19, and in similar clauses in the NASA FAR supplement, when applicable.

8. **General.** This Agreement constitutes the entire understanding of the parties and revokes and supersedes all prior agreements, oral or written, between them and may not be modified or amended except in a writing signed by both parties hereto that specifically refers to this Agreement. This Agreement shall take precedence over any other documents that may be in conflict herewith. If any one or more provisions contained in this Agreement are held by any court or tribunal to be invalid, illegal, or otherwise unenforceable, each and every other provision shall remain in full force and effect.

Installation Instructions

*T*he *Starting an Online Business For Dummies* CD contains software and Web links to help you start and run your online business. The following steps explain how to install the items from the CD to your hard drive. However, in order to run some of the programs on the CD, you may need to keep the disc inside your CD-ROM drive. (These installation steps are for Microsoft Windows users only. If you use a Macintosh, see the appendix for your installation instructions.)

1. **Insert the CD into your computer's CD-ROM drive.**

2. **Windows 95/98/NT users: Choose Start⇨Run. Windows 3.*x* users: From Program Manger, choose File⇨Run.**

3. **In the dialog box that appears, type** D:\SETUP.EXE.

   If your CD-ROM drive uses a different letter, replace *D* with the proper drive letter.

4. **Click on OK.**

5. **Read through the License Agreement and then click the Accept button if you want to use the CD.**

6. **Click anywhere on the Welcome screen.**

7. **To view the items within a category, just click the category's name.**

8. **For more information about a program, click the program's name.**

   Sometimes, a program has its own system requirements or requires you to do a few tricks on your computer before you can install or run the program, and this screen tells you anything special you may need to do.

9. **To install a program, click on the appropriate Install button.**

10. **To install other items, repeat Steps 7, 8, and 9.**

11. **When you finish installing programs, click on Quit.**

    You can eject the CD now. Carefully place it back in the plastic jacket of the book for safekeeping.

For more information about installing and using the CD, see the "About the CD" appendix.

IDG BOOKS WORLDWIDE
BOOK REGISTRATION

Register This Book and Win!

We want to hear from you!

Visit **http://my2cents.dummies.com** to register this book and tell us how you liked it!

- ✔ Get entered in our monthly prize giveaway.

- ✔ Give us feedback about this book — tell us what you like best, what you like least, or maybe what you'd like to ask the author and us to change!

- ✔ Let us know any other ...*For Dummies*® topics that interest you.

Your feedback helps us determine what books to publish, tells us what coverage to add as we revise our books, and lets us know whether we're meeting your needs as a ...*For Dummies* reader. You're our most valuable resource, and what you have to say is important to us!

Not on the Web yet? It's easy to get started with *Dummies 101*®: *The Internet For Windows*® *98* or *The Internet For Dummies*®, 5th Edition, at local retailers everywhere.

Or let us know what you think by sending us a letter at the following address:

...*For Dummies* Book Registration
Dummies Press
7260 Shadeland Station, Suite 100
Indianapolis, IN 46256-3945
Fax 317-596-5498

FOR DUMMIES™

BESTSELLING
BOOK SERIES
FROM IDG